Categorically Unequal

Categorically Unequal

The American Stratification System

ॐ

Douglas S. Massey

A Russell Sage Foundation Centennial Volume

Russell Sage Foundation
New York

The Russell Sage Foundation

The Russell Sage Foundation, one of the oldest of America's general purpose foundations, was established in 1907 by Mrs. Margaret Olivia Sage for "the improvement of social and living conditions in the United States." The Foundation seeks to fulfill this mandate by fostering the development and dissemination of knowledge about the country's political, social, and economic problems. While the Foundation endeavors to assure the accuracy and objectivity of each book it publishes, the conclusions and interpretations in Russell Sage Foundation publications are those of the authors and not of the Foundation, its Trustees, or its staff. Publication by Russell Sage, therefore, does not imply Foundation endorsement.

Library of Congress Cataloging-in-Publication Data

Massey, Douglas S.
  Categorically unequal : the American stratification system / Douglas S. Massey.

    p. cm. — (A Russell Sage Foundation centennial volume)
  Includes bibliographical references.
  ISBN 978-0-87154-585-5 (HB)   ISBN 978-0-87154-584-8 (PB)

  1. Equality--United States. 2. Social stratification—United States.
3. United States—Social conditions—1945- I. Russell Sage Foundation.
II. Title.

  HN90.S6M36 2007

  305.0973--dc22   2006038385

Text design by Suzanne Nichols.

RUSSELL SAGE FOUNDATION
112 East 64th Street, New York, New York 10065
10 9 8 7 6 5 4

Dedicated to my mother,
born Ruth Sylvia Matson to immigrant parents,
who taught me the importance of education,
and the importance of using it for good.

CONTENTS

ABOUT THE AUTHOR

DOUGLAS S. MASSEY is Henry G. Bryant Professor of Sociology and Public Affairs at the Woodrow Wilson School and president of the American Academy of Political and Social Science.

THE RUSSELL SAGE
CENTENNIAL VOLUMES

America Works: Critical Thoughts on the Exceptional U.S. Labor Market
Richard B. Freeman

Categorically Unequal: The American Stratification System
Douglas S. Massey

Social Science for What? Philanthropy and the Social Question in a World Turned Rightside Up
Alice O'Connor

FOREWORD

On April 19, 2007, the Russell Sage Foundation will celebrate its centennial, 100 years to the day since Margaret Olivia Sage dedicated the foundation, in her husband's name, "to the improvement of social and living conditions in the United States of America." From the outset, social research played a key role in the foundation's mission—both by providing vivid descriptions of the social problems that called out for reform in a newly industrialized, urbanized America and by assessing the effectiveness of the foundation's early programs designed to improve the lot of the disadvantaged. As the foundation's enterprise matured after World War II, the Russell Sage trustees realized that to better serve the emerging mass society social science would require significant development—in its analytic tools, its sources of data, and its theoretical capacities. Accordingly, the trustees decided that a foundation the size of RSF could contribute to the general social welfare most effectively by investing directly in the development and application of social science. This has been the foundation's unique objective ever since.

Over the past sixty years, the foundation has sought to shape and strengthen the social sciences in a wide variety of ways. It has invested in new disciplines, among them the sociology of medicine and law, and a new brand of economics based less on presumed rationality and more on evidence about how economic decisions are actually made. It has pushed to create new sources of social data, such as the General Social Survey, and to improve the analysis of existing data sources, principally by means of its long-standing analysis of social trends revealed by the U.S. Census. Russell Sage has also worked to support and disseminate promising new methodologies, such as statistical techniques for synthesizing multiple research studies of a given social policy or program to achieve more reliable generalizations about what works.

The foundation's recent activities have sustained its traditional aims of bringing social science more effectively to bear on describing social problems and analyzing the causes and consequences of social change. RSF has developed research programs on the social consequences of changing gender roles in the wake of the civil rights movement, on the vexing persistence of poverty and the rise of economic inequality in the United States over the past three decades, on the declining fortunes of minority workers in the inner-city economies of the 1980s and early 1990s, and on the tectonic shifts in the U.S. labor market since the early 1980s that have put workers with limited education and bargaining power at such a distinct and growing disadvantage. Russell Sage has also devoted substantial attention to understanding the social consequences of recent demographic change. The foundation's fifteen-year program of research on the continuing wave of immigration to the United States provides a rich source of information about the impact the new immigrants are having on the country and the problems that immigrants and their children face as they try to make their way in American society. A related research program has addressed the changes in American life brought on by the increased diversity of the U.S. population—from the growing complexity of relations between racial and ethnic groups to the problems that American institutions encounter as they attempt to accommodate a more diverse citizenry.

The Russell Sage Foundation's hundredth birthday offers a unique moment to pause and take stock of this work, even as the enterprise continues. The three volumes commissioned for the centennial illustrate and reflect upon the use of social science to deepen our understanding of American life. They do not recapitulate the work of the foundation. They seek instead to push the work ahead. Over its long history, Russell Sage has struggled repeatedly to understand the social costs of the rough and tumble American labor market, the systemic roots of persistently high levels of inequality in the United States, and the political difficulties of establishing an effective role for social research in the formation of social policy.

The three centennial volumes take up these themes with innovative and provocative arguments that demonstrate again the power of social research to move debate beyond conventional wisdom, to give society fresh ways to see itself, and to recommend new strategies for improving national life. No doubt these arguments will provide rich grounds for debate. But since social science is, after all, a continuing contest founded on a shared commitment to honest evidence and reasoned argument, that is just as it should be.

Eric Wanner
President
Russell Sage Foundation

PREFACE

In her presidential address to the American Sociological Association, Barbara Reskin (2003) called for social scientists to forgo their obsession with the modeling of motives in favor of a new focus on mechanisms. She noted that considerable progress has been made in documenting the existence of social and economic disparities with respect to race and gender, but that there has been less progress in explaining them; she attributed the latter to the misguided attempt to explain variation in outcomes in terms of people's motivations. In her view, "this approach has been inconclusive because motive-based theories cannot be empirically tested" and because they lead to a "reliance on individual-level data and the balkanization of research on ascriptive inequality into separate specialities." For her, "explanation requires including mechanisms in our models—the specific processes that link groups' ascribed characteristics to variable outcomes such as earnings" (Reskin 2003, 1).

This book responds to Reskin's call for a focus on mechanisms by undertaking a systematic analysis of how inequality is produced in the United States along three categorical boundaries—race, class, and gender. According to the view advanced here, inequality is rooted in the human proclivity to think in categorical terms—that is, to divide the world into conceptual categories associated with different attributes and meanings, which are then translated into social organization and action. Drawing on experimental results from the fields of social cognition and social neuroscience, I show how basic features of human social perception make stratification possible and even likely.

Given the categorical organization of the social world in human cognition and its expression in human institutions, inequality is produced by specific institutional mechanisms that are all variations on two basic strategies, exploitation and opportunity hoarding, which are commonly observed as discrimination and exclusion. Categorical mechanisms are embedded within the infrastructure of the social institutions, cultural practices, and conceptual understandings upon which markets rest. Markets create the potential for inequality by producing a larger pie, but because there is no single architecture for a capitalist market, there is no single degree of inequality associated with a market society. It is not market competition that determines how the pie is divided up, but the nature of the institutions that undergird the market and make competition possible. Depending on how a market is structured and organized institutionally, it can produce more or less inequality and lead to greater or lesser stratification.

Over the past thirty years, markets in the United States have been restructured institutionally to produce rising levels of inequality with respect to income, wealth, and social well-being. The United States is now vastly more unequal than it was in 1975 and vastly more unequal than other advanced industrial societies in the world today. This book describes the historical evolution of the categorical mechanisms responsible for this remarkable outcome, focusing on how inequality is generated with respect to the intertwined social categories of race, class, and gender. Racially based mechanisms of stratification are explored by a detailed examination of the multiple means by which African Americans and Mexican Americans have been and continue to be exploited and excluded in U.S. society. The mechanisms of class stratification are exposed by showing how the rules and organization of the U.S. political economy have changed over the past three decades to favor the affluent at the expense of others. And the peculiar fashion by which gender operates to stratify Americans is documented by comparing the contrasting fates of women at the top and bottom of the class distribution.

The evidence marshaled in these exercises reveals that the contemporary political economy of the United States is riddled with categorical mechanisms that produce unequal distributions of material, symbolic, and emotional resources along the lines of race, class, and gender, which together combine to yield extreme stratification. Attentive readers will develop a clear idea of how inequality is produced in America today and appreciate why unless actions are taken to change the structure and organization of the political economy, inequalities of wealth, power, and income will continue to be reproduced and grow more extreme. It is hoped that improved knowledge about the mechanisms of stratification will change the motivations of readers and inspire them to political action. While motives may not be central to modeling or explaining the rise of American inequality, they are critical to bringing about the social and political actions required to reverse it.

Douglas S. Massey
Princeton, New Jersey
October 29, 2006

✦ CHAPTER 1 ✦

HOW STRATIFICATION WORKS

A ll human societies have a social structure that divides people into categories based on a combination of achieved and as-cribed traits. Achieved characteristics are those acquired in the course of living, whereas ascribed characteristics are set at birth. The categories defined within a social structure may be nominal or graduated—that is, they may assign labels to people on the basis of shared qualitative attributes, or they may rank people along some quantitative continuum (see Blau 1977). Ascribed social categories include nominal groupings such as gender, in which people are la-beled male or female on the basis of inherited physical traits (ulti-mately, the possession of one versus two X chromosomes), as well as graduated categories such as age, in which people are classified according to the amount of time elapsed since birth. Achieved sta-tuses may also be nominal—being a member of a fraternal lodge such as the Moose or Elks—or graduated—being a member of an income class.

Stratification refers to the unequal distribution of people across social categories that are characterized by differential access to scarce resources. The resources may be material, such as income and wealth; they may be symbolic, such as prestige and social standing; or they may be emotional, such as love, affection, and, of course, sex. The term "stratification" comes from the Latin *stratum*, which in the geological sense refers to an identifiable layer of sedi-ment or material in the ground. Over time, changing environmen-tal conditions produce identifiable layers within the earth's crust,

1

known as strata, which are distinctive in composition and can be associated temporally with different geological eras. In an analogous manner, societies may be conceptualized as having social strata, different layers that are distinctive in composition and characterized by more or less access to material, symbolic, and emotional resources.

Stratification systems order people vertically in a social structure characterized by a distinct top and bottom. The distance from the top to the bottom of any society is indicated by the size of the gap in access to resources between those in the uppermost and lowermost social categories. As the distance between the top and the bottom of a social structure increases, and as the distribution of people across social categories shifts toward the extremes, a society is said to become more stratified—literally having more socially defined layers with more people distributed among them at greater distances from one another. The degree of social stratification is often measured in terms of inequality, which assesses the degree of variability in the dispersion of people among ranked social categories.

Human societies differ greatly with respect to their degree of social inequality. In general, small foraging societies in which people hunt and gather for a living tend to be quite egalitarian (Kelly 1995). Social categories are defined mainly on the basis of gender, age, and kinship, categorical perceptions that appear to be hardwired into human social cognition (Macrae and Bodenhausen 2000). Among hunters and gatherers there is little inequality in access to material resources. The stratification that does exist is mainly expressed as unequal access to symbolic or emotional resources. Among men, prestige and sexual access derive not simply from skill at hunting and successful food provision but also from generosity and sharing within the group. Selfishness and hoarding are discouraged through a variety of informal leveling mechanisms that involve ridicule, shaming, and humor, which are often enforced through prescribed rituals (Gamble 1999).

The most common form of stratification in foraging societies occurs on the basis of gender. Stratification between males and females derives primarily from the amount of time that men spend alone together, typically on a hunt, and is thus determined by local

2

ecology (Massey 2005a). Societies where men spend large amounts of time away from women hunting large game tend to be more gender-stratified. During the time they are away on their own, males reinforce male predispositions and tendencies to become more aggressive and domineering (Macoby 1998). At the same time, females left by themselves reinforce female predispositions and tendencies to become more caring and nurturing. The end result is a divergence in gender-specific attitudes and behaviors that works to the detriment of females once the two sexes reunite (Macoby 1998; Sanday 1981). Compared with foraging societies built around the hunting of large mammals, societies that rely on aquatic resources, gathering and scavenging, or the pursuit of small game tend to be much lower in gender inequality.

Sedentary agrarian societies are more stratified than foraging societies (Sjoberg 1960). The domestication of plants and animals around ten thousand years ago enabled farmers to produce more food than they themselves consumed, and thus a very small number of people could stop toiling each day to procure the calories needed for survival. Instead, these fortunate few pursued other, non-food-producing activities such as trade, manufacturing, politics, religion, and soldiering (Chant and Goodman 1999).

Given a pre-industrial agrarian technology, the food surplus was necessarily meager, and to support even a small class of non-food-producing specialists, crops had to be collected over a large area and assembled at a fixed location for redistribution to people who had no direct role in their cultivation; these fixed locations were the first cities (Chandler and Fox 1974). Since peasant households do not willingly hand over the fruits of their labor to others, social structures came into existence to effect and legitimate the confiscation, leading to the formation of ruling and working classes in addition to peasant farmers (Sjoberg 1960). Noble and priestly families based in cities enjoyed favored access to material, symbolic, and emotional resources; workers, tradesmen, and artisans made do with whatever the ruling classes granted them; and peasants were heavily taxed to support both sets of urban dwellers.

Although the distance between the top and bottom rungs of society was large compared with foraging societies and mobility between classes was minimal, the total amount of inequality was constrained by the small size of the food surplus produced with a pre-industrial technology (Massey 2005a). In the world of agrarian urbanism, which prevailed from 8000 B.C. to around 1800 A.D., no more than 5 percent of the inhabitants within any society ever lived in cities, and among urban dwellers only a tiny fraction belonged to the ruling elite. The typical member of a pre-industrial agrarian society was an illiterate peasant whose access to resources was the same as that of most of the rest of the population. Despite the existence of privileged classes, total inequality was actually quite modest by contemporary standards.

Beginning around 1800, however, the industrial revolution breached the technological cap that had limited inequality for millennia. Mechanization enabled a dramatic increase in agricultural productivity so that for the first time fewer than 5 percent of humans could produce enough food for everyone else (Berry 1973). Industrial societies urbanized, and the vast majority of people came to inhabit cities and work in non-agricultural occupations. As the share of workers employed in manufacturing and services grew, the number and range of occupations expanded rapidly to produce new social forms of differentiation. In the United States, for example, the variance in the distribution of people across occupational categories increased by a factor of four between 1850 and 1950 (Massey 2005a).

Industrialization also enabled an unprecedented increase in material well-being, dramatically widening the absolute distance between the top and the bottom of human social structures. Between 1850 and 1950, the total value of goods and services produced in the global economy rose from $939 trillion to $5,336 trillion (Maddison 2003), and the largest private fortune in the United States rose from $1 million to $1.6 billion (Phillips 2002). This increased distance between the top and bottom of the social hierarchy and the proliferation of categories in between made possible a new burst of stratification and inequality that lasted well into the twentieth century (Williamson 1980).

In the United States the restructuring of the political economy in the wake of the Great Depression and the Second World War compressed the distribution of earnings and substantially reduced levels of inequality, beginning in the 1930s (Goldin and Margo 1992). From 1945 to 1975, under structural arrangements implemented during the New Deal, poverty rates steadily fell, median incomes consistently rose, and inequality progressively dropped as a rising economic tide lifted all boats (see Burtless and Smeeding 2001; Danziger and Gottschalk 1995; Freeman 2001; Levy 1998; Smeeding, O'Higgins, and Rainwater 1990).

During the 1970s, however, a new *post-industrial* economy arose, one based on the creation of knowledge and manipulation of information rather than the production of goods and services or the cultivation of food (Devine and Waters 2004; Svallfors 2005). Once again occupational differentiation increased and the distance between the top and the bottom of the social hierarchy grew. Whereas the largest private fortune in the United States stood at $3.6 billion in 1968, by 1999 it had reached $85 billion, raising the distance between the top and bottom of the social structure by a factor of 24 in just thirty years (Phillips 2002). Likewise, from 1975 to 2000 wealth inequality increased by 11 percent while income inequality rose by 23 percent (Keister 2000; Massey 2005a). At century's end, the richest 1 percent of Americans controlled 40 percent of the nation's total wealth.

Categorical Inequality

Despite the radical transformation of human societies over time—from foraging societies through agrarian urbanism into industrial urbanism and on to our current post-industrial world—the fundamental mechanisms producing stratification have not changed much. Although the number and range of categories in the social structure may have risen dramatically, and the stock of material resources may have accumulated to new heights, the basic means by which people are granted more or less access to scarce material, emotional, and symbolic resources have remained remarkably similar through the ages. Indeed, all stratification processes boil down to a combination of two simple but powerful mechanisms: the allocation of people to social categories, and the institutionalization of practices that allocate resources unequally across these categories. Together, these two social processes produce what Charles Tilly (1998) calls "categorical inequality"—a pattern of social stratification that is remarkably "durable" in the sense that it is reproduced across time and between generations.

The Basic Mechanisms of Stratification

Given socially defined categories and people being distributed among them, inequality is generated and perpetuated by two basic mechanisms: exploitation and opportunity hoarding (Tilly 1998). *Exploitation* occurs when people in one social group expropriate a resource produced by members of another social group and prevent them from realizing the full value of their effort in producing it. *Opportunity hoarding* occurs when one social group restricts access to a scarce resource, either through outright denial or by exercising monopoly control that requires out-group members to pay rent in return for access. Either way, opportunity hoarding is enabled through a *socially defined process of exclusion*.

The most extreme form of categorical inequality ever invented by human beings is slavery, wherein the labor of one socially defined group is expropriated in its entirety by another, whose members simultaneously and drastically restrict the access of the enslaved to material, symbolic, and emotional resources. The Jim Crow social system that replaced slavery in the American South after 1876 used sharecropping as a new institutional means of exploitation and carrying out exclusion and opportunity hoarding (Foner 1988). Until quite recently, racial stratification in the southern United States was extreme and social mobility for African Americans was limited.

Within any social structure, exploitation and opportunity hoarding are, in turn, reinforced by two other social processes that work over time to institutionalize categorical distinctions and lock them into place (Tilly 1998). The first is *emulation*, whereby one group of people copies a set of social distinctions and interrelationships from another group or transfers the distinctions and interrelationships from one social setting to another. The second is *adaptation*: social relations and day-to-day behaviors at the microsocial level become oriented toward ranked categories, so that decisions about who to befriend, who to help, who to share with, who to live near, who to court, and who to marry are made in ways that assume the existence and importance of asymmetric social categories. In the words of Tilly (1998, 10): "Exploitation and opportunity hoarding favor the installation of categorical inequality, while emulation and adaptation generalize its influence."

In the Jim Crow South, for example, if legislation to enforce racial segregation that was invented in one southern state was successful, it would be imitated by other southern states, such that by 1920 all the states of the former Confederacy came to have remarkably similar legal codes on the issue of race (Packard 2002; Woodward 1955; Wormser 2003). At the same time, faced with violence and coercion, blacks came to "know their place" in the southern social order and adapted to it in ways that reinforced their subjugation. Whites throughout the South likewise adapted their behaviors according to the formal and informal rules of Jim Crow, which allowed them to intimidate, victimize, and punish African Americans with impunity. As a result, racial segregation was enforced not only formally in public settings but also informally in private practice through a racial etiquette negotiated daily by black and white southerners.

The Psychology of Social Classification

Although obvious and glaring, in principle the mechanisms of stratification employed in the Jim Crow South are quite general and operate at some level in all human societies. They are ultimately social in origin and predate the emergence of the market as a means of organizing human production and consumption (Massey 2005a). Instead, they follow naturally from the pursuit of core social motives common to all human beings (Fiske 2004). What has changed dramatically is the societal context within which the core social motives play out. Human interactions increasingly occur within urban

7

environments of great size, density, and heterogeneity, and the ecological settings that individuals find themselves adapting to—psychologically, socially, culturally, and physiologically—vary greatly depending on whether the individuals are rich or poor, light or dark, male or female.

In a very real way, stratification begins psychologically with the creation of cognitive boundaries that allocate people to social categories. Before categorical inequality can be implemented socially, categories must be created cognitively to classify people conceptually based on some set of achieved and ascribed characteristics. The roots of social stratification thus lie ultimately in the cognitive construction of boundaries to make social distinctions, a task that comes naturally to human beings, who are mentally hardwired to engage in categorical thought (Fiske 2004). Indeed, recent work shows that human intelligence works more through pattern recognition and inductive generalization than deductive logic or mathematical optimization (Dawes 1998). In contrast to the software and hardware of a digital computer, which work together to make decisions using a strict Boolean logic, the "wetware" of the human brain is messy, inconsistent, and often quite "illogical" in a strictly deductive sense (Dawes and Hastie 2001; Kahneman and Tversky 1973, 1979). Instead, human "rationality" has been shaped by evolution to depart in characteristic ways from strict adherence to the principles of logic and probability that are assumed by most rational choice models (Dawes 1998; Kahneman and Tversky 2000).

Our natural capacity for categorical thought evolved in this fashion because the human brain is an energy sink. Constituting just 2 percent of the body's weight, the brain uses 20 percent of its total energy (Donald 1991). In the course of thousands of years of evolution, therefore, human beings evolved ingrained mental shortcuts to conserve cognitive resources. Operating with deductive rigor to consider all possible combinations, permutations, and contingencies before making a decision is possible for a powerful electronic computer contemplating a single problem, but if the brain were to adopt such an approach to decide the myriad of choices that human beings face in daily life, humans would waste a lot of scarce energy pondering routine situations and everyday actions that have little effect on survival. Most decisions made by humans are not perfect or optimal in any real sense; they are just "good enough" to get by and live another day, yielding the human practice of "satisficing" rather than optimizing (Simon 1981).

For this reason, human beings function mentally as "cognitive misers." They take a variety of characteristic mental shortcuts and use simple rules of thumb and shorthands to make everyday judgments (Fiske and Taylor 1991). As organisms, we tend to "satisfice" rather than optimize (Newell and Simon 1972), and we are wired cognitively to construct general categories about the world in which we live and then to use them to classify and evaluate the stimuli we encounter. These conceptual categories are collectively known as *schemas*. They represent cognitive structures that serve to interconnect a set of stimuli, their various attributes, and the relationships between them (Fiske 2004).

Since human memory is finite and cannot be expanded, if the brain is to remember more things it must combine or "chunk" bits of information into larger conceptual categories (schemas), using common properties to classify a much larger number of people, objects, and experiences into a small number of readily identifiable categories for recall. Ultimately schemas are nothing more than well-established neural pathways that have been created through the repeated firing of particular constellations of synapses, leading to the formation of an integrated assembly of neurons that function together according to a specific sequence along specific routes to produce a consistent mental representation (LeDoux 2002).

People use schemas to evaluate themselves and the social roles, social groups, social events, and individuals they encounter, a process known as social cognition (Fiske 2004). The categories into which they divide up the world may change over time and evolve with experience, but among mature human beings they always exist and people always fall back on them when they interpret objects, events, people, and situations (Fiske 2004), and they are especially reliant on categorical judgments under conditions of threat or uncertainty. Human beings are psychologically programmed to categorize the people they encounter and to use these categorizations to make social judgments.

9

Social schemas do not exist simply as neutral mental representations, however; they are typically associated with emotional valences. The human brain is composed of two parallel processors that, while interconnected, function independently (Carter 1998; Konner 2002; Panksepp 1998). The emotional brain is rooted in a set of neural structures that are common to all mammals and are known collectively as the limbic system, whereas the rational brain is centered in the prefrontal cortex and other areas of the neocortex (Damasio 1994, 1999). The two portions of the brain, labeled system 1 and system 2 by Daniel Kahneman (2003), are neurally interconnected, but the number and speed of the connections running from the limbic system to the neocortex are greater than the reverse, so that emotional memories stored in the limbic system, which are typically unconscious or implicit, greatly affect how human beings make use of categories that exist within the rational, conscious brain (LeDoux 1996; Zajonc 1998).

Emotions stored in the limbic system may be positive or negative, but when they are associated with particular classes of people or objects they contribute to *prejudice*, which is a predetermined emotional orientation toward individuals or objects (Fiske 2004). A prejudicial orientation for or against some social group thus contains both conscious and unconscious components (Bargh 1996, 1997). On the one hand, people may be principled racists who consciously believe that African Americans are inferior and thus rationally seek to subordinate them, consistent with their explicit beliefs. On the other hand, a person may quite sincerely believe in equal opportunity and racial justice and yet harbor unconscious anti-black sentiments and associations that were created through some process of conditioning (such as the repeated visual pairing of violent crime scenes with black perpetrators on television), even though this prejudice may be inconsistent with the person's explicit beliefs.

All human beings, whether they think of themselves as prejudiced or not, hold in their heads schemas that classify people into categories based on age, gender, race, and ethnicity (Stangor et al. 1992; Taylor et al. 1978). They cannot help it. It is part of the human condition, and these schemas generally include implicit memories that yield subconscious dispositions toward people and objects, leading to stereotypes (Fiske 1998). Moreover, although stereotypical notions are always present, people are more likely to fall back on them in making judgments when they feel challenged, face uncertainty, or experience sensory overload (Bodenhausen and Lichtenstein 1987; Bodenhausen and Wyer 1985).

In making stereotypical judgments about others, human beings appear to evaluate people along two basic psychological dimensions: warmth and competence (Fiske et al. 2002). Warmth is how likable and approachable a person is. We are attracted to people we view as high on the warmth dimension, and we seek to interact and spend time with them. We find people who are low on the warmth dimension to be off-putting, and we generally avoid them and seek to minimize the number and range of our social contacts with them; we don't like them and find them "cold." In addition to these subjective feelings of attraction and liking, we also evaluate people in terms of competence and efficacy—their ability to act in a purposeful manner to get things done. We may or may not like people who are highly competent, but we generally respect them and admire their ability to achieve.

These two dimensions of social perception come together in the *stereotype content model*, which argues that human social cognition and stereotyping involve the cognitive placement of groups and individuals in a two-dimensional social space defined by the intersection of independent axes of warmth and competence (Fiske et al. 2002). As shown in figure 1.1, the social space for stereotyping has four quadrants. The top-right quadrant contains people within the person's own group, along with members of groups perceived to be similar to one's own. Naturally, we think of members of our own social group as warm and competent and, hence, approachable and worthy of respect. The relevant emotion associated with in-group social perceptions is esteem or pride.

The intersection of the two dimensions yields three distinct kinds of out-groups, however, which vary in terms of approachability and respect. The bottom-right quadrant contains those groups that are viewed socially as competent but not warm. They are respected but not liked, and the relevant emotion that people

Figure 1.1   The Stereotype Content Model

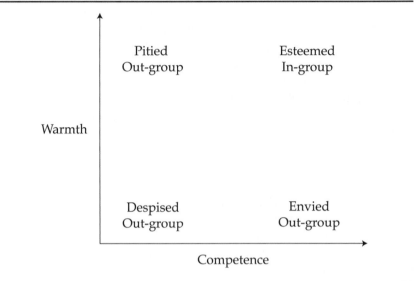

Source: Author's compilation.

feel toward them is envy. This quadrant embraces the classic middleman minorities, such as Jews in medieval Europe, Chinese in Malaysia, Tutsi in Rwanda, and Indians in East Africa. In a stable social structure, people show public respect for and defer to members of envied out-groups, but if the social order breaks down, these out-groups may become targets of communal hatred and violence because they are not liked and are not perceived as people "like us."

The top-left quadrant includes out-groups that are viewed as warm, and thus likable, but as not competent. Those falling into this category include people who have experienced some misfortune but are otherwise perceived as "people like me," such as the disabled, the elderly, the blind, or the mentally retarded. One could imagine being in their shoes but for an accident of fate, and so the relevant emotion is pity. We like the members of these out-groups, but recognizing their lack of competence, we also feel sorry for them and do not respect them. In a stable social structure, members of pitied out-groups tend to be looked after and cared for, but in times of social disorder they may suffer from neglect (as seen in the aftermath of Hurricane Katrina in New Orleans), though they generally do not become targets of intentional hatred or communal violence.

Finally, social groups occupying the bottom-left quadrant are perceived simultaneously as low in warmth and low in competence. Being neither likable nor capable, people within these out-groups are socially despised, and the dominant emotion is disgust. This quadrant contains social outcasts such as drug dealers, lazy welfare recipients, sex offenders, and the chronically homeless. It also includes members of groups that have been subject to an ideological process of group formation and boundary definition that questions their humanity. African Americans in the Jim Crow South were perceived by whites as neither competent nor warm. They were socially labeled as inferior, even subhuman, and because they were perceived as less than fully human, they could be exploited, segregated, humiliated, and killed with near impunity.

Recent work in neuroscience has implicated a particular region of the brain as central to the process of social cognition (see Harris and Fiske 2006). Whenever individuals perceive a stimulus as a human being and therefore a potential social actor, an area of the brain known as the *medial prefrontal cortex* lights up when observed under functional magnetic resonance imagery (fMRI). Lasana Harris and Susan Fiske (2006) pretested a number of photographic images of social actors to establish the quadrant into which they fell; then they showed these images to experimental subjects so that each person saw a total of eighty images—twenty of in-group members, twenty of envied out-groups, twenty of pitied out-groups, and twenty of despised out-groups.

As they viewed the various social images, the brains of subjects were scanned under fMRI and centers of activity recorded. As expected, the investigators found that images of people representing in-groups, envied out-groups, and pitied out-groups triggered clear reactions in the medial prefrontal cortex. Startlingly, however, images of despised out-groups did not (Harris and Fiske 2006). Whereas out-groups triggering feelings of pity and envy were instantly perceived as human beings and social actors, those that were despised were not seen in social terms at all—at the most fundamental level of cognition. Despised out-groups thus become dehumanized at the neural level, and those who harbor these feelings thus have a license, in their own minds, to treat members of these out-groups as if they are animals or objects.

This basic feature of human social cognition provides the psychological foundations for exploitation and opportunity hoarding in the real world. It is reinforced by another characteristic feature of human psychology known as the *fundamental attribution error*, "the general tendency to overestimate the importance of personal or dispositional factors relative to environmental influences" in accounting for behavior (Ross, Greene, and House 1977, 184). In evaluating others, all human beings have a natural tendency to attribute behavioral outcomes to characteristics of the people involved rather than the structure of the situation. Thus, the poor are poor because they are lazy, lack a work ethic, have no sense of responsibility, are careless in their choices, or are just plain immoral, not because they lost their job or were born into a social position that did not give them the resources they needed to develop. Because of the fundamental attribution error, we are all cognitively wired and prone to blame the victim—to think that people deserve their location in the prevailing stratification system.

In parallel fashion, human beings have an opposite bias when they make attributions about themselves, at least with respect to negative outcomes. Rather than blaming themselves—something about their disposition or character—they tend to attribute personal misfortunes to specific features of the situation, a proclivity known as the *actor-observer effect* (Jones and Nisbett 1972). When *someone else* ends up on welfare, it is because he or she is lazy, careless, or irresponsible; when *I* end up on welfare, however, it is through no fault of my own but because of events beyond my control: I lost my job, got sick, was injured, got pregnant accidentally, got divorced, was widowed. Because of the actor-observer effect,

14

we are also cognitively prone to explain our own misfortunes and outcomes in terms of the structure of the situation.

The Creation of Capital

The position of a group within the social space defined by warmth and competence is not fixed but malleable, varying across time, space, and culture (Leslie, Constantine, and Fiske 2006). Although social categories are ultimately constructed and maintained by individuals within their own minds, the process by which boundaries are expressed is ultimately social. Group identities and boundaries are negotiated through repeated interactions that establish working definitions of the categories in question, including both objective and subjective content, a process that sociologists have labeled *boundary work* (Gieryn 1983; Lamont and Molnar 2002). When social actors succeed in establishing the limits and content of various social categories in the minds of others, psychologists refer to the process as *framing* (Kahneman and Tversky 2000). In essence, boundary work involves defining categories in the social structure, and framing involves defining them in human cognition.

People naturally favor boundaries and framings that grant them greater access to material, symbolic, and emotional resources, and they seek to convince others to accept their favored version of social reality (Lakoff 2002; Lakoff and Johnson 2003). In general, social actors who control more resources in society—those toward the top of the stratification system—have the upper hand in framing and boundary work. Whites historically have perpetuated negative stereotypes of African Americans as unintelligent, violent, hypersexual, and shiftless, and rich people likewise have promoted a view of the poor as lazy, unmotivated, undisciplined, and undeserving. To the extent that such stereotypes become a part of everyday social cognition, individual members of the stereotyped outgroup tend to experience discrimination and exclusion.

Nonetheless, exclusionary social distinctions and demeaning framings are always contested by people on the receiving end

(Barth 1969). Those subject to exploitation by a particular framing of social reality work to oppose it and substitute an alternative framing more amenable to their interests. Likewise, when they encounter categorical boundaries that prevent them from accessing a desired resource, people work actively to resist and subvert the social definitions as best they can. Members of subjugated groups have their own expectations about how they should be perceived and treated, and even if they outwardly adapt to the social preconceptions of more powerful others, they generally work inwardly to undermine the dominant conceptual and social order in small and large ways.

Through such two-way interactions, however asymmetric they may be, people on both sides of a stratified social divide actively participate in the construction of the boundaries and identities that define a system of stratification. No matter what their position in the system, people seek to define for themselves the content and meaning of social categories, embracing some elements ascribed to them by the dominant society and rejecting others, simultaneously accepting and resisting the constraints and opportunities associated with their particular social status. Through daily interactions with individuals and institutions, people construct an understanding of the lines between specific social groups (Barth 1981).

The reification of group boundaries within human social structures creates two important resources that are widely deployed in the process of social stratification: social capital and cultural capital (Bourdieu 1986). In classical economics, of course, capital refers to anything that can be used in the production of other resources, is human-made, and is not fully consumed in the process of production (Ricardo 1996). Common examples are *financial capital*, which can be invested to generate income, and *physical capital*, which can be applied in production to increase output. Economists later generalized the concept by defining *human capital* as the skills and abilities embodied in people, notably through education and training (Schultz 1963). By investing in education, parents and societies thus create human capital in their children, and when individuals forgo

16

income and incur costs to gain additional training, they invest in their own human capital. Individuals recoup this investment through higher lifetime earnings; societies recoup it through higher taxes and enhanced productivity; and parents recoup it by enjoying the economic independence and financial security of their adult children (Becker 1975).

Sociologists have broadened the concept of capital to embrace resources derived from social ties to people and institutions (Bourdieu 1986; Coleman 1988). *Social capital* comes into existence whenever a social connection to another person or membership in a social organization yields tangible benefits with respect to material, symbolic, or emotional resources, such as getting a job that offers higher income, greater prestige, and more access to attractive sexual partners. Most "good" jobs are not found through formal mechanisms such as paid advertisements but through informal connections with other social actors who provide information and leads (Granovetter 1974). Because ties to friends and family do not extend very far and mostly yield redundant information, weak ties to casual acquaintances are generally more important in getting a job than close relationships to close friends or kin (Granovetter 1973).

The use of framing and boundary work to construct an advantaged social group with privileged access to resources and power creates the potential for social capital formation. Having a tie to a member of a privileged elite increases the odds of being able to access resources and power oneself. Elites implicitly recognize this fact and generally take steps to restrict social ties to other members of the elite. Marriage outside the group is discouraged; friendships are turned inward through exclusive organizations such as clubs, fraternities, and lodges; and rules of inheritance conserve elite status along family lines. To the extent that group members are successful in confining social ties to other group members, they achieve *social closure*. Outsiders trying to break into elite circles are labeled bounders or interlopers, and they are derided for acting "uppity" or "above their station."

Social closure within elite networks and institutions also creates the potential for another valuable resource known as *cultural capital*

17

(Bourdieu 1986). In contrast to human capital, which includes knowledge, skills, and abilities that make people directly productive as individuals, cultural capital consists of knowledge and manners that do not make individuals more productive in and of themselves, but that permit them to be more effective as actors within a particular social context—in this case, elite settings. Because members of an elite tend to go to the same schools, read the same books, peruse the same periodicals, learn the same stylized manners, follow the same fashions, and develop the same accents and speech patterns, they are easily able to acquire a common set of socially defined markers that designate "good taste" and "high class," so that elite members are quickly recognizable to one another and to the masses.

The possession of cultural capital makes an individual more productive not because he or she can perform a given operation better or faster, but because he or she can navigate structures of power with greater ease, feeling relaxed and comfortable in the social settings they define and thus interacting with other persons of influence to get things done. Cultural capital represents a symbolic resource that privileged groups can manipulate through opportunity hoarding to perpetuate stratification and increase inequality.

Spatial Boundaries

To this point, I have argued that stratification stems from a social process wherein individuals form categorical mental representations of in-groups and out-groups through framing; translate these representations into social categories through boundary work; and then establish institutional structures for exploitation and opportunity hoarding that correspond to categorical boundaries, thereby generating unequal access to resources such as financial capital, human capital, social capital, and cultural capital. To function, this system need only exist in the social and cognitive spheres. Position in a cognitively and institutionally defined social order need not correspond to any real location in physical space. If, however, social boundaries can be made to conform to geographic boundaries through a systematic process of segregation, then the fundamental processes of stratification become considerably more efficient and effective (Massey 2005a).

If out-group members are spatially segregated from in-group members, then the latter are put in a good position to use their social power to create institutions and practices that channel resources away from the places where out-group members live, thus facilitating exploitation. At the same time, they can use their social power to implement other mechanisms that direct resources systematically toward in-group areas, thus facilitating opportunity hoarding. Spatial segregation renders stratification easy, convenient, and efficient because simply by investing or disinvesting in a place, one can invest or disinvest in a whole set of people (Massey and Denton 1993).

Stratification thus becomes more effective to the degree that social and spatial boundaries can be made to overlap. When members of an out-group are well integrated spatially, stratification is more difficult and costly because disinvestment in the out-group must occur on a person-by-person, family-by-family basis. Throughout history, therefore, whenever the powerful have sought to stigmatize and subordinate a particular social group, they have endeavored to confine its members to specific neighborhoods by law, edict, or practice (Wirth 1928).

The overlapping of social, cultural, economic, and spatial boundaries yields what Peter Blau (1977) calls a *consolidation of parameters*. When social parameters are consolidated—when social, economic, and spatial characteristics correlate strongly with one another—the process of stratification becomes sharper and more acute. Within a hypothetical social space made up of cells defined by the intersection of spatial status, social status, economic status, and cultural status, within-cell relations intensify and between-cell interactions attenuate. Over time, inter-cell mobility withers, social categories reify and reproduce themselves, and the social structure as a whole grows rigid. A society defined by consolidated parameters is thus one in which the categorical mechanisms of inequality operate very effectively and social boundaries are salient and difficult to cross, yielding "durable inequality," a structural state wherein stratification replicates and reproduces itself more or less automatically over time.

Markets and Stratification

The mechanisms of stratification described so far do not presuppose any particular economic system. They can function in a command economy, where property is owned by the state and decisions about production and consumption are made by central planners, or in a capitalist economy, where property is privately held and decisions about production and consumption are made by free and autonomous agents working through markets. Stratification and inequality are not created by capitalism, and the existence of markets does not guarantee inequality; nor does their absence preclude it. Markets are a human invention, and until recently most transactions occurred outside the market. Stratification has been with us, however, for millennia (Massey 2005a).

Markets are basically competitions between people that occur within socially constructed arenas according to socially defined rules using a socially accepted medium of exchange (Massey 2005b). By building the competitive arenas, defining the rules of play, and defining the media of exchange, societies bring markets into existence to facilitate the production, consumption, and distribution of goods and services. If markets are socially constructed by actors within the societies in which they are embedded, then there is no inherently correct number, distribution, or nature of markets. As societies change socially, demographically, and culturally, as new technologies emerge, and as new knowledge is created, the nature and number of markets change.

For transactions to occur, buyers and sellers must come together within a mutually accepted arena. Sometimes the arena is delimited physically (such as the trading pit in the New York Stock Exchange), and at other times it is geographically diffuse (as with NASDAQ, where securities are traded electronically in hyperspace). But competitive arenas are always defined *socially* by mutually agreed-upon rules, both formal and informal, that govern transactions. As markets have evolved and expanded, the rules have increasingly shifted from the informal to the formal realm (Carruthers and Babb 2000).

Formal rules are laws and regulations that are written down by political authorities to recognize private property, define the rights of buyers and sellers, establish a basis for the execution and enforcement of contracts, and define acceptable behaviors within a competitive arena. Informal rules are unwritten codes of conduct and practice that are implicitly understood by market participants and reinforced through mechanisms of enforceable trust such as ridicule, gossip, shaming, exclusion, and ostracism. Whereas some markets are predominantly formal (such as U.S. mortgage markets), others remain highly informal (for example, the global diamond trade). Most markets, however, remain mixtures of formal and informal mechanisms (jobs and hiring).

In addition to being supported by a social infrastructure of laws, regulations, expectations, and conventions, competitive arenas often require a physical infrastructure (Massey 2005b). The necessary infrastructure may be erected by public or private efforts, but it is generally achieved by a mixture of the two. Whereas private interests may finance the construction of factories to produce consumer goods, for example, the public builds highways and ports and subsidizes air and rail travel, which enables producers to bring the goods to market. A core responsibility of the state is to make sure, by some combination of public and private means, that the physical and social infrastructure necessary for markets is created and maintained.

The final task of the state is to establish a secure medium of exchange (Massey 2005b). The invention of something called "money" is not inherent in the logic of the market. Rather, the idea of money was invented independently and then imposed on markets through a long series of trials and errors that only gradually revealed the most effective course of action (Davies 2002). The earliest economic exchanges between human beings occurred through bartering, but as societies grew in size and scale and the volumes of the goods, services, and commodities being exchanged rose, bartering became increasingly cumbersome and inefficient.

The first coins were minted around 2,700 years ago, and for most of the past 2,000 years precious metals were used to define the media of exchange in most societies. With the advent of metal-backed currency, the value of any good, service, or commodity could be expressed according to a common metric. Price did not have to be negotiated independently for each exchange, nor did two sets of goods or commodities have to be shipped: one party could simply send money in payment for the later shipping and delivery of materials by the other party. As a result, transaction costs were dramatically reduced, transparency was increased, and the efficiency of markets was greatly enhanced.

Although the use of precious metals to create common currencies and consensual standards of exchange constituted a great advance over bartering, a major problem was that the money supply remained tied to the arbitrary supply of a particular metal rather than the needs of the market or its participants (Williams 1998). Economic expansion could be stunted if supplies of precious metals did not keep pace with the demand for currency, and inflation tended to follow from the discovery and exploitation of new ore deposits irrespective of the needs of the economy. Following the theoretical work of Milton Friedman (1956), governments around the world eventually abandoned precious metal standards and adopted monetarist policies that linked the supply of money to the level of economic output in the economy; in so doing, they were able to gain control over the relative inflation or deflation of the currency, thus solving a problem that had long bedeviled market economies.

Markets came into existence because human beings created social structures, innovated cultural understandings, built competitive arenas, defined formal and informal rules of competition, and specified media of exchange to allow for the production, distribution, and consumption of goods and services. Because markets are always embedded within a particular constellation of social institutions and cultural conventions (Granovetter 1985; Swedberg 2003), there is no single way to create a functioning market society and no unique architecture for successful market relations (Fligstein 2001; Hall and Soskice 2002; Whitley 1999). It all depends on the institutional context within which a market is working (Massey, Sanchez, and Behrman 2006).

From the viewpoint of stratification, the competitive arenas, rules of competition, and media of exchange may be structured by social actors so as to produce more or less inequality—either to maximize the opportunities for exploitation and opportunity hoarding or to minimize them. Whatever their institutional foundations, however, markets enhance the *potential* for stratification by increasing the total stock of material resources and multiplying the number of social categories across which they are distributed. Having more resources spread across a larger number of social categories yields greater inequality, and history has clearly shown that markets produce more wealth and income than other economic systems, other things equal.

Although economic growth under market mechanisms may increase the potential for stratification and inequality by accelerating income accumulation, wealth creation, and social differentiation relative to other economic systems, *how* the resulting wealth is distributed across categories within the underlying social structure is not predetermined. The distribution of material resources depends very much on choices made by social actors in creating the institutions and practices that underlie the market. Exploitation and opportunity hoarding may be built into the way a market functions if they are embedded within the institutional matrix that contains the market (Massey 2005b).

Categorical inequality results whenever those in power enact policies and practices to give certain groups more access to markets than others; offer competitive advantages to certain classes of people within markets; protect certain groups from market failures more often than others; invest more in the human capital of certain groups than others; and systematically channel social and cultural capital to certain categories of people. Historically, many social groups in the United States were excluded from markets as a matter of both formal policy and informal practice.

The U.S. Constitution, of course, was originally written to authorize the imposition of chattel slavery upon persons of African ancestry, thereby excluding them entirely from markets (Higgin-botham 1980, 1996). After the abolition of slavery, laws in southern states were written explicitly to prevent the formation of competitive labor markets in agriculture and, instead, to indenture black sharecroppers to white planters and landowners (Foner 1988). Women were effectively excluded from many occupations and markets until quite recently, as were various ethnic and racial groups (Farkas and England 1986; Schaefer 2005; Tilly 1994).

Even when they were allowed to participate in markets, moreover, minorities and women were often forced socially to compete on unfavorable terms, yielding wage discrimination, price discrimination, and a variety of categorical barriers to occupational mobility. Before the 1960s, it was perfectly legal to pay women and minorities less than white men for the same work; to deny public services to members of specific racial or ethnic groups; to prevent the entry of women into prestigious occupations; to prohibit the membership of women and minorities in favored social organizations; to refuse to rent or sell dwellings to people on the basis of race, ethnicity, or gender; and to deny credit and capital to people based on the same characteristics (Perlmutter 1999). Not only were these practices legal, but they were common and widely accepted by the American public (see Schuman et al. 1998).

Before people can compete effectively in markets, of course, they must be prepared for competition through the deliberate cultivation of human, social, and cultural capital. Human capabilities are generally created through some mixture of public and private auspices. The private institution most fundamentally and universally involved in producing capable human beings is the family (Folbre 2001). Within families, children are born, fed, housed, clothed, and taught. Within the confines of the family, people learn to walk, speak, behave, and think. As a result of structured instruction and unstructured emulation, children learn to value and follow certain patterns of thought and action and to devalue and shun others.

As the size and complexity of human populations have increased, however, other social institutions have assumed larger roles in the creation and enhancement of human capabilities, and in the last quarter of the twentieth century the importance of nonfamily institutions increased dramatically (Massey 2005a). Industrialization created new needs for literate workers and led governments to require and provide primary and secondary schooling to citizens on a mass basis. The recent shift to a knowledge-based information economy has further accelerated the rate of investment in post-graduate education, research, and lifetime training. In advanced market societies, a critical responsibility of government is to ensure levels of education and training that not only will permit citizens to participate effectively in a growing array of complex markets but also will promote the sustained growth of income and the continued creation of wealth in a competitive global economy.

For much of American history, most African Americans were relegated by law to a separate educational system that was poorly funded, meagerly staffed, and badly organized; the huge racial differentials in the quantity and quality of education that resulted left most black citizens unprepared for successful competition within markets. Although the legal foundations of school segregation were eliminated beginning in 1954, a variety of de facto mechanisms continue to operate to deny African Americans, Latinos, the poor, and other social groups equal access to education (Anderson and Byrne 2004). The lack of equal access to high-quality education continues to be a major engine of stratification in the United States (Kozol 1991, 2005).

In addition to inculcating knowledge, the other major investment that governments make in creating human capital comes in the form of health. As educational levels have risen, post-industrial societies have spent higher shares of their wealth and income to prolong life and improve health, thus protecting their investment in human capital and lengthening the period over which this investment is amortized. In the United States, however, spending on health care continues to be uneven, displaying large inequities by race, class, and ethnicity (Quadagno 2005; Smedley, Stith, and Nelson 2002), and these categorical inequities are associated with large intergroup differentials with respect to morbidity, mortality, and life expectancy (Kawachi and Kennedy 2002).

Finally, markets can never achieve all the goals that citizens would like to see accomplished, nor are they foolproof mechanisms for the seamless production, distribution, and consumption of resources. The history of capitalism is replete with examples of failed, missing, and ineffective markets. Although improvements in institutions and technology have reduced the depth and frequency of market failures, the hazard can never be eliminated entirely from a capitalist economy. In response, most developed nations have erected social "safety nets"—aid programs such as unemployment insurance, welfare payments, medical insurance, old-age benefits, and food subsidies—to prevent citizens from falling too far down the economic ladder. Once again, however, the eligibility rules and regulations for social benefits in the United States were historically written to exclude certain social groups and favor others. In enacting most of the social welfare provisions of the New Deal, for example, laws were written in such a way as to minimize participation by African Americans (Katznelson 2005; Quadagno 1994).

Understanding Stratification

In the United States, as in other countries throughout the world, markets did not arise out of neutral institutional matrices that guaranteed equal opportunity to all; instead, they were embedded in a social structure that was itself riddled with categorical inequalities based on race, class, and gender. Indeed, much of the nation's history consists of a struggle to eradicate exploitation and opportunity hoarding along group lines and move the United States toward greater conformity with its founding principles. It took a bloody civil war to end slavery and a violent civil rights struggle to dismantle Jim Crow, and it has only been about forty years since exclusion and discrimination on the basis of race, gender, and national origin were formally prohibited from most markets and institutions.

In the next chapter, I set the stage for a more systematic evaluation of the mechanisms of American stratification by examining trends in market outcomes, paying particular attention to differentials along the traditional axes of categorical inequality—race, class, and gender. In two subsequent chapters, I go on to consider how the categorical mechanisms that produce and reproduce racial inequality have evolved in recent years, focusing first on African Americans and then on Mexican Americans. In the following chapter, I describe the institutional foundations of class inequality by contrasting the structure and organization of the American political economy before and after 1975. In the subsequent chapter, I build on this understanding to analyze the institutional underpinnings of gender inequality and how they have changed since the 1970s. In the final chapter, I conclude by considering how race-based, class-based, and gender-based mechanisms of stratification combine in the present day to make the United States the most unequal society in the developed world.

❧ Chapter 2 ❧

The Rise and Fall
of Egalitarian Capitalism

The twentieth century was notable for its accelerated rate of change. Never in the course of a mere one hundred years did human beings have to adapt to so many technological, social, cultural, and economic shifts. Empires that had existed for hundreds and even thousands of years collapsed; new empires came into existence and themselves crumbled; vast areas of the earth were colonized and then decolonized; new nations proliferated in the wake of collapsed empires and decolonized lands; nations industrialized; the world urbanized; new transnational institutions came into existence; and in the course of these massive transformations millions upon millions of people died through warfare, genocide, starvation, and disease (Gilbert 2001).

The initial decade of the twentieth century witnessed the culmination of a first wave of globalization. Between 1800 and 1914, the international circulation of goods, capital, people, and resources grew steadily as industrialization spread across the face of Europe and hopscotched to its extensions overseas (Hatton and Williamson 1998; Kenwood and Lougheed 1992; O'Rourke and Williamson 1999). Economic interconnection between nations grew faster than their political integration, however, and the rudimentary multilateral institutions of 1914 proved unable to manage the shifting balances of power, leading to a catastrophic world war that staggered the first global economy.

As the fog of war lifted, nations experimented with a variety of new political structures in an effort to overcome the perceived defects of laissez-faire capitalism (Timmer and Williamson 1998). Germany, Italy, and Japan embraced a state-centered system known as fascism; the Soviet Union adopted a command economy under communism; and Western democracies all adopted protectionist policies in a vain attempt to create autonomous economies insulated from the troubles of the world (James 2001). The erection of barriers to trade, investment, and immigration backfired, however, and ultimately triggered the serial collapse of all national economies, bringing the global economy to a standstill and setting the stage for another world war, even bloodier than the first, in which communist and capitalist nations joined forces to defeat fascism.

In the new world order that emerged from the Great Depression and the Second World War, the United States assumed the mantle of global leadership and took the initiative in building a new set of national and international institutions. Within the nation, President Franklin D. Roosevelt transformed the American political economy in ways that simultaneously promoted greater economic growth and more equality. Tax rates on the rich were increased, and the resulting revenues were used to support the expansion of the federal government into a range of new domains—regulating markets, managing industrial relations, assisting workers, protecting consumers, increasing education, promoting research, and erecting a rudimentary but functional safety net for the elderly and the poor.

On the international scene, President Harry S. Truman saw to the creation of a new set of multilateral institutions to promote global peace while achieving national prosperity through trade, investment, and the movement of ideas and people across borders. While the United Nations and its various agencies worked to prevent the catastrophe of another world war and to promote greater international cooperation, the World Bank financed the reconstruction of Europe and Japan and then began to promote economic development in the developing world. The International Monetary Fund (IMF) guaranteed the convertibility of currencies and ensured international liquidity to prevent recurrent monetary crises, and the General Agreement on Tariffs and Trade (GATT) worked to lower barriers to the international exchange of goods, capital, commodities, and services.

From 1945 to the mid-1970s, both national and international institutions functioned remarkably well to prevent global war, increase trade and investment, and promote economic growth, first in the United States and then in Europe, Japan, and Australia, and finally in portions of the developing world, notably Asia. Postwar progress rested on a political economy that invested heavily in financial, human, and social capital to produce standardized industrial goods that were sold on mass consumer markets at home and abroad. Standards of living rose rapidly in core capitalist nations, median incomes increased, inequality fell, and average citizens came to know the benefits of what John Kenneth Galbraith (1958) called "the affluent society" and Lane Kenworthy (2004) has labeled "egalitarian capitalism."

Beginning in the 1970s, however, simultaneous revolutions in telecommunications and computation combined with a global energy crisis to transform advanced nations from industrial to post-industrial societies. In the new political economy, wealth was not created by producing standardized manufactured goods for mass consumer markets, but by developing new knowledge and manipulating information to produce a range of specialized goods and services targeted to specific niches within a new global marketplace (Harvey 1991). With the collapse of the Soviet Union, the decisive turn of China away from a command economy, and the institutionalization of multilateral trade through the World Trade Organization (WTO), economic activity was for the first time integrated on a truly global scale (Friedman 2000, 2005).

The growing size of product markets and the increasing scale of financial markets interacted with falling costs of transportation and communication as well as dramatic increases in computing power to produce a new and remarkable burst of wealth creation (Phillips 2002). These dramatic shifts, however, put new pressure on social institutions that had been developed in the industrial era to promote popular welfare within self-sufficient and relatively autonomous nation-states. Although vastly more wealth and income were being created through the global spread of technology, the revival of international trade, and the application of post-industrial social organization to production, the material resources being created were distributed much more unequally than before, bringing about an abrupt end to four decades of egalitarian capitalism.

The Great U-Turn

The 1970s was the watershed period in this transformation, which was rooted in three powerful developments: computerization, market expansion, and fragmentation. The cybernetic revolution profoundly altered the nature and organization of economic production. During the 1970s and early 1980s, computerization swept through manufacturing. Older factories that had once employed thousands of well-paid, unionized workers were replaced by new, capital-intensive plants where a few workers operated automated, continuous-flow production lines monitored by computers assisted by robots. Manufacturing productivity soared, and those plants that could not compete either closed their doors or relocated to low-wage areas overseas. Employment in manufacturing plummeted, especially in older urban areas (Kasarda 1995), and as industrial jobs declined, so did union membership, thus undercutting the bargaining position of workers (Freeman 1993).

While manufacturing bore the brunt of the cybernetic revolution during the 1970s and early 1980s, the technological steam roller hit the service sector in the late 1980s and early 1990s (Rifkin 1995). Large, bureaucratic organizations filled with midlevel white-collar workers gave way to reengineered, downsized, and flattened organizations that were "lean and mean" (Harrison 1995). Making use of new, ultra-fast computer chips and fiber optics, programmers wrote software that obviated the need for human intervention; service workers were replaced with canned algorithms and user-friendly interfaces controlled directly by managers or consumers. Armed with these new cybernetic tools, one modestly trained technician could perform all of the tasks formerly carried out by scores of expensive, white-collar workers, often in a fraction of the time and usually at a fraction of the cost. During the 1990s, the era of the gray flannel suit gave way to the period of the pink slip as corporations shed midlevel bureaucrats by the thousands (Uchitelle 2006).

As computers transformed productivity in manufacturing and services, they also expanded the geographic reach of markets during the 1980s and 1990s, leading to the globalization of factor markets. As investors scoured the world incessantly looking for companies and countries that offered higher returns to their capital, workers in developed nations found themselves competing in a global hiring hall that pitted them against billions of ambitious but much poorer workers in the developing world.

The globalization of markets for capital and labor was facilitated by the rising speed of telecommunications, the declining costs of transportation, the growing ease and rapidity of international movement, the increasing importance of smaller and lighter products, and the rising importance of knowledge and information in the productive process (Friedman 2005). If the owners of capital could find more attractive prospects in one nation or disliked developments in another, they had the ability to shift billions of dollars across international borders in a nanosecond (Friedman 2000). Likewise, if producers based in developed nations needed to reduce labor costs, they could easily relocate factories to developing nations overseas—or they could simply wait for immigrants from these countries to show up at their factory gates.

A final feature of the post-industrial economic order is the fragmentation of consumer markets (Harvey 1991). From 1870 to 1970, nations in general and the United States in particular prospered because companies were able to manufacture and sell standardized goods to mass markets of middle-class consumers whose incomes were rising but whose tastes were homogeneous. Products became more affordable because economies of scale reduced their price, and consumer markets grew because mass production required armies of well-paid, unionized workers to staff the manufacturing apparatus and legions of salaried, white-collar workers to administer it (Maddrick 1995).

Since the 1970s, however, international competition, technological innovation, and demographic shifts have fragmented formerly integrated and homogeneous mass markets. In response, firms have developed new strategies to cater to small, specialized bundles of consumers, relying on innovative techniques of flexible production, just-in-time delivery, outsourcing, subcontracting, and continuous-flow production. Under the old industrial regime, companies were large, hierarchies were deep, authority was rigid, markets were massive, tastes were homogeneous, and companies were slow to respond to shifts in consumer demand. In the new post-industrial order, companies became lean, hierarchies flattened, authority grew more flexible, markets segmented, and demand diversified. Successful companies were those that could move quickly to anticipate constantly shifting demand, yielding an intense segmentation of labor markets and downward pressure on wages (Harrison 1995).

The forces of computerization, market expansion, and fragmentation operated in a mutually reinforcing fashion, feeding off one another to bring about a profound change in the economic structure of particular nations and the world. The depth of this shift is suggested by figure 2.1, which draws upon data developed by Thomas Piketty and Emmanuel Saez (2003) using special tabulations of U.S. income tax returns to estimate the share of income going to different segments of the taxpaying distribution. Specifically, the figure shows the percentage of income going to the three wealthiest segments of U.S. taxpayers over eight decades from 1922 to 2002: the top 10 percent, the top 5 percent, and the top 1 percent. The higher the percentage of income going to each of these categories, the more unequal the distribution of income.

The period has been divided into four broad eras for heuristic purposes, beginning with the era of laissez-faire capitalism in the 1920s. During this period, the richest 10 percent of American taxpayers earned about 45 percent of all income, the top 5 percent earned 30 to 35 percent, and the top 1 percent earned 15 to 20 percent. Those at the top of the income distribution were doing very well indeed, but the Roaring Twenties came to a sudden end with the collapse of the American stock market in late 1929, which triggered the Great Depression of the 1930s, which, in turn, brought about a political realignment in the United States that yielded twenty years of Democratic administrations, first under Franklin D.

Figure 2.1   Share of Income Earned by Top Segments of
              Taxpayer Income Distribution, 1922 to 2002

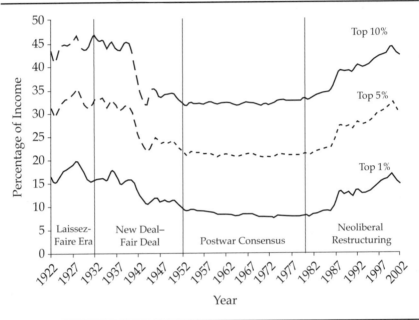

Source: Piketty and Saez (2003).

Roosevelt and his New Deal and then under Harry S. Truman and his Fair Deal.

The economic policies of both "Deals," in combination with strong deflationary pressures during the 1930s and the Second World War, led to a remarkable compression of the income distribution and a sharp decline of inequality during the 1940s (Goldin and Margo 1992). By 1952, when Republicans finally reoccupied the White House, the share of income going to the top 10 percent of taxpayers had fallen from 45 percent to 32 percent; that going to the top 5 percent had dropped from 35 percent to 21 percent; and that accruing to the top 1 percent had declined from 20 percent to 10 percent. These figures represent respective declines of roughly 30, 40, and 50 percent from the peak levels of inequality in 1928 measured by Piketty and Saez.

Despite the return to Republican Party rule, however, a bipartisan consensus prevailed with respect to economic policy, and despite periodic attempts to roll back policies enacted under Roosevelt and Truman, the political economy of the New and Fair Deals remained largely intact and enjoyed broad public, bipartisan support through the Eisenhower presidency (McCarty, Poole, and Rosenthal 2006). There was no return to the elevated levels of inequality that had prevailed in the era of laissez-faire capitalism. Indeed, for three decades, from 1942 through 1972, the shares of income going to the top 10 percent and top 5 percent of taxpayers held fairly steady at 30 to 32 percent and 20 to 21 percent, respectively, while the share going to the top 1 percent trended slowly downward to reach 7.7 percent in 1973. In the prior year, the share of income going to the top 5 percent reached its lowest level ever at 20.4 percent, and two years before that the share going to the top 10 percent reached its nadir at 31.5 percent. After 1973, there would be no further declines in the share of income going to the three top categories.

Indeed, over the remainder of the 1970s the share of income going to wealthy taxpayers edged slowly upward and then exploded in the 1980s and 1990s, a shift that Bennett Harrison and Barry Bluestone (1988) call "the Great U-Turn." The rate of change increased after Ronald Reagan's election to the presidency, moderated somewhat under George H. W. Bush, and then accelerated once again under President Bill Clinton. The share of income going to the top 10 percent of taxpayers rose from 32.9 percent in 1980 to 38.6 percent in 1988, then crept up to 39.6 percent in 1992 before rising rapidly to 43.9 percent in the year 2000, roughly the percentage that prevailed in the late 1920s. Rising inequality after 1973 was thus a bipartisan affair, stemming from deep structural changes in the political economy rather than monetary or fiscal policies associated with a particular administration, be it Democratic or Republican.

After 1973, the higher up in the income distribution one looks, the greater the reconcentration of income. Whereas the share of income earned by the top 10 percent of taxpayers grew by 31 percent between 1973 and 2000, the share going to the top 5 percent rose by 45 percent, and that going to the top 1 percent nearly doubled, rising by 91 percent. In simple but stark terms, by the end of the twentieth century all of the declines in inequality achieved under the New and Fair Deals had been wiped out and the United States had unambiguously returned to levels of inequality not seen since the laissez-faire era of the 1920s.

Stratification's Holy Trinity

The foregoing analysis clearly suggests that *something* very dramatic happened in the U.S. political economy in the 1970s. Something must have occurred to cause the great U-turn. As outlined in the opening chapter, high levels of income inequality are neither necessary nor inevitable by-products of a market economy, irrespective of whether that market is global or national in scope. Inequalities in the distribution of material resources substantially predate the advent of markets and are rooted in categorical mechanisms that operate on specific social groups to extract their labor under exploitative terms and to channel opportunities, resources, and benefits toward favored categories. The difference between a market society and other political economies is that under capitalism categorical mechanisms of inequality, in addition to existing outside the market, are often built into the social organization of the market itself—they are embedded within its laws, regulations, conventions, understandings, and institutions, both formal and informal.

An accurate understanding of any system of stratification necessarily begins with the identification of *which* social groups experience the categorical mechanisms of exploitation and exclusion. Having specified which social groups are likely to be subject to such inequality-producing mechanisms, we find that it becomes much easier to identify and describe the institutional manifestations and social practices that effect them. At least we will know where to look. Thus, a natural place to begin a study of stratification in the United States is to consider trends in the economic status of social groups known to have suffered historically from exclusion and discrimination. Social structures and processes are characterized by considerable inertia and do not change overnight. As a result, groups that experienced inequality in the past are likely to continue to do so in the future, even though the stratifying mechanisms may change.

As Rogers Smith (1997) points out, a curious paradox of U.S. history is that a large fraction of Americans have historically been denied political and economic rights in a nation ostensibly dedicated to individual liberty and equality under the law. Well into the nineteenth century, states and localities restricted voting rights to property owners and taxpayers, thus disenfranchising the poor. African Americans, of course, were enslaved without any political or social rights until 1865, and women did not acquire the right to vote until 1920. It was perfectly legal to discriminate against both groups in markets for labor, housing, services, insurance, credit, and capital until the 1960s and 1970s, and the poor as well as minorities were routinely disenfranchised politically through poll taxes and literacy tests.

Given this set of historical realities, researchers have traditionally focused on three categorical distinctions that together make up the holy trinity of stratification—race, class, and gender. The importance of these dimensions within the United States is indicated by the structure of the American Sociological Association, an organization whose members largely devote themselves to studying stratification. Although stratification is arguably the subject area of greatest interest to sociologists, the ASA does not have a section on the sociology of stratification. What the association does have are sections on the sociology of sex and gender, Asians and Asian Americans, Latinos and Latinas, and racial and ethnic minorities and one section devoted specifically to the interaction of race, gender, and class. Understanding the American stratification system must therefore begin with an appreciation for ongoing inequalities between majority and minority, men and women, rich and poor.

Race

No cleavage looms larger in U.S. history than the chasm of race. To illustrate this fact, figure 2.2 plots median incomes (in constant 2002 dollars) earned by white, black, and Latino households between 1972 and 2002. (Because annual income data for Asians are not

Figure 2.2   Median Household Income, 1967 to 2003

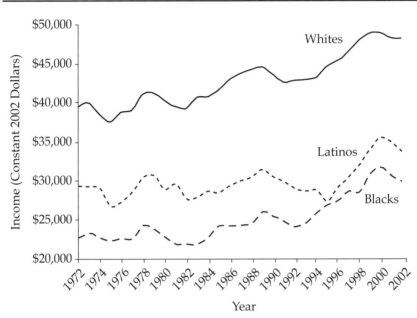

Source: U.S. Bureau of the Census.

available until the 1990s, they are not considered here.) Although white and black households both experienced rising incomes over the period, very little progress was made in closing the racial gap, despite policies and programs instituted during and after the civil rights era. In real terms, the size of the racial gap actually *grew* from 1972 to 1988, going from $16,700 to $19,700 before falling back to $18,000, around which it has fluctuated ever since. In other words, three decades of affirmative action efforts and antidiscrimination policies have not closed the gap between black and white incomes. To put it bluntly, racial inequality remains a basic feature of the U.S. stratification system.

Since the civil rights era, of course, the United States has changed demographically in rather dramatic ways, and Latinos recently overtook African Americans as the nation's largest minority. Historically, Latinos occupied a position in the American stratification system somewhere in between whites and blacks. As of 1972, for example, white households earned a median income of $39,300 compared with a black median of $22,600, and Latinos fell close to the midpoint of this gap at $29,300. (The true midpoint was $30,950.) This intermediate position was maintained until 1989, when Latino income began to fall even as black income rose, leading to convergence in the two medians around 1995.

Although Latino fortunes improved somewhat thereafter, the income growth was not enough to compensate for ground lost earlier, and as of 2002 the Latino-black income gap stood at $3,300 in constant dollars, compared to a differential that was twice as large ($6,600) thirty years earlier. These data are consistent with corresponding figures on poverty. Poverty rates of African Americans and Latinos have been virtually identical since 1993, whereas before that date the rate for Latinos was five to six points lower than the black rate. Apparently the place of Latinos in the American stratification system changed in the late 1980s and early 1990s. *Something* happened to depress the incomes of Latinos and push them downward in the income distribution to a position much closer to that of African Americans.

Class

The taxpayer data summarized earlier clearly showed that after 1973 the rich got progressively richer. But what of the poor and the middle classes? Figure 2.3 answers this question by showing mean incomes (in constant dollars) reported by households at the top, middle, and bottom segments of the income distribution. These data refer to all households in the United States. The bottom segment of the distribution is represented by the 20 percent of U.S. households with the lowest incomes, the middle is indicated by the median household income (the fiftieth percentile), and the top is indicated by the 20 percent of U.S. households with the highest incomes. The very top of the distribution is represented by the 5 percent of U.S. households with the highest incomes.

The divergent fortunes of upper-, middle-, and lower-class

Figure 2.3   Average Constant Income Earned by Households at
               Different Points in the Income Distribution, 1967 to
               2002

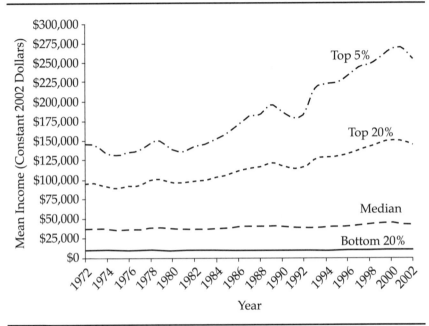

Source: U.S. Bureau of the Census.

households after the great U-turn are clearly indicated in the figure. Whereas the incomes of households at the bottom of the distribution stagnated and the median inched slowly upward, incomes at the top of the distribution rose dramatically. Among households in the lowest quintile, for example, average income stood at $8,800 in 1972 and had risen to $10,200 by 2002, an increase of $1,400, or 16 percent, in twenty years. Those at the middle of the income distribution fared little better. Over three decades, the median household income grew from $37,000 to $43,400, for a real gain of $6,400, or 17 percent. In contrast, average income for the highest quintile increased by 66 percent, going from $88,700 in 1972 to $147,000 in 2002, for a real gain of $58,300.

Figure 2.3 illustrates a basic feature of inequality in the post-industrial era: the higher up in the income distribution one goes, the greater the economic improvement over time. Whereas the top 20 percent of households enjoyed a 66 percent increase in income from 1972 to 2002, the top 5 percent of households were blessed with a 77 percent gain. According to Piketty and Saez (2003), taxpayers in the ninetieth to ninety-fifth percentiles increased their share of total income by 3 percent between 1980 and 1998, those in the ninety-fifth to ninety-ninth percentiles increased theirs by 14 percent, and the share for those in the top 1 percent rose by 36 percent. These figures do not include capital gains, and once this source of income is taken into account, the top 1 percent are found to have increased their share of income by a remarkable 80 percent over eighteen years!

Thus, against a backdrop of persisting stratification between blacks and whites and growing inequality between Latinos and whites, class stratification has risen even more. Although poor and middle-class households may not have gotten much poorer in absolute terms after 1973, they steadily lost ground to earners at the top of the distribution and fell much further behind in relative terms. In post-industrial America, the rich got richer while the poor languished and the middle class struggled to keep up. The intensity of their struggle is difficult to appreciate from these data, however, because household incomes do not reveal how many people worked or for how many hours. To understand these dynamics, we must turn to trends in personal income, a topic approached here through the lens of gender stratification.

Gender

As already noted, well into the twentieth century women were second-class citizens politically, and only since the 1960s have they not been second-class citizens economically. Until the 1960s, women were routinely excluded from high-paying professions such as law, business, and medicine, as well as from skilled blue-collar jobs, especially those represented by unions. Women instead were confined to the "pink-collar ghetto" of occupations devoted to personal service and "caring labor"—work that served the emotional, physical, or developmental needs of others (England 1992, 2005).

Under this regime, poor women generally worked as maids, waitresses, or nannies, and middle-class women worked as nurses, secretaries, or teachers (Charles and Grusky 2004). Within any job category, the higher the percentage of women the lower the wages paid, holding constant numerous attributes of the job and the workers themselves (Kilbourne et al. 1994; Karlin, England, and Richardson 2002; England, Thompson, and Aman 2001).

To assess the economic progress of women during the second half of the twentieth century, figure 2.4 presents the median incomes of males and females from 1947 to 2002. Figure 2.5 complements these data by displaying the ratio of female-to-male median income over the same period. Figure 2.4 reveals that the postwar economic boom improved income for both men and women as each gender category experienced a rising median income. It is quite clear, however, that male incomes rose much faster than female incomes, causing women steadily to lose economic ground to men until the mid-1960s. Whereas the female median income rose by 18 percent between 1947 and 1967, going from $7,100 to $8,400, male income rose much faster, going from $15,600 to $25,900, an increase of 66 percent. This differential caused a precipitous drop in the ratio of female-to-male income. Whereas the average woman received almost half of what the average man did in 1947 (46 percent), by 1967 she got only one-third as much (32 percent).

The good news is that after the 1960s female incomes began rising relative to those of males—slowly at first, but with increasing speed during the 1970s and 1980s. From a value of 0.32 in 1967, the ratio of female-to-male income climbed steadily to reach .57 in 2002. The bad news is that this improvement occurred not because of any significant growth in female income but because of the stagnation of male incomes. Female income was essentially flat between 1973 and 1982, and male income actually declined in real terms. Growth resumed for females from 1982 to1992, but not for males. Only after 1990 did male incomes begin to improve once again, and those received by females rose more quickly, so women continued to pick up ground on men.

In terms of gender stratification, therefore, women's gains since 1970 have come less from real improvements in their own status

Figure 2.4   Median Personal Income Earned by Males and
Females, 1947 to 2002

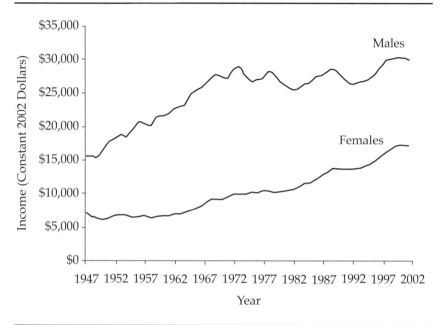

Source: U.S. Bureau of the Census.

than from a deterioration in the economic position of men. In 1973 the median personal income for males stood at $28,900; thirty years later it was only $29,900, a real increase of only $1,000, or 3.5 percent. Among women, median personal income rose from $10,000 in 1973 to $17,300 in 2003, an increase of $7,300, or 73 percent. Although this pay raise is nothing to scoff at, thirty years of progress still leaves the average woman receiving less income than the average male got back in 1951, and 43 percent less than that of the average male today.

Earlier we noted that median household income rose by 17 percent from 1972 to 2002. Given that male median income rose by only 3.5 percent over the same period, there is only one reasonable explanation for the continued increase in household income during

Figure 2.5   Female Personal Income as a Proportion of Male
                Personal Income, 1947 to 2002

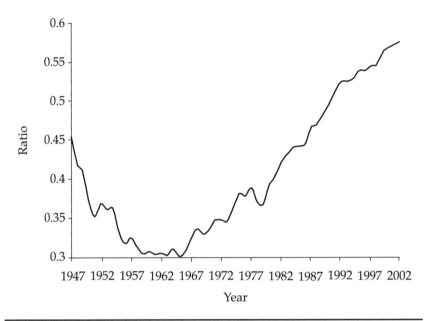

Source: U.S. Bureau of the Census.

a period of stagnant male income: female household members entered the labor force in large numbers to generate additional income that offset the declining fortunes of men. Although middle-
income households managed to achieve modest income gains after
the great U-turn, more household members—usually wives—had
to work to do so. In other words, in the post-industrial political
economy of the United States, it increasingly requires two earners
for a household to remain in the middle class.

The importance of having two incomes is illustrated in figure 2.6,
which shows the change in median income since 1987 among one-
and two-earner households. Naturally, two-earner households
have more income than those with one breadwinner, but we are in-
terested in relative change, not absolute amounts, so each series has
been divided by its value in 1987 to indicate proportional growth

Figure 2.6   Incomes of One- and Two-Earner Households
                Relative to Their Values in 1987

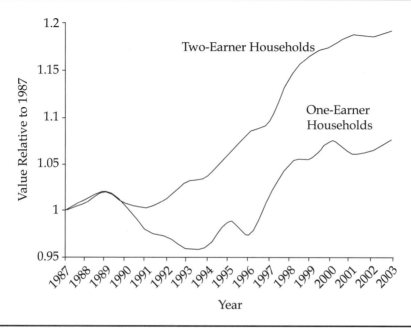

Source: U.S. Bureau of the Census.

since that date. As can be seen, from 1987 through 1990 the incomes of one- and two-earner households moved together, but thereafter they began to depart. The recession of the early 1990s hit all households hard, but whereas two-earner households saw their incomes drop, they never dipped below the median for 1987, and by 1992 they had begun to rebound. In contrast, the median income of one-earner households fell to 96 percent of the 1987 value and did not make it back to parity until 1997. Thus, one-earner households experienced an entire decade with no growth in income, whereas two-earner households were able to hang on during the recession and increase their incomes by 10 percent by 1997. By the year 2003, two-earner households enjoyed a median income that was 19 percent above what they reported in 1987, whereas the median income earned by one-worker households was only 8 percent more.

Women did not enter the workforce only to offset the declining incomes of husbands, brothers, and fathers, of course. Female education rose, the age of marriage declined, fertility fell, and feminism legitimated and encouraged women's labor force participation (Bianchi and Spain 1986). At the same time, divorce rates rose: women could no longer assume that a husband would support them throughout their lives (Becker 1991). Among American women, these changes increased the opportunity costs of *not* working. Nonetheless, elevated rates of male unemployment and stagnant male incomes provided a strong additional incentive for married women to enter the labor force, whatever was happening in terms of the women's liberation movement.

Reflecting this material incentive, rates of female labor force participation increased most rapidly during and after periods of male income stagnation. Moreover, once a higher rate had been achieved, female participation did not go back down when male earning prospects improved; it only increased at a somewhat slower pace. This interplay between male income and female employment is shown in figure 2.7, which plots median male income relative to its 1987 value, along with the annual rate of female labor force participation relative to its 1987 value. The stagnation of male incomes is indicated by the fact that from 1973 through 1997 men experienced no increase in real personal income at all. Over the same period, the rate of female labor force participation increased by roughly one-third, going from 42 percent in 1973 to 60 percent in 1997.

Despite the relative stagnation in male income over time, however, there were nonetheless peaks and valleys in the trend. As shown in the figure, local peaks in male income growth occurred in 1978, 1989, and 2000. In each case, as male income rebounded, the increase in female labor force participation fell off; after male incomes once more declined and bottomed out, rapid growth in female labor force participation resumed. In particular, the surge in male incomes during the 1990s was accompanied by a marked slowing down and leveling off of female labor force expansion, despite the fact that after 1996 welfare mothers were being pushed by new public policies into the workforce.

Figure 2.7   Trends in Female Labor Force Participation and
              Male Personal Income

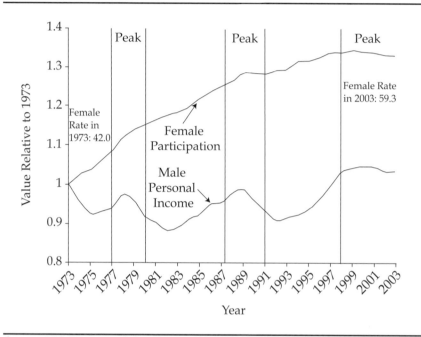

Source: U.S. Bureau of the Census.

America's New Inequality

The purpose of this chapter has been to provide a general description of what happened to Americans with respect to income stratification during the twentieth century. As we have noted, the past one hundred years have been tumultuous for both the world and the United States, including two periods of globalization, both accompanied by massive shifts in trade, investment, population, and social structure. The first era of globalization was accompanied by high levels of inequality that in the United States peaked in the late 1920s, when the effects of the First World War, isolationism, and protectionism brought national and global economies crashing down.

The ensuing depression, political realignment, and a second world war brought about a marked change in the structure and organization of the market and ushered in a long period of egalitarian capitalism during which inequality fell, economies grew, and the incomes of the poor and middle classes increased relative to those of the affluent. Inequality fell sharply in the 1930s and 1940s and continued to edge slowly downward throughout the 1950s and 1960s. Income rose for workers no matter what segment of the distribution they belonged to. The political economy enacted during the New Deal and Fair Deal enjoyed bipartisan and widespread public support as it promoted economic expansion while mitigating the pressures for inequality emanating from the market.

The era of egalitarian capitalism came to an end in the 1970s as inflation raged, real incomes stagnated, unemployment rose, and inequality stopped declining. The 1970s brought about a dramatic U-turn in American stratification, and thereafter income inequality rose at an accelerating pace until at century's end all the equality-producing achievements of the New and Fair Deals had been wiped out and levels of income inequality had returned to those last seen in the heyday of laissez-faire capitalism during the 1920s. The United States is now vastly more unequal than it was just thirty years ago.

The forces of computerization, market expansion, and segmentation structurally transformed the United States and other nations into post-industrial societies characterized by the centrality of knowledge, information, and services to economic growth. This transformation, along with a demographic shift to older age structures, put new pressure on the political, economic, and social structures that had been developed in the industrial era to protect the poor and middle classes from the market's downside. Consistent with the conceptualization of inequality as resulting from categorical mechanisms of exploitation and exclusion embedded within the institutions that undergird the market, the benefits and hardships of the new political economy have not been shared equally across social groups.

As a result, in the years since 1973 the economic fortunes of people at the top, middle, and bottom of the income distribution have increasingly diverged. Households in the top 20 percent of earners experienced steadily rising incomes, and the higher up in the income distribution one goes, the greater the increase in material well-being. After experiencing stagnant incomes during the 1970s, households in the middle of the income distribution were able to eke out modest gains thereafter, but only because of the massive entry of women into the labor force to bolster sagging male incomes, which in real terms fell and did not come back to their 1973 value until the end of the 1990s. The bottom fifth of the income distribution experienced little income growth after 1973, irrespective of the number of earners. Although the poor and middle classes may not have been growing poorer in absolute terms, they were falling further and further behind those in the top fifth of the income distribution. Class stratification had returned with a vengeance.

In addition to the poor, two other social groups have historically been vulnerable to the processes of categorical inequality in the United States: women and minorities, especially African Americans. It is thus not surprising that economic fortunes after the great U-turn also diverged substantially by race, ethnicity, and gender. Despite the passage of federal legislation to outlaw discrimination on the basis of race, along with the implementation of affirmative action policies to overcome the legacy of exclusion, racial stratification has proved remarkably tenacious and the black-white income gap has hardly changed. If anything, it widened slightly during the 1970s and early 1980s, going from around $16,000 to $18,000. Although Latinos historically occupied an intermediate position in the American stratification system, during the late 1980s and early 1990s their economic situation deteriorated until they were roughly on par with African Americans.

Even during the golden years of egalitarian capitalism, moreover, the economic status of working women deteriorated relative to that of working men because of wage discrimination and exclusion from the most lucrative occupations. As noted, from 1947 to 1967 the ratio of female-to-male wages fell sharply, from 46 percent to 32 percent. This fact, along with de facto discrimination against minorities in the North and legalized discrimination in the South, suggests that the egalitarian capitalism created under the New and

Fair Deals was in many ways not all that egalitarian. Until the 1960s, rising incomes and declining inequality were confined mainly to households headed by white males and came at the expense of subordinated women and minorities.

After 1967 women's rates of labor force participation rose along with their personal incomes. The labor force participation rate for women rose from 44 percent to 60 percent between 1973 and 2003, while median personal income grew from $10,000 to $17,000. Over the same period, female incomes relative to those of males increased from 35 percent to 58 percent. In terms of personal income, therefore, men and women came to be substantially more equal. Unfortunately, this improvement came as much from the stagnation of male incomes as from an improvement in female incomes. As of 2003, the average female worker was making as much money in real terms as the average male had achieved way back in 1951.

One of the paradoxical features of the new inequality is that over the past three decades membership in the middle class, and even in the affluent classes, has come increasingly to require two incomes generated by jointly working husbands and wives—at a time when rates of marital dissolution were rising, out-of-wedlock births were increasing, and single-parent households were proliferating. Given that women bear a disproportionate share of the burden in bearing, raising, and supporting children, and that African Americans display far higher rates of unwed childbearing and marital dissolution than other groups, both of these groups are at elevated risk of poverty, a fact that underscores the centrality of the trinity of race, class, and gender in understanding the system of American stratification.

❧ CHAPTER 3 ❧

REWORKING THE COLOR LINE

The American civil rights movement came together in the 1950s, culminated in the 1960s, and wound down in the 1970s. The bookend events that define this era in U.S. history are the 1954 *Brown v. Board of Education* decision, in which the Supreme Court overturned the doctrine of "separate but equal," and the 1977 Community Reinvestment Act, in which Congress outlawed the practice of redlining—denying people mortgages because of the race of their neighbors. In the nearly quarter-century between these two legal landmarks, nearly all of the nation's major civil rights initiatives were enacted.

Most of the action occurred in the 1960s. The 1964 Civil Rights Act prohibited discrimination in employment, outlawed discrimination in services, and mandated faster action on school desegregation. The 1965 Voting Rights Act affirmed black political rights and empowered federal authorities to intervene at the state level to guarantee them. The 1968 Fair Housing Act forbade discrimination in the rental or sale of housing. In 1969 Richard Nixon took Lyndon Johnson's executive order mandating "affirmative" hiring in federal employment and applied it to private contractors to make hiring targets and race-sensitive recruitment methods standard in American labor markets (Skrentny 1996).

Progress continued in the 1970s, though at a slower pace. In 1974 Congress passed the Equal Credit Opportunity Act, which outlawed discrimination in home lending, and followed up in 1975 with the Home Mortgage Disclosure Act, which required banks to publish data on the location of properties for which loans had been granted and denied. The Community Reinvestment Act of 1977 provided the final icing on the civil rights cake by banning the color coding of neighborhoods for creditworthiness based on racial composition. The civil rights revolution was complete.

At least so it seemed to many. Discrimination had been prohibited in public and private practice, and black political rights were federally protected. So profound did the civil rights revolution appear that some took to calling it "the second reconstruction" (Bartley 1975; Donaldson 1999; Marable 1984). By the 1980s, most white Americans had come to believe that Gunnar Myrdal's (1944) *American Dilemma* had finally been resolved. Optimists in the white community, in particular, looked forward to the steady erosion of long-standing categorical mechanisms of racial stratification. African Americans, however, were less convinced of racism's imminent demise. Whereas 60 percent of whites in 1985 believed that racial inequality was *not* due to discrimination, 80 percent of black Americans insisted that racial disparities were still caused by discriminatory mechanisms (Schuman et al. 1998). Likewise, among African Americans surveyed in Atlanta, Boston, Detroit, and Los Angeles in the early 1990s, a clear majority—between 57 and 69 percent—perceived "a lot" of discrimination against blacks, but only 19 to 33 percent of whites held a similar view (Kluegel and Bobo 2001).

African Americans, of course, have sound historical reasons for skepticism, given the systematic reinstitutionalization of racism that occurred after the first reconstruction (Foner 1988). History aside, there are also good social scientific reasons to expect that categorical mechanisms of racial stratification will prove resistant to change. We know, for example, that once learned, cognitive structures do not simply disappear. Racial schemas honed over generations tend to persist in the minds of adults and get passed on to children in conscious and unconscious ways. Likewise, institutions and practices that have evolved over centuries do not just cease to exist when laws change. As William Ogburn (1922) long ago realized, human societies are characterized by considerable inertia, or what he termed "cultural lag."

Given what we know about the durability of cognitive structures and social institutions, therefore, it is not realistic to believe that racial stratification will just end with a simple declaration that it is all over. In the social as well as the physical world, structures do not change unless energy is brought to bear, and history has shown that the energy required for change in public policy and private practice must come from the federal government. (For a demonstration of the effectiveness of civil rights enforcement in labor markets, see Heckman and Payner 1989.) Federal interventions into state-level affairs, however, carry significant costs on a variety of fronts—higher taxes, more burdensome regulations, and greater restrictions on white freedom. Citizens may not be willing to pay these costs, for both racial and nonracial reasons. As a result, for elected representatives, actions taken to force an end to racial stratification carry a very real price tag.

In addition to the inertia common to all human ideational and social structures, there is also the powerful force of self-interest. Although most whites are reluctant to admit it, the simple fact of the matter is that categorical mechanisms of racial inequality worked to their advantage for most of the twentieth century. Ending racial stratification, therefore, not only requires the direct expenditure of public resources but also imposes significant costs on people who benefited under the old racial regime. (For a demonstration of how whites benefited from residential segregation, see Massey 1990.) A significant failure of the civil rights movement was that it never developed a political plan to manage the white losses of material, symbolic, and emotional resources entailed in the ending of racial stratification (Massey 2005b).

The foregoing considerations led Stanley Lieberson (1985, 191–92, emphasis in original) to adopt "a radically different perspective" on what it would take to end racial inequality:

> Let us hypothesize that racial or other interest groups will tend to take as much as they can for themselves and will give as little as necessary to maintain the system and avoid having it overturned. In this case, whites will give blacks as little as they

can. Under such circumstances, one would assume that observed interrelations between income gaps and features such
as education … describe … the current pathways leading from
a specific causal force to the outcome of that force. If so, a com-
plicated causal analysis of factors contributing to the racial
gaps in income has not the causal value one might have assumed. It describes the given set of events at a given time; it describes what a black person might well follow as a get-ahead
strategy if he or she can assume that not many other blacks will
follow the same strategy and hence the basic [social] matrix
will remain unaltered. But there is no assurance that this matrix
will continue to operate—indeed, there is virtual certainty that
the matrix will not continue to operate if some superficial factor that *appears* to cause the income gap is no longer relevant
(for example, if the groups end up with the same educational
distribution). In which case, new rules and regulations will operate; the other regression coefficients will change in value in
order to maintain the existing system.

In other words, whether whites care to admit it or not, they have
a selfish interest in maintaining the categorical mechanisms that
perpetuate racial stratification. As a result, when pushed by the
federal government to end overt discriminatory practices, they are
likely to innovate new and more subtle ways to maintain their privileged position in society (Massey 2005c). If one discriminatory
mechanism proves impossible to sustain, whites have an incentive
to develop alternatives that may be associated only indirectly with
race and therefore not in obvious violation of civil rights law. The
specific mechanisms by which racial stratification occurs can thus
be expected to evolve over time as practices and institutions shift in
response to civil rights enforcement and other societal changes.

This pessimistic analysis suggests that the American dilemma is
not likely to be resolved easily or quickly by passing a few reforms
and calling it a day. Racial stratification is a moving target (Massey
2005c). One cannot simply ban a prevailing set of discriminatory
practices and declare the struggle for racial equality won. Given the
historical depth and institutionalized longevity of racism in the

United States, it is only logical to assume that new mechanisms of racial subordination will emerge as others are eliminated. Under these circumstances, ending racial discrimination in U.S. markets is likely to require a sustained, dedicated effort over a prolonged period of time. To understand why, one must appreciate in some detail the system of racial stratification that the civil rights movement sought to overturn.

Racial Stratification Before the Civil Rights Era

Categorical mechanisms of racial inequality prevailed throughout the United States until the 1960s, but the means by which exploitation and exclusion were achieved differed in the North and the South. In southern states, of course, African Americans were second-class citizens by law and custom, subordinated by the system of racial separation known as Jim Crow (Packard 2002; Woodward 1955; Wormser 2003). Public services were racially segregated by law, with separate facilities for black and white southerners not just in education but in theaters, hotels, restaurants, government offices, parks, pools, clinics, hospitals, washrooms, buses, trains, and even drinking fountains.

Formal segregation naturally required a legal definition of who was black and who was white, and in response southern legislatures came to define "black" according to a "one-drop rule" in which virtually any discernible African ancestry placed one on the wrong side of the color line (Higginbotham 1996). Intermarriage between the races was prohibited, and despite the Fifteenth Amendment to the U.S. Constitution, black political power was suppressed through a variety of legal and quasi-legal subterfuges, including poll taxes, literacy requirements, grandfather clauses, gerrymandering, and voter intimidation (Higginbotham 1996).

The formal apparatus of segregation was enforced by a criminal justice system run almost entirely by white men (Waldrep 1998). African Americans were barred from service as jurors or judges,

55

and all law enforcement officers—from the town policeman to the county sheriff to state troopers and National Guardsmen—were white. "Loitering" laws prohibited African Americans from gathering and organizing and required them to hold contracts for labor during harvest season while forbidding growers to bid against one another for black labor. White southerners thus arranged the political economy explicitly to prevent the emergence of a competitive labor market for black workers (Foner 1988). African Americans could be criminally victimized with virtual impunity because all-white juries would not convict a white citizen for any crime—be it fraud, larceny, assault, rape, or murder—perpetuated against a person of color (Dray 2002).

In addition to the formal apparatus of segregation erected by southern legislatures, racial subordination was maintained by a host of informal social practices and cultural understandings that were built into the fabric of daily life throughout the South. Indeed, much of the "justice" administered to African Americans occurred outside the judicial system entirely, most commonly in the form of a lynch mob (Dray 2002). The extrajudicial execution of African Americans was a gruesome public spectacle of extended torment that remained common throughout the South until the 1950s, with the number of lynchings coming and going in waves that corresponded to the ups and downs of cotton prices and white status insecurities (Tolnay and Beck 1995).

In the sphere of employment, African Americans were excluded from all but the meanest occupations. In rural areas of the South, the vast majority of men worked as farmhands or as sharecroppers under terms of debt peonage that were barely above slavery (Royce 1993). In cities, they took menial jobs as janitors, shoeshine boys, waiters, busboys, chauffeurs, and washroom attendants or worked as unskilled laborers in construction and manufacturing (Silver and Moeser 1995). The vast majority of employed black women, whether rural or urban, worked in domestic service as maids, cooks, and nannies. Both sexes worked long hours for pitifully low wages (Farley and Allen 1989), which were fixed more by custom than by competitive markets (Packard 2002).

In sum, Jim Crow was a system that institutionalized categorical inequality between blacks and whites at every level in southern society, with exploitation and opportunity hoarding built into virtually every social, economic, and political interaction between the races. Although many northerners looked southward in horror, their hands were hardly clean. Racism may not have been as overt or violent in the North, but in many ways it was just as brutal, and in the end it was just as effective in denying African Americans access to material, symbolic, and emotional resources. The principal difference in the way that exploitation and opportunity hoarding were institutionalized in the North was that categorical inequality was constructed under private rather than public auspices, though the balance shifted as black populations grew in northern cities (Massey and Denton 1993).

As a result of this difference, state involvement in racial subordination was passive rather than active in the North. State and local officials there simply refrained from enforcing black social, economic, and political rights so that private discriminatory practices could do their work. Until the civil rights era, discrimination was rampant in virtually all northern markets—those for jobs and work, homes and apartments, mortgages and loans, and goods and services. Discrimination was normative in civil society as well, with African Americans excluded from white clubs and social organizations and frozen out of white social networks.

As a result, interracial contact in the North was extremely limited—much more limited than in the South—and whatever interpersonal contact did occur was highly asymmetric, with whites enjoying greater wealth, power, prestige, and authority in the interaction. This asymmetry was how white Americans liked it. In surveys from the 1940s, 68 percent of *all* white Americans said that blacks and whites should attend separate schools, 54 percent said that blacks should be segregated in public transportation, and 55 percent said that white people should have the first chance at jobs (Schuman et al. 1998). During the 1950s, 63 percent of whites said that they would not vote for a black presidential candidate, and 96 percent opposed black-white intermarriage as a matter of principle. As late as 1963, a clear majority of whites, some 60 percent, opined that they "have a right to keep blacks out of their neighborhoods, if they want to, and blacks should respect that right" (Schuman et al. 1998).

The linchpin of racial inequality in the North was residential segregation (Pettigrew 1979). From institutionalized discrimination in housing markets, other forms of racial separation naturally followed: racially separate schools, racially separate churches, racially separate stores, racially separate services, racially separate social networks, racially separate jobs, and a geographically isolated and politically subordinate black population. In cities with large black communities, such as New York, Philadelphia, and Chicago, blacks and whites rarely came into contact with one another unless they left their neighborhoods, and relatively few African Americans dared venture into the central business district. Before the civil rights era, blacks and whites in northern cities inhabited parallel societies (Drake and Cayton 1945).

As urban black populations in the North began to grow through migration out of the rural South after 1900, the residential color line was initially maintained through violence—vandalism, arson, beatings, gunshots, and bombings targeted at African Americans who were bold enough to seek homes in "white" neighborhoods (Massey and Denton 1993). Urban black populations surged during the First World War (see Grossman 1989; Spear 1967), and densities in ghetto neighborhoods rose to unprecedented heights, putting intense pressure on the residential color line, which in the end proved uncontainable. With nowhere else to live, black home-seekers spilled over into adjacent white neighborhoods (Duncan and Duncan 1957; Taeuber and Taeuber 1965), triggering a wave of communal white-on-black violence that spread from city to city after 1917 and culminated in the great Chicago Race Riot of 1919 (Massey and Denton 1993).

Faced with such violence and the accompanying destruction of property, the real estate industry responded by institutionalizing racial discrimination in northern housing markets during the 1920s (Massey and Denton 1993). Henceforth, black demand would be systematically channeled away from white areas, and whenever the entry of black home-seekers became inevitable within a white area because of black population growth, the pioneer settlers would be targeted to predesignated neighborhoods where racial turnover could be professionally managed by real estate agents without violence and at considerable profit.

Realtors took the lead in organizing "neighborhood improvement associations" to resist black entry and then invented deed restrictions to prevent the resale of covered properties to nonwhites. During the 1920s, the National Association of Real Estate Brokers revised its code of ethics to state that "a realtor should never be instrumental in introducing into a neighborhood … members of any race or nationality … whose presence will clearly be detrimental to property values in that neighborhood" (see Massey and Denton 1993, 37).

Perhaps the most important tool innovated by realtors during this period was the racially restrictive covenant, a legal agreement among homeowners in a particular area not to rent or sell their homes to African Americans (Massey and Denton 1993). The Chicago Real Estate Board went so far as to create a "model covenant" that was approved by the National Association of Real Estate Brokers. It was subsequently copied by agents throughout the country and tailored to local circumstances. Once a majority of property owners signed a restrictive covenant, it became binding, and violators could be sued in state court to force removal of the black tenant or home buyer.

Institutionalized discrimination in the real estate industry, when combined with rampant private discrimination in labor markets, functioned quite effectively to exploit African Americans while reserving resources and opportunities for whites. This private system of racial stratification prevailed everywhere in the North through the 1940s. As white suburbanization accelerated after 1945, however, and as the number of black city dwellers again surged because of black out-migration from the rural South (Lemann 1991; Marks 1989), the ghetto expanded enormously in size, alarming northern white leaders, who turned to the government for help in maintaining the color line. In the political economy of the 1940s and 1950s, of course, government help meant federal programs and resources.

Most white Americans do not appreciate the degree to which the welfare state created by the New Deal was itself riddled with categorical mechanisms intended to perpetuate racial stratification. The political coalition that brought Franklin Roosevelt to power was an alliance between northern workers, East Coast liberals, western progressives, and, most critically, southern populists. Given one-party democratic rule in the South and the allocation of congressional leadership positions on the basis of seniority, southerners occupied virtually all key committee posts in the House and Senate and had the final say on all federal legislation during the period (Moore 2000). As a result, the institutions bequeathed to postwar America by the New Deal were systematically and quite intentionally "racialized" to exclude African Americans (Lieberman 1998; Katznelson 2005).

Southern senators and representatives were willing, even eager, to support the populist economic goals of the New Deal—but only so long as those goals did not threaten the racial status quo, a view generally shared by representatives of blue-collar constituencies in the North. As a result, *every* piece of New Deal legislation was carefully crafted to exclude blacks from coverage or, failing that, to delegate to the states the authority to exclude, yielding what Robert Lieberman (1998) calls "discrimination by design."

The Federal Housing Administration (FHA), for example, actively promoted racial exclusion in federally guaranteed real estate lending (Jackson 1985). The FHA *Underwriting Manual* explicitly stated that "if a neighborhood is to retain stability, it is necessary that properties shall continue to be occupied by the same social and racial classes," and the agency went on to recommend the use of restrictive covenants to "protect" FHA mortgages (Massey and Denton 1993, 54). When the Supreme Court declared such covenants unenforceable and contrary to public law in 1948, FHA officials continued to insist on their use in federally backed mortgages until litigation by the NAACP forced them to stop the practice in 1950.

The FHA also helped institutionalize the practice of redlining by requiring banks to use "residential security maps" in determining eligibility for federal loan guarantees (Jackson 1985). These maps, initially developed by the Home Owners' Loan Corporation (HOLC), the predecessor to the FHA, color-coded city neighborhoods to indicate creditworthiness. Invariably, areas that had black residents or were located adjacent to existing black neighborhoods were coded red, making homes within them ineligible for government-backed mortgages (Jackson 1985).

The FHA mortgage program was wildly successful and hugely popular with politicians and the public. Because of it and other federal loan programs, homeownership became accessible to the vast majority of American households, and the homeownership rate rose markedly, going from 44 percent in 1934 to 63 percent in 1969 (Massey and Denton 1993, 53). Home equity soon became the single most important source of wealth for middle-class families—at least for those who were white. African Americans were, for all practical purposes, excluded from this great engine of wealth creation. Even today, whereas three-quarters of all white families own their homes, the figure is under half for black families (Ross and Yinger 2002).

The racialization of the New Deal was so complete that even its centerpiece—the Social Security Act of 1935—was carefully worded to exclude African Americans. At the insistence of southern congressional representatives, for example, the original act was amended to exclude agricultural and domestic workers from coverage, two segments of the American workforce that in the 1930s were overwhelmingly black (Katznelson 2005; Quadagno 1994). In this way, millions of African Americans were left outside the New Deal's old-age insurance system, the program most responsible for reducing old-age poverty in the postwar era (Preston 1984).

The Social Security Act also established two relief programs for the poor: Aid to Dependent Children (for widows and divorced mothers) and Old Age Survival and Disability Insurance (for the elderly and infirm). For practical reasons, it was not possible to amend these portions of the legislation to achieve the wholesale exclusion of African Americans, so the southern delegation took a different tack: they made sure the act left the setting of standards for eligibility and the size of payments to the states, knowing that in the South state officials would rarely find an African American qualified for relief, at least not during harvest season; in the rare event that a black worker did qualify, the relief payments would be so low as to make their receipt barely worthwhile (Katznelson 2005; Quadagno 1994). As a result, throughout the postwar era millions of African Americans fell through holes in the American social safety net that were deliberately put there to allow them pass through.

A third provision in the Social Security Act was its creation of an unemployment insurance program, and in this case southerners were successful both in excluding black workers and in delegating terms of eligibility and payments to states (Lieberman 1998; Quadagno 1994). As with Social Security's retirement program, southerners worded the legislation carefully to exclude domestics and farmworkers from coverage, and as with Aid to Dependent Children and Old Age Survivors and Disability Insurance, the eligibility criteria and the size of unemployment payments were put in the hands of state officials.

The racial intent of all of these provisions was clearly laid out by Florida congressman James M. Wilcox on the floor of the House of Representatives:

> There has always been a difference in the wage scale of white and colored labor. So long as Florida people are permitted to handle the matter, the delicate and perplexing problem can be *adjusted*; but the Federal Government knows no color line and of necessity it cannot make any distinction between the races. We may rest assured, therefore, that when we turn over to a federal bureau or board the power to fix wages, it will prescribe the same for the Negro that it prescribes for the white man. Now, such a plan might work in some sections of the United States but those of us who know the true situation know that it will just not work in the South. *You cannot put the Negro and the white man on the same basis and get away with it.* (quoted in Katznelson 2005, 60, emphasis added)

As if exclusion from unemployment insurance were not enough, farmworkers and domestics also were excluded from coverage under the National Labor Relations Act of 1935 and the Fair Labor

Standards Act of 1938, the two pieces of New Deal legislation most responsible for strengthening the bargaining position of workers in the postwar economy. Moreover, even among black workers covered by these acts, the legislation was worded to permit segregated black and white unions and separate employment contracts (Katznelson 2005). As before, southerners acted preemptively to forestall the emergence of a competitive labor market for black workers and to prevent their unionization.

One of the most important legacies of the New Deal was the Selective Service Readjustment Act, better known as the GI Bill of Rights, which in many ways served as the "model welfare system" of the postwar era (Levitan and Cleary 1973). Of men born during the 1920s, some 80 percent were eligible for benefits under the GI Bill (Katznelson 2005). Between 1944 and 1971, the amount invested in former soldiers totaled $95 billion; in the end, more money was spent on veterans' educational benefits alone than on the entire Marshall Plan in Europe (Katznelson 2005). Once again, however, owing to the influence of southern congressional representatives, the GI Bill of Rights was thoroughly racialized and, for all intents and purposes, "earmarked 'For White Veterans Only'" (Bolte and Harris 1947, 20).

The point person for racializing the GI Bill was Mississippi congressman John Rankin, chair of the House Committee on World War Legislation. He began by brokering a deal to guarantee that VA hospitals in the South would be racially segregated, and then he inserted language ensuring that state and not federal officials would be the ones who determined eligibility for the bill's educational benefits (Katznelson 2005). The coup de grâce in the disenfranchisement of black veterans was the decision of the Veterans Administration to employ the same standards and criteria in allocating mortgages as the FHA, thus preventing black former servicemen who had served honorably in time of war from following the same path to housing wealth as their white counterparts, not just in the South but throughout the country.

The importance of the GI Bill in creating the great American middle class cannot be overestimated. In the words of Ira Katznelson (2005, 113):

> With the help of the GI Bill, millions bought homes, attended college, started business ventures, and found jobs commensurate with their skills. Through these opportunities, and by advancing the momentum toward suburban living, mass consumption, and the creation of wealth and economic security, this legislation created middle-class America. No other instrument was nearly as important.

No other instrument may have been as important to *whites*, but for all intents and purposes, it was closed to African Americans.

Although the pervasive racialization of the New Deal reflected the South's desire to preserve Jim Crow and maintain white supremacy in the states of the former Confederacy, other federal policies were racialized at the behest of northerners. As noted earlier, the massive expansion in the physical size of the ghetto after the Second World War overpowered the ability of private actors in real estate and banking to control racial turnover and protect place-bound white interests, such as hospitals, museums, business districts, and universities (Bauman 1987; Hirsch 1983). In response, business, civic, and political leaders turned to Congress and the federal government for help.

Assistance came from the Housing Acts of 1949 and 1954, which authorized the creation of local development authorities and gave them powers of eminent domain. The acts also set aside funds for these authorities to acquire slum properties, assemble them into large tracts, clear them of existing structures, and turn them over to private entrepreneurs for "redevelopment." Under the banner of urban renewal, black neighborhoods whose existence or expansion threatened important white districts were systematically torn down and converted to other uses—institutional or upper-class residential—thereby blocking the path of black population growth and "saving" white districts from the "blight" of the ghetto. In practice, urban renewal literally became "Negro removal" (Hirsch 1983; Massey and Denton 1993; White 1980).

In order for urban renewal to proceed, however, redevelopment authorities had to guarantee an adequate supply of replacement housing for displaced families, and so they drew upon other provisions of the Housing Act to construct public housing projects (Hirsch 1983). During the 1950s and 1960s, in city after city, authorities would tear down one black neighborhood for "renewal" while razing another to construct a public housing project that would then be used to house both sets of displaced residents. In this way, poor African Americans came to be stacked on top of one another in high-rise projects, yielding a new "second ghetto, solidly institutionalized and frozen in concrete," in which "government took an active hand not merely in reinforcing prevailing patterns of segregation, but in lending them a permanence never seen before" (Hirsch 1983, 252–54).

Barriers to Racial Change

As the foregoing section indicates, ending racial stratification in the United States was bound to be a daunting task and would involve much more than simply banning legal segregation in the South. In the North, it required ending an entrenched, institutionalized, decades-old system of private racial discrimination. In the South, it required concrete actions to neutralize systemic, informal practices that subordinated African Americans in association with the formal practices of Jim Crow. Throughout the nation, ending racial stratification required undoing the hidden mechanisms of racial stratification that were built into federal programs during the New Deal.

All of these actions carried significant costs, both directly in terms of the government resources necessary to bring about change and indirectly in terms of the losses that white Americans could expect to experience as racial stratification was brought to an end. Whereas ending legal segregation imposed few costs on whites outside of the South, ending racial stratification nationally imposed a significant burden on virtually all white Americans. This fact helps to explain the emergence of a large gap in white racial attitudes—a growing gulf between their considered view on racial equality in principle and their subjective feelings about racial equality in practice. Whereas a large majority of white Americans have come to abjure racism in the abstract, they nonetheless remain unwilling to support government efforts to do anything to combat it. Likewise, in the race-blind society they purport to favor in principle, whites somehow do not wish to interact with very many black people.

The shift in principle is clearly evident in national survey data. As noted earlier, during the late 1950s the large majority of white Americans disapproved of racial intermarriage, said they would not vote for a black presidential candidate, advocated legal prohibitions on intermarriage, said they had a right to keep blacks out of their neighborhoods, and preferred racially separate schools. Support for such positions fell drastically in the 1970s and 1980s, however, and by the late 1990s only 33 percent disapproved of interracial marriage, only 5 percent said they would not vote for a black presidential candidate, just 13 percent supported prohibitions on intermarriage, the same share said they had a right to keep blacks out of their neighborhoods, and only 4 percent advocated school segregation (Schuman et al. 1998, 104–8).

In light of these attitudinal shifts, and given the multitude of civil rights bills enacted between 1954 and 1977, white Americans came to view America's racial problems as "solved"—at least that was what they told themselves and survey interviewers. By the 1990s, only 34 percent of white Americans said that the lower socioeconomic standing of African Americans could be attributed to continued discrimination. In contrast, 52 percent blamed the lack of racial progress on the absence of motivation among blacks, with 65 percent saying that African Americans just needed to "try harder." Fully 81 percent of whites believed that a black job applicant had the same chance of getting a job as a white applicant, and 82 percent said that housing discrimination was no longer a problem (Schuman et al. 1998).

Given these views, it is unsurprising that white Americans were reluctant to support governmental actions to promote civil rights. By the 1990s, 77 percent of whites said that blacks deserved "no special favors in society," and upwards of 50 percent said that government had no obligation to overcome persisting racial inequalities (Schuman et al. 1998, 172–73). In terms of programs designed specifically to help African Americans, whites were adamant: 65 percent opposed affirmative action in college admissions, and 88 percent opposed it in hiring and promotion (Schuman et al. 1998, 174–75). Some 28 percent of white respondents went so far as to say that the government was spending too much money on African Americans (Schuman et al. 1998, 172–73).

These ambivalent white attitudes are closely mirrored in the civil rights legislation that emerged from Congress during the 1960s and 1970s (Moore 2000). In bill after bill, the original text submitted by civil rights supporters contained strong enforcement provisions that empowered federal authorities to monitor markets for discrimination and to prosecute perpetrators whenever such evidence was found, but invariably in the final text these tough enforcement provisions were amended out of existence and replaced with a weaker, complaint-based system of private enforcement. Rather than empowering federal authorities to look for, identify, and forcefully eradicate discrimination, the legislation merely authorized individuals who believed they had been discriminated against to file suit in federal court and collect modest awards if they could prove discrimination. Federal authorities themselves were authorized to do little more than investigate, mediate, and exhort. In effect, Congress asked individual Don Quixotes to step forward from the ranks of subordinated minorities and tilt at the powerful windmills of institutionalized racial discrimination.

The legislative history of the Fair Housing Act offers a case study in how antidiscrimination provisions were systematically eliminated and deliberately watered down (Dubofsky 1969; Metcalf 1988). The original bipartisan bill, introduced by Democratic senator Walter Mondale of Minnesota and Republican senator Edward Brooke of Massachusetts (the Senate's only black member), not only banned discrimination in the marketing of *all* housing but also authorized the secretary of Housing and Urban Development (HUD) to investigate allegations of discrimination, issue complaints against perpetrators, hold hearings, and publish cease-and-desist orders. The attorney general was specifically empowered to prosecute real estate agents who engaged in a pattern and practice of racial discrimination, and individual victims were authorized to file suit for significant damages and punitive awards, as well as to recover court costs and attorneys' fees.

When the bill finally emerged from the Senate, however, a "compromise" introduced by Senator Everett Dirksen of Illinois had reduced the bill's coverage to 80 percent of the nation's housing units; eliminated HUD's authority to hold hearings, issue complaints, or publish cease-and-desist orders; lowered the maximum fine to $1,000 per violation; and limited awards to actual damages incurred (Massey and Denton 1993). As weak as these provisions were, when the Senate legislation reached the House of Representatives, minority leader Gerald Ford sought to water it down further. He offered an amendment, ultimately not adopted, to permit *legal* racial discrimination in the sale of single-family homes upon the written request of the homeowner (Metcalf 1988).

Even in its weakened state, the bill probably would not have cleared the House had the Rev. Martin Luther King Jr. not been assassinated, compelling legislators to make a dramatic gesture in favor of civil rights. King's blood thus paid for passage of the Fair Housing Act, but it emerged from Congress an emasculated version of its former self. In return for declaring racial discrimination in housing to be against the law of the land, Congress prohibited the federal government from doing anything to enforce the precept. Although housing discrimination was forbidden in principle, it could continue in practice, for in the words of one fair housing lawyer, "Congress made a promise in 1968 that the Fair Housing Act cannot keep" (Schwemm 1989, 47). In the final decades of the twentieth century, little federal action would be taken to end racial discrimination in housing—or in any other market in the United States.

Corresponding to the inertia inherent in social institutions and interpersonal practices is an inertia in the cognitive structures that white Americans carry around in their heads. As noted in the first chapter, cognitive schemas have two components—a rational component rooted in the neocortex and an emotional component rooted in the limbic system. Although white Americans have clearly moved away from conscious, rational support for principled racism, it does not necessarily follow that they feel comfortable with African Americans in practice or want the government to ensure that civil rights laws are obeyed. Although whites may no longer be principled racists, conscious adherence to the abstract principle of racial equality does not automatically translate into acceptance and liking; nor does it imply that negative beliefs about African Americans—prejudicial stereotypes—will simply vanish. On the contrary, the negative feelings and demeaning stereotypes attached to African Americans over the centuries have proved to be remarkably resilient.

For example, the Russell Sage Foundation's Multi-City Study of Urban Inequality, which was fielded in the early 1990s, asked whites in four metropolitan areas to evaluate various out-groups with respect to common stereotypes. In Los Angeles, 48 percent of whites agreed that blacks were less intelligent than whites, and 75 percent believed that blacks preferred welfare to work (Bobo and Johnson 2000); in Detroit the respective figures were 52 percent and 73 percent (Farley, Danziger, and Holzer 2000), and in Atlanta they were 50 percent and 75 percent (Clayton et al. 2000). In Boston, 45 percent of whites viewed African Americans as less intelligent than whites, 64 percent saw them as preferring welfare to work, and 62 percent said they were more prone to involvement with drugs and gangs (Bluestone and Stevenson 2000).

A comprehensive analysis of the structure of white attitudes by Lawrence Bobo and Michael Massagli (2001) found that white stereotypes had a common conceptual organization across all four metropolitan areas and that harsh antiblack stereotypes did not flow from a simple us-versus-them mentality. Rather, the target group mattered a great deal, and African Americans were always perceived more negatively than other groups. Bobo and Massagli (2001, 131) therefore concluded that "stereotypes are grounded in social structure and shaped by direct social learning and the acquisition of group culture."

Using national-level data for 1990, Bobo and James Kluegel (1997) found that 47 percent of whites rated blacks as lazy, and 54 percent said they were prone to violence. Paul Sniderman and Edward Carmines (1997) estimated that at least one-fifth of white Americans hold *uniformly* negative views of African Americans across all dimensions—intelligence, motivation to work, proclivity toward violence, drug use, and criminality. Obviously, despite their endorsement of racial equality in principle, substantial shares of white Americans still adhere to negative stereotypes about African Americans, seeing them as stupid, lazy, violent, and drug-addicted. (In fact, blacks abuse drugs at lower rates than whites do; see Johnston et al. 2004.)

If anything, the foregoing data understate the true incidence of racist sentiment, owing to the influence of social desirability bias: because public expressions of racism are no longer publicly acceptable, people who hold negative stereotypes are reluctant to voice them openly (Bobo 2001; Sniderman and Piazza 1993) and work actively to suppress them (Richeson and Trawalter 2005). In addition, as we have seen, stereotypes are encoded unconsciously (Bargh 1996, 1997; Devine 1989; Fiske 1998). Within American society especially, stereotypical depictions of African Americans are constantly being displayed in newspapers, magazines, television, and films (Biagi and Kern-Foxworth 1997; Dates and Barlow 1983; Entman and Rojecki 2000). Especially on local television news, crime, violence, and disorder are reported at rates many times their actual incidence in real life (Fishman and Cavender 1998; Gilliam and Iyengar 2000; Glassner 2000; Radford 2003), and blacks are very disproportionately paired with these negative stimuli relative to their actual levels of involvement in the population (Holtzman 2001; Lester and Ross 2003).

Under these circumstances, it is difficult for people *not* to form implicit associations between African Americans and negative stimuli such as crime, violence, welfare use, drug addiction, homelessness, illicit sex, unwed childbearing, and so on (Rome 2004). The constant pairing of black faces and bodies with negative circumstances and outcomes is guaranteed to produce implicit associations that are below the level of consciousness but that nonetheless have powerful effects on conscious attitudes and behavior (Banaji and Greenwald 1994; Banaji and Hardin 1996; Bargh 1989; Fiske 2004). Holding negative stereotypes of African Americans strongly predicts less support for race-targeted policies (Bobo and Kluegel 1993), increases aversion to welfare programs (Gilens 1999), and hardens attitudes toward crime and punishment (Hurwitz and Peffley 1997).

Not surprisingly, given persistent stereotypes about African Americans, large numbers of whites express a desire not to associate with them (Bobo 1989; Bobo and Zubrinsky 1996). As already noted, one-third of white Americans disapprove of black-white intermarriage, and the same share say they would *not* try to change the rules of a club they belonged to if it refused to admit black members. Even now, nearly one-quarter of whites say they would feel uncomfortable with a black dinner guest, and although few would object to sending their children to a school containing a "few" blacks, most would refuse to send them to a majority-black school (Schuman et al. 1998).

This reluctance to associate with African Americans and the link between this reluctance and negative stereotyping have been most clearly documented with respect to residential preferences. Whites may be willing to tolerate a few black neighbors, but their tolerance wanes quickly as the potential number increases. Whereas 82 percent of white respondents to a 1992 survey in Detroit said they would feel comfortable living in a neighborhood that was 7 percent black, the figure dropped to 56 percent at one-third black, and to 35 percent at half black (Farley, Danziger, and Holzer 2000). In Boston the respective figures were 97 percent, 63 percent, and 40 percent (Bluestone and Stevenson 2000), and in Los Angeles they were 92 percent, 71 percent, and 46 percent (Charles 2000). In other words, the greater the number of potential black neighbors, the greater the discomfort experienced by whites. When it comes to sharing residential space with African Americans, whites have a limited "comfort zone" (Charles 2002).

The most comprehensive data on neighborhood preferences come from the 2000 General Social Survey (GSS), which offers a unique window on the racial attitudes of a nationally representative sample of white Americans. When asked to state the percentage of different racial and ethnic groups that would be present in their "ideal" neighborhood, the average white respondent offered up a neighborhood that was 57 percent white, 17 percent black, 13 percent Hispanic, and 13 percent Asian (Charles 2003). On average, therefore, whites preferred to live in neighborhoods where they constituted the clear majority. In contrast, blacks and Hispanics expressed an average preference for neighborhoods in which they were *not* the majority.

Although white preferences do yield an average neighborhood that is 17 percent black—an improvement over earlier surveys—this figure conceals the fact that some 25 percent of whites in 2000 said their ideal neighborhood would contain *no blacks whatsoever* (Charles 2003). Thus, as we enter the twenty-first century, one-quarter of all white Americans express a very clear and firm preference *not* to live near *any* African Americans, a figure that, once again, probably understates the true incidence because of social desirability bias.

Camille Charles (2003) sought to identify the determinants of white aversion to black neighbors by estimating the degree to which this sentiment was related to the desire of whites to live among their own kind, the degree to which they perceived African Americans to be of lower economic status, and the degree to which they held negative racial stereotypes. She found that the effect of stereotyping was four times that of in-group attachment and seven times that of class, replicating earlier work (Bobo and Zubrinsky 1996). Likewise, in her comprehensive analysis of data from all four metropolitan areas covered by the Multi-City Study of Urban Inequality, Charles (2001) showed that racial stereotypes played by far the most important role in determining neighborhood preferences—as antiblack stereotypes became more negative, acceptance of black neighbors systematically declined.

In her most detailed statistical analysis, based on data from the Los Angeles Survey of Urban Inequality, Charles (2006) not only confirmed the strong influence of negative stereotyping on white neighborhood preferences but also found that white aversion to black neighbors was determined by perceived social distance from African Americans and the degree to which blacks were viewed as a competitive threat. Nonetheless, when all factors were included in a multivariate regression along with a battery of social, demographic, and economic controls, negative racial stereotyping outperformed all other variables by a sizable margin. Its standardized effect was four times that of class, twice that of perceived threat, and 72 percent greater than that of social distance. Moreover, in this analysis the effect of in-group attachment was essentially zero. Whites do not avoid black neighbors because they prefer their own kind, but because they do not like people who are black.

In another model, Charles (2006) showed that neighborhood racial preferences had a powerful and very statistically significant effect in determining the racial composition of the census tracts where whites actually lived, thus confirming the connection between attitudes and outcomes. Although Charles made certain statistical adjustments to infer that racial attitudes led to residential outcomes rather than the reverse, her data nonetheless originated from a cross-sectional survey. A stronger, experimental demonstration of the power of stereotyping on white residential behavior was accomplished by Michael Emerson, George Yancey, and Karen Chai (2001).

These investigators conducted a factorial experiment that systematically manipulated the racial composition of hypothetical neighborhoods along with other social characteristics. Respondents were told to imagine that they had two school-age children, were in the process of house-hunting, and had finally found a home that they liked better than any other, that was close to work, and that was in their price range. Then they were given additional information about the quality of schools in the neighborhood, the crime rate, trends in property values, and racial-ethnic composition. Values for these variables, however, were randomly assigned so that their independent effects could be measured.

After hearing the neighborhood described with randomly assigned traits, respondents were then asked if they would buy the home. As expected, the likelihood of buying fell sharply as school quality declined, crime rose, and home values decreased. Holding constant these effects, however, the presence of blacks strongly and significantly lowered the likelihood of purchasing a home in the hypothetical neighborhood. The fact that the presence of Hispanics and Asians had no significant influence on the odds of purchase suggests that it was negative sentiments toward blacks, not a preference for white neighbors, that drove the decision.

This conclusion is consistent with the work of Lincoln Quillian and Devah Pager (2001), who showed that the percentage of young black men in a neighborhood is itself positively associated with perceived crime risk, holding constant the actual rate of crime and other relevant neighborhood traits. Not surprisingly, given this fact, Emerson, Yancey, and Chai (2001) found that whites were extremely unlikely to buy a home in any neighborhood that was more than 15 percent black, no matter what its level of school quality, property values, or crime. Race—more than class, crime, schools, or property values—continues to be the dominant organizing principle in U.S. housing markets.

Post–Civil Rights Era Discrimination

Despite the remarkable shift in white attitudes away from principled racism and the embrace of an ideal of equal rights, substantial numbers of white Americans continue to hold explicitly negative racial stereotypes, and an even larger number probably harbor implicit prejudices of which they are not fully aware. Cognitive structures built up over the centuries do not change overnight, and despite waning support for segregation and discrimination in the abstract, in practice whites retain negative beliefs about and feelings of aversion toward African Americans; these translate into a lack of comfort in their presence, which in turn places distinct limits on whites' tolerance for interracial contact in neighborhoods and other intimate social settings.

Scholars have attempted to convey the contradictory nature of contemporary white racial attitudes using a variety of conceptual labels: symbolic racism (Kinder and Sears 1981), modern racism (McConahay 1983), laissez-faire racism (Bobo, Kluegel, and Smith 1997), color-blind racism (Bonilla-Silva 2003), and aversive racism (Dovidio and Gaertner 2004). What all these terms have in common is the recognition that white attitudes are now segmented— between a conscious rejection of principled racism, on the one hand, and the persistence of negative sentiments and beliefs about African Americans, on the other. Inwardly, this contradiction is expressed in terms of an ongoing cognitive struggle to avoid admitting prejudice (Richeson and Trawalter 2005). Outwardly, it is expressed by a willingness to accept African Americans in small numbers, but to withdraw from or avoid settings as their numbers increase.

Given such an attitudinal structure, we would expect to observe different levels of residential segregation in metropolitan areas with large and small black populations. If we define integration as an even distribution of blacks and whites across neighborhoods, then in a perfectly integrated city each neighborhood has the same black percentage as the urban area as a whole (see Massey and Denton 1988). If the overall percentage of blacks in an urban area is small, therefore, the cognitive structures prevailing in white America predict a trend toward greater integration. If an urban area is only 3 percent black, for example, then perfect integration yields a residential configuration where every neighborhood is, on average, 3 percent black, which is well within the comfort zone of most whites.

The situation is reversed, of course, in urban areas where African Americans make up a large share of the population. If an urban area is 30 percent black, movement toward integration is not at all assured, for perfect integration would mean that every neighborhood would be 30 percent black, which is outside the comfort zone of most white Americans. Metropolitan areas with large black populations are therefore predicted to remain segregated.

These theoretical expectations are borne out by actual trends in residential segregation since 1970. Metropolitan areas with small black percentages (such as Tucson, Albuquerque, Seattle, San Jose) have progressed substantially toward greater racial integration, whereas those with large black communities (Chicago, Detroit, Philadelphia) remain segregated at extremely high levels that have hardly changed since the passage of the Fair Housing Act (Krivo and Kaufman 1999; Massey and Gross 1991). Despite shifts toward integration in some metropolitan areas, therefore, race remains a dominant dimension of stratification in American housing markets.

This conclusion is underscored by the weak influence of economic status on racial segregation and the disparate outcomes experienced by black and white Hispanics in U.S. housing markets. Unlike other racial and ethnic groups, the degree of segregation experienced by African Americans does not vary by socioeconomic status. Affluent black households are just as segregated as poor black households—indeed, they are more segregated even than the poorest Hispanic and Asian households (Iceland and Wilkes 2006; Massey and Fischer 1999). At the same time, the degree of segregation experienced by Hispanics varies markedly by skin color, with darker-skinned Hispanics being more segregated than their lighter-skinned counterparts, and black Hispanics being just as segregated as African Americans (Denton and Massey 1989; Massey and Bitterman 1984).

The evidence adduced to this point implies that racial discrimination persists in American housing markets, but the data so far have been indirect. Residential outcomes are what we would expect if discriminatory mechanisms were operating, but the discrimination itself has not been directly observed. Differential residential outcomes among blacks and whites *could* stem from other, nonracial factors, such as differences in tastes and resources, or the influence of unmeasured variables. Fortunately, social scientists have made significant advances in measuring discrimination using experimental approaches, and a growing body of work has accumulated on the extent of racial discrimination within a variety of different markets (Massey and Blank, forthcoming).

Housing Markets

The passage of the Fair Housing Act in 1968 did accomplish one thing: it stopped overt discrimination in housing. After 1968, no sales or rental agent would be so foolish as to tell a black homeseeker, "We don't market to people like you," "No blacks allowed," "Whites only," or something even cruder. Openly racist expressions would invite a lawsuit and yield much aggravation, expense, and bad publicity no matter what the outcome of the litigation. Thus, if discrimination persists in the post–civil rights era world, it is not likely to be open. Rather, it will be expressed in subtle and clandestine ways that are not readily observable and thus will be unlikely to trigger legal action or invite public opprobrium.

Fair housing advocates soon realized this fact and began to de-

76

velop techniques to measure discrimination unobtrusively. The initial efforts were pioneered by local fair housing organizations, but social scientists ultimately got involved in refining and perfecting the methods, which have come to be known as audit studies (Blank, Dabady, and Citro 2004). In an audit study, units being marketed for sale or rent are randomly selected and separate teams of white and black auditors posing as home-seekers are sent to inquire about the availability of the advertised units, the number of other units available, and the terms under which units might be obtained. Auditors are assigned similar personal, social, and economic characteristics by the researcher and carefully trained to present themselves in a neutral fashion and to ask standard questions about the housing being marketed. Afterward, each auditor fills out a form describing the nature and outcome of the encounter without knowing what happened to the other auditor (see Yinger 1986, 1989).

These forms are then collated across white and black auditors and sampled agents and tabulated to see whether there were discernible differences in treatment by race. Early results obtained by fair housing groups generally indicated that discrimination in the post–civil rights era persisted in a variety of guises. Black auditors might be told that no units were left even though whites were informed that units were still for rent or sale. Black auditors might be shown fewer units than their white counterparts, or they might be offered different terms, with larger deposits or down payments, higher rents or interest rates, and larger fees for making the application and undergoing a credit check. They might simply be treated more brusquely and not have their phone calls returned.

Local fair housing organizations undertook a variety of audit studies in both rental and sales markets after 1968, with varying degrees of rigor. In 1987 George Galster (1990a, 172) wrote to more than two hundred organizations and obtained reports of seventy-one audit studies. Despite differences in measures and methods, he concluded that "racial discrimination continues to be a dominant feature of metropolitan housing markets in the 1980s." Using a conservative measure of racial bias, he found that blacks averaged a 20 percent chance of experiencing discrimination in home sales markets and a 50 percent chance of discrimination in rental markets on any given encounter with a real estate agent.

In addition to limiting housing access, discrimination may also channel black and white home-seekers to different *kinds* of neighborhoods, a practice known as steering. Steering is indicated, for example, whenever black auditors are shown or offered units in neighborhoods that are poorer, blacker, more dilapidated, and closer to existing black neighborhoods than those presented to whites (Pearce 1979; Saltman 1979). Galster (1990b) examined the behavior of six real estate firms in Cincinnati and Memphis and found that racial steering occurred in roughly 50 percent of the transactions, with African Americans being directed differentially toward areas that already contained black residents or that were near established black areas. Agents were also likely to make positive comments about white neighborhoods to white clients but not to black clients. In his review of thirty-six audit studies conducted by local fair housing groups, Galster (1990c) discovered that selective commentary by agents was more common than the systematic showing of different houses and neighborhoods to white and black auditors.

Although audit studies continue to be carried out by local fair housing groups, beginning in the late 1970s the U.S. Department of Housing and Urban Development got into the act. To date, HUD has implemented three nationwide housing audits—in 1977, 1988, and 2000—that have attempted to measure the incidence and severity of discrimination in rental and sales markets using a representative sample of U.S. metropolitan areas (Turner, Ross, et al. 2002; Wienk et al. 1979; Yinger 1995). The first study compared the treatment of blacks and whites, the second added Hispanics to the mix, and the third estimated discrimination against Asians and Native Americans as well.

All three studies found significant discrimination against African Americans in the rental and sale of housing (Turner, Ross, et al. 2002). A comparison of results from the 1977 and 1988 audits uncovered little evidence of change, but between 1988 and 2000 analysts detected a shift in the nature of housing discrimination against African Americans (Charles 2003). Specifically, the incidence of white-favored treatment dropped over the period, but the likelihood of racial steering rose; in addition, the decline in white favoritism was greater in sales than in rental markets (Ross and Turner 2004). Thus, the overall picture of progress in housing discrimination was one of two steps forward and one step backward.

The HUD audits were based on in-person visits to real estate agents, but in real life initial contacts between agents and home-seekers generally occur by telephone. Recent research indicates substantial potential for phone-based discrimination on the basis of linguistic cues, a discriminatory process that has come to be known as "linguistic profiling" (Squires and Chadwick 2006). Phone-based discrimination can take a variety of forms, some of which parallel those forms characteristic of face-to-face encounters. An agent may tell a black-sounding caller that a unit is rented or sold when it really is not, and even when the agent acknowledges the availability of the advertised unit, he or she may not mention that other units may be available.

In addition, however, phone inquiries offer new opportunities for discrimination that are not present in personal encounters. Specifically, in an era of rampant voice mail, when many inquiries about the availability of rental units are intercepted by answering devices, agents can profile prospective tenants linguistically simply by not returning calls from people who leave a message that "sounds black," a new form of passive discrimination that does not require any direct interaction between perpetrator and victim.

It is segregation itself that paradoxically makes linguistic profiling possible. One consequence of historical segregation in the United States is that a large share of African Americans speak a distinctive version of English, with different rules of pronunciation, diction, grammar, and syntax compared to that ordinarily spoken by whites (Baugh 1983; Labov 1972; Labov and Harris 1986). Research shows that white Americans are capable of making accurate racial attributions on the basis of very short speech fragments (Feagin 1994). Not only are they quick to identify the race of someone speaking black English, but they are able to identify the race of code-switching blacks—those who speak mainstream English but with a "black" pronunciation of certain words (see Doss and Gross 1994).

Thomas Purnell, William Idsardi, and John Baugh (1999) examined how black and white speech affected the likelihood of receiving an appointment to look at an advertised unit in the San Francisco Bay Area. They found that black-sounding callers were significantly less likely to obtain an appointment than white-sounding callers and that the effect was strongest for listings in predominantly white areas. In our study of rental housing in the Philadelphia metropolitan area, Massey and Lundy (2001) found that black-sounding callers were significantly less likely than whites to receive callbacks or to be told that units were available and that they were more likely to have credit raised as a complicating issue or be required to pay up-front fees for a "credit check."

Massey and Lundy (2001) also found significant interactions with gender and class, such that lower-class black females experienced by far the least access to housing in the Philadelphia rental market. Whereas 76 percent of white middle-class males reached an agent and were told that a unit was available, only 38 percent of poor black females achieved the same result. In a follow-up study, Fischer and Massey (2004) found that blacks had less access to housing in suburban areas than in the central city, that blacks' access to units marketed by professional agents was lower than it was to units marketed by private landlords, and that the odds of discrimination fell as distance to the closest black neighborhood increased.

The findings of audit studies lend credence to the numerous complaints of discrimination filed by African Americans every year. When the National Fair Housing Alliance compiled data from local fair housing groups, HUD, the U.S. Department of Justice, and state and local government agencies, it found that race was by far the most common basis for complaints of housing discrimination, accounting for 32 percent of the 23,557 complaints filed in 2001 (National Fair Housing Alliance 2002). Not surprisingly, substantial pluralities of African Americans surveyed in national polls have reported experiencing housing discrimination—around one-quarter in a *USA Today* survey, a figure that rose to 36 percent among black respondents with incomes over $50,000 (Massey and Denton 1993). African Americans who report experience with discrimination are less likely to own a home (Pol et al. 1981), suggesting, as Massey and Denton note in *American Apartheid* (1993, 109), that "seeing the cards so obviously stacked against them, it is no wonder that many otherwise qualified African Americans simply abandon their quest to purchase a home without really trying."

Lending Markets

Housing segregation is perpetuated not only by discrimination in the rental and sale of housing but also by discrimination in home lending. It was this realization that prompted Congress to pass the Equal Credit Opportunity Act, the Home Mortgage Disclosure Act, and the Community Reinvestment Act. Lending discrimination may be direct, as when black applicants are denied loans at higher rates than similarly qualified white applicants, or it may be indirect, as when black applicants are denied loans not because they themselves are black or economically unqualified, but because the neighborhood surrounding the property they seek to mortgage contains black residents, the practice known as redlining.

Direct discrimination against African American mortgage applicants became front-page news in 1989 when the *Atlanta Constitution* analyzed 10 million loan applications nationwide and found that black applicants were twice as likely to be turned down as whites. Whereas the black rejection rate was 24 percent, the rate for whites was only 11 percent. The investigation also found that high-income African Americans were more frequently rejected even than the lowest-income whites (Dedman 1988, 1989). An investigation by the *New York Times* using different data found the same thing. The Manufacturers Hanover Trust Company of New York rejected 43 percent of applications from high-income blacks but just 18 percent from high-income whites (Quint 1991).

A more systematic and better-controlled study carried out by the Federal Reserve Bank of Boston found that after holding constant creditworthiness and a variety of other personal characteristics, minorities were denied loans at a rate of 17 percent compared with 11 percent for whites (Munnell et al. 1996) and that minorities received systematically lower credit ratings than whites with the same ob-

81

jective characteristics (Carr and Megbolugbe 1993). Other studies have revealed that African Americans are likely to experience less favorable treatment before they even file a loan application, getting fewer actual quotes, higher estimated payments, longer proposed repayment periods, and greater interest rate offers (Smith and De-Lair 1999).

Margery Turner, Fred Freiberg, and their colleagues (2002) found that, in Los Angeles, African Americans received significantly less coaching from agents than whites when preparing loan applications and that they were systematically pushed toward FHA financing rather than conventional loans. In Chicago the same authors found that black home-seekers were often denied even the most basic information about loan amounts and were generally offered fewer products and that they received less coaching than whites. In his review of banking practices, John Yinger (1995) discovered that African Americans were also less likely than whites to obtain private mortgage insurance. Harold Black and Robert Schweitzer (1985) likewise determined that black loan applicants were offered systematically higher interest rates and shorter repayment periods than whites, controlling for a variety of social, economic, and neighborhood factors.

The most comprehensive study of mortgage discrimination done to date is that of Stephen Ross and John Yinger (2002, 12), who systematically investigated in considerable detail every methodological and substantive criticism that had ever been leveled against the Boston Federal Reserve study; they concluded that "the large minority-white disparity in loan approval found by the Boston Fed Study cannot be explained by data errors, misclassification, omitted variables, or the endogeneity of loan terms." After compiling the most detailed and comprehensive dataset yet assembled, they undertook a sophisticated and well-controlled statistical analysis to determine whether racial disparities could be attributed to the use of different underwriting standards across lenders. Although their analysis confirmed that underwriting standards did vary from lender to lender, they nonetheless found "that accounting for this variation has no impact on the estimated loan approval disparity" (12).

In short, black home-seekers continue to experience significant racial discrimination at virtually all phases of a housing market transaction: when they contact agents by phone, when they meet with agents in person, when they are shown units in different neighborhoods, when they apply for loans, when they are evaluated for credit, when they receive private mortgage insurance, and when their interest rates and repayment periods are set. In addition to experiencing discrimination because of their own skin color, moreover, African Americans continue to be denied mortgages because of the color of their neighbors.

In their survey of lending practices in Boston during the 1970s, Harriet Taggart and Kevin Smith (1981) found that residential security maps dating back to the 1930s were still being used routinely by banks to classify minority neighborhoods as "high-risk areas" with "adverse environmental factors" and "questionable economic viability," thus rendering these areas ineligible for loans. Once racial data on lending became available after 1975, researchers began to estimate statistical models to predict the number and size of loans made to different neighborhoods based on their geographic location, housing characteristics, economic status, and social composition. In our review of this research, Massey and Denton (1993, 106) concluded that "despite the diverse array of characteristics that have been controlled in different studies, one result consistently emerged: black and racially mixed neighborhoods receive less private credit, fewer federally-insured loans, fewer home improvement loans, and less total mortgage money than socioeconomically comparable white neighborhoods."

In their analysis of neighborhood lending patterns, Katharine Bradbury, Karl Case, and Constance Dunham (1989) found a 24 percent unexplained gap in lending rates between black and white areas of Boston. Richard Hula (1981, 1982) found that black inner-city neighborhoods in Dallas experienced a relative deficit in loans compared to what their socioeconomic characteristics would predict—and that the size of the apparent deficit increased as black proportion rose. Gregory Squires and William Velez (1987) also found that the frequency of loans made to different neighborhoods in Milwaukee was strongly influenced by the percentage of black residents.

Greater attention by federal regulatory authorities has nonetheless been successful in reducing mortgage discrimination, especially on federally backed loans. Samantha Friedman and Gregory Squires (2005) showed that across U.S. metropolitan areas, the higher the share of financial institutions covered by the Community Reinvestment Act, the more likely African Americans were to own homes in white neighborhoods. As federal scrutiny has increased, however, lending institutions have shifted away from FHA mortgages, except for use with minority borrowers. According to Anne Shlay (1983), by the early 1980s FHA mortgages were increasingly being channeled to inner-city minority neighborhoods while conventional mortgages flowed mainly to suburbs and gentrifying city areas.

Increasingly, bankers may be discriminating less on the basis of access and more on the basis of price, by charging black loan applicants and borrowers from minority neighborhoods higher interest rates. Thus, Richard Williams, Reynold Nesiba, and Eileen Diaz McConnell (2005) reported a sharp increase in "predatory lending" in recent years: they showed that lending to African American residential areas increased during the 1990s, but that more than half of the gain was in the form of "subprime" loans that charged higher interest rates, offered shorter payment periods, assessed greater penalties for missed payments, and required more money down. Clearly the lending industry has not yet been cleansed of categorical mechanisms that exploit African Americans, and some new ones appear to have been invented.

Labor Markets

Owing to racial discrimination, the wages earned by black workers have historically lagged well behind those earned by white workers. In 1940, for example, the average black male earned just 40 percent of what the average white male earned (Holzer 2001). Owing to labor scarcities as well as federal civil rights provisions imposed on defense industries during the Second World War, the relative wages of African Americans improved markedly from 1940 to 1950, going from 40 percent of the white male wage, on average, to 52 percent.

The pace of improvement slowed markedly during the 1950s, with the black-white wage ratio moving from 52 percent at the beginning of the decade to 55 percent at the end. Thereafter, it accelerated markedly in the 1960s and 1970s to reach 76 percent in 1975.

A detailed econometric analysis by James Heckman and Brook Payner (1989) showed that federal antidiscrimination efforts during the 1960s and 1970s played a central role in raising the earnings and employment of African Americans and was primarily responsible for closing the racial gap. After the mid-1970s, however, as the economy deteriorated and federal enforcement efforts waned, further improvements in the relative wages of blacks ceased; since that time, a persistent 25 percent wage gap between white and black men has prevailed (Holzer 2001).

Although this gap might well reflect the continuation of subtle processes of discrimination, it could also stem from objective differences in human capital and other labor market inputs. Yet even when we adjust for the influence of such variables as education, veteran and marital status, region, urban residence, number of children, and hours worked, a significant racial gap of 20 percent persists. Among those with ten or fewer years of work experience, black males earn 82 percent of what comparably qualified white males make, and among those with eleven or more years of experience, blacks earn about 84 percent of what whites do (Holzer 2001).

The persistence of black-white earnings differentials despite the application of statistical controls suggests the persistence, either directly or indirectly, of racial discrimination in U.S. labor markets. Direct discrimination occurs when employers fail to hire a worker or when they pay a person less simply because he or she is black. Indirect discrimination occurs when employers avoid workers with characteristics that are strongly associated with being black, such as location, but do not discriminate on the basis of race itself. This form of discrimination is called *statistical discrimination* because it takes advantage of statistical correlations between race and certain socioeconomic characteristics (Blank, Dabady, and Citro 2004). By screening applicants on those characteristics, employers can effectively exclude African Americans from the pool of potential workers.

One survey of employers in Chicago during the mid-1980s found extensive racial coding of workers on the basis of place of residence and race, made possible by the high degree of segregation of blacks and whites in that city. Employers systematically dismissed residents of housing projects and poor neighborhoods on the city's South and West Sides as unemployable without necessarily mentioning the race of the people who lived there (Kirschenman and Neckerman 1991).

Employer surveys done in association with the Multi-City Study of Urban Inequality also uncovered substantial evidence of statistical discrimination against African Americans. According to Philip Moss and Chris Tilly (2001, 152), although few employers "are willing to endorse a sweeping statement that some jobs are better suited to certain racial or ethnic groups … about 20 percent agree that inner-city workers are poorer performers." Another 20 percent of employers expressed reservations about hiring minority workers because they believed their customers had racial biases.

Moreover, even though employers were reluctant to express prejudicial views of blacks in standardized survey questions, their comments to interviewers during in-depth interviews were more forthcoming. Some 46 percent criticized either the hard or soft skills of African American workers in open-ended comments, singling out a lack of motivation as a particular weakness of black employees. Moss and Tilly (2001, 153) reported that employers "typically attributed African Americans' shortcomings as workers to the pernicious influences of single motherhood, the welfare system, or the inner city environment."

Such perceptions appear to make a significant difference in actual hiring. In his analysis of employer attitudes and behaviors based on the Multi-City Study of Urban Inequality, Harry Holzer (1996) found that the screening criteria used at most firms routinely excluded African Americans from consideration. Among employers seeking to fill entry-level jobs, 73 percent required a high school degree, 70 percent required general work experience, 63 percent required specific work experience, and 31 percent said they performed a criminal background check.

On the basis of these data, Holzer (1997, 127, emphasis added) concluded that most employers "seem reluctant to hire workers with unstable work histories, especially those *they suspect* of having criminal records." Multivariate regressions estimated by Holzer showed that blacks were more likely to apply to city employers, who generally demand higher skills, and that these employers were more likely to hire black applicants, even though they had fewer skills than their counterparts in the suburbs, leading him to conclude that since "task requirements are generally a bit higher in the central city than in the suburban areas, while the relative credentials of black applications in central cities are probably not higher, the data strongly suggest greater discriminatory behavior by suburban employers" (104).

The foregoing analyses are based on cross-sectional surveys, of course, and being non-experimental they do not necessarily prove that employers are discriminating, either directly or indirectly. Although housing audits began in the late 1960s, audit methodologies were not applied to labor markets until the late 1980s, and their initial application was to test for discrimination against Hispanics in the wake of immigration reform legislation, not discrimination against African Americans in violation of civil rights law (Cross et al. 1990). The first systematic audit study of employment using African American testers was that of Margery Turner, Michael Fix, and Raymond Struyk (1991), who studied the market for entry-level jobs in Washington and Chicago. They found that black applicants were significantly less likely to receive an interview than whites, that the interviews they received were much shorter, and that they received significantly more negative remarks in the course of the exchange. Under these circumstances, it is not surprising that black applicants were less likely to be offered a job and, among those who received a job offer, to receive a less desirable position.

More recently, Marianne Bertrand and Sendhil Mullainathan (2004) implemented a creative large-scale field experiment by sending résumés in response to 1,300 help-wanted ads placed in Boston and Chicago newspapers. They created a bank of experimental résumés by downloading actual examples from two well-known job search websites (www.careerbuilder.com and www.americasjob

bank.com), rendering them anonymous, and then dividing them into high-skill and low-skill pools. Then they sent two résumés from each pool in response to each job ad and randomly assigned race using "black-sounding" names (Ebony, Darnell) on some and "white-sounding" names (Allison, Brad) on others. Addresses were also randomly assigned to avoid inferences about race from residential location.

The authors found that applicants with white-sounding names received 50 percent more callbacks than those with black-sounding names. Thus, the callback rate was 12 percent for "whites" but only 7 percent for "blacks." They also found greater returns to skill among white than black applicants. Among those with white-sounding names, those in the high-skill pool had a 14 percent callback rate, compared with only 10 percent among those in the low-skill pool. Among "black" applications, however, the callback rates hardly differed: 7.7 percent for high-skill applications versus 7.0 percent for low-skill applicants. In other words, a low-skill white applicant generated significantly more interest from employers than a high-skill black applicant.

Devah Pager (2003) audited Milwaukee's unskilled labor market using a methodology similar to that developed by Turner, Fix, and Struyk (1991). She selected two white and two black twenty-three-year-old men matched on appearance and style of presentation to serve as auditors. Each person was assigned a comparable educational background and work history, and one of each pair was randomly assigned a "criminal record" in the form of a conviction for a nonviolent drug offense. The auditors were then sent out to apply for entry-level jobs advertised in the Sunday classified section of the *Milwaukee Journal Sentinel*, where entry-level positions were defined as those requiring no prior work experience and no more than a high school education.

As expected, Pager (2003) found that a criminal record decreased the likelihood of receiving a callback. More surprising was the fact that the effect of race was even stronger than that of criminality. Whereas 34 percent of noncriminal whites received a callback, the figure was only 17 percent for those with a criminal record; the callback rate even for *noncriminal* African Americans, however, was just 14 percent, implying that in terms of attractiveness to employers, a noncriminal black candidate was on a par with a white criminal, and perhaps even a little less attractive (the three-point gap was not statistically significant). Black criminals, of course, experienced by far the lowest fraction of callbacks—just 5 percent.

The segmented nature of white racial attitudes revealed in most surveys is exemplified by the contrast between what employers say and what they do. As part of the Milwaukee study, the employers selected for unobtrusive audits were also interviewed by telephone about their hiring practices. Some 63 percent of employers said they were likely or very likely to hire someone with a criminal record, a figure that was the same whether the hypothetical applicant was black or white, but only 17 percent actually called back the white criminal applicant, and just 5 percent called back the black ex-offender (Pager and Quillian 2005). There was thus a large gap between employers' stated willingness to hire ex-offenders and the rate at which they actually did so, and the gap was significantly larger when the ex-offender was black. Whether this larger gap reflects social desirability bias (employers really do not want to hire a black ex-offender but are afraid to say so) or implicit discrimination (employers are not aware of their prejudice against black ex-offenders) is impossible to say.

Pager and Bruce Western (2006) recently replicated Pager's audit study in New York City by arranging for teams of black and white auditors to apply for 1,470 entry-level jobs over ten months in 2004. Once again they found a significant difference in callback rates for black and white applicants: 23 percent of the former were called back, but only 13 percent of the latter. Once again race trumped criminality in determining employer interest: the callback rate for a white felon was exactly the same as for African Americans in general—13 percent.

From the available audit evidence it seems clear that racial discrimination persists in U.S. labor markets at significant levels. Judging from the accumulated results of Bertrand and Mullainathan (2004), Pager (2002), and Pager and Western (2006), the employment prospects of black job-seekers are roughly half those of equally qualified whites and are lowered even further by the stigma of a criminal record. Moreover, based on the findings of Bertrand and Mullainathan (2004), the severity of discrimination seems to rise rather than fall as skill increases. This finding implies that more education and training among African Americans, by themselves, will not erase racial differences in employment outcomes unless actions are also undertaken to eliminate categorical mechanisms of inequality from American labor markets.

Product Markets

In a capitalist society such as the United States, markets not only allocate homes, capital, and jobs but also goods and services. Given the cyclical and unstable nature of markets and their sensitivity to exogenous shocks, life in a capitalist society is risky and access to insurance is critical to the maintenance of social and economic well-being. Without access to insurance, one's life savings may be wiped out by an unexpected illness, an ill-timed layoff, a destructive fire, or a serious accident. In housing markets especially, insurance coverage is essential, for no lender will mortgage a property unless it is insured up to the value of the loan.

Studies have documented a host of discriminatory practices in insurance underwriting, including reports of explicit instructions to avoid writing policies for African American individuals and minority neighborhoods (Lynch 1997; Ritter 1997). Consistent with this anecdotal evidence, Gregory Squires, William Velez, and Karl Taeuber (1991) found that the relative number of insurance agents per neighborhood was negatively related to the percentage of African American residents within it. Similarly, in her survey of homeowners in metropolitan Rochester, New York, Barbara Van Kerkhove (2005) found that respondents from minority neighborhoods paid higher premiums, even after adjusting for home value, and that they held policies that offered less comprehensive coverage.

Biased marketing practices, in turn, yield racial disparities in access to insurance that are geographically structured. When Squires and Velez (1987) analyzed the distribution of homeowner policies across neighborhoods of Milwaukee, they found that the number of policies per owned dwelling fell significantly as the black percentage rose, holding constant the age of the housing stock, average household income, property values, residential turnover, and prior insurance loss ratios. A more recent analysis using 1999 data suggested that little had changed (Squires, O'Conner, and Silver 2001).

In his analysis, Robert Klein (1995, 1997) analyzed the distribution of insurance policies across communities in thirty-three metropolitan areas. He uncovered significant disparities in coverage by racial composition after controlling for past loss records and other socioeconomic and demographic characteristics of the neighborhood. Although Jay Schultz (1997) found that the number of owner-occupied housing units—and thus the size of the home insurance market—did fall as the minority proportion rose across zip codes in St. Louis, the number of insurance agencies fell off at an even faster rate. Thus, the number of agents per owned housing unit fell from a ratio of 3.9 among zip codes in the lowest quintile nonwhite (average 2 percent nonwhite) compared with a ratio of 0.33 in the highest quintile nonwhite (77 percent nonwhite).

Multivariate statistical analysis of geo-coded insurance data thus confirms a process of insurance redlining parallel to that identified in the lending industry. Neighborhoods containing African Americans do not get the insurance coverage we would expect given their social and economic characteristics, and the degree of undercoverage increases as the black percentage rises. But such analyses are once again cross-sectional and therefore subject to questions about the direction of causality and the confounding influence of unmeasured variables. To document more conclusively the operation of discriminatory processes, therefore, researchers have begun to apply audit methods to the insurance industry.

Shana Smith and Cathy Cloud (1997), for example, sent matched pairs of auditors to inquire about the availability of insurance for homes in a nationwide sample of cities. They found that auditors from black neighborhoods were less likely to be offered insurance and that when they did receive an offer the price quoted was above that of comparable white locations. Agents were also less responsive to auditors from black neighborhoods in returning phone calls, making follow-up calls, providing written quotes, and making encouraging versus discouraging comments. Overall rates of discrimination—transactions in which minority auditors experienced some form of discrimination—were 83 percent in Chicago, 67 percent in Atlanta, 62 percent in Toledo, 58 percent in Milwaukee, 56 percent in Louisville, 44 percent in Cincinnati and Los Angeles, 37 percent in Akron, and 32 percent in Memphis.

Douglas Wissoker, Wendy Zimmermann, and George Galster (1998) likewise trained auditors to pose as first-time buyers of homes in black versus white neighborhoods and then sent them to randomly selected insurance agents in three New York City boroughs. Whereas 82 percent of the auditors from white neighborhoods received a quote, the figure was 78 percent for those from black neighborhoods; there was also a four-point difference favoring white neighborhoods in the offering of replacement cost coverage for the dwelling (96 percent versus 92 percent). Moreover, although 46 percent of auditors from white neighborhoods were offered replacement cost coverage on the contents of the home, only 39 percent were offered this coverage. Testers with homes in white neighborhoods were also six percentage points more likely to receive both written and verbal quotes rather than verbal quotes alone (18 percent versus 12 percent).

Squires and Jan Chadwick (2006) found that the "linguistic profiling" uncovered by Massey and Lundy (2001) in real estate rental markets also prevailed in insurance markets. Over the phone, white-sounding callers were generally quoted prices and offered policies with considerable enthusiasm, but black-sounding callers were told that no agent was currently available and asked to call back later. People sounding African American were significantly less likely to receive a quote over the phone, more likely to be told that an inspection was required, and more likely to be referred to a publicly administered insurance pool. In contrast to the enthusiastic salesmanship lavished on white-sounding callers, agents were much less likely to return messages left by those with black-sounding voices.

Audit methodologies have recently been applied to the study of racial discrimination in consumer sales markets. Ian Ayres and Peter Siegelman (1995), for example, sent 19 pairs of black and white auditors, male and female, to 153 randomly selected Chicago-area car dealerships. The auditors were instructed to bargain for nine specific car models within a few days of each other. The testers were trained to follow a bargaining script in which they informed the dealer that they would not need financing and then pursued one of two strategies: one dependent on the behavior of the seller and another independent of seller behavior. They found that the initial offers made to white males averaged $935 less than those made to black males, and that black females received initial offers that were $220 greater than initial offers to white females. After bargaining, the final offers were lower across the board, but the gaps remained very similar. On average, white males got the best deal, followed by white females ($92 more), black females ($410 more), and black males ($1,100 more).

Although taxi service may not be as critical as insurance, mortgage lending, or car sales, being unable to get a taxi while watching cabs pass by empty is aggravating and humiliating (Feagin and Sikes 1994). To test for discrimination in the Washington, D.C., taxi cab market, Stanley Ridley, James Bayton, and Janice Outtz (1989) assigned white and black auditor pairs to preselected downtown locations and had them attempt to hail a cab from nearby locations. Over the course of two hundred trials, black auditors were passed up 20 percent of the time compared with 3 percent for white auditors. It also took longer for drivers to stop for African Americans than for white testers, and drivers were quite likely to refuse to take the auditor to an address in a black neighborhood, irrespective of whether the auditor was black or white.

The Color of Justice

In many ways, discrimination in housing, lending, labor, and product markets simply continues long-standing and well-established practices of racial exclusion, albeit under more subtle guises. In the wake of civil rights legislation, discrimination moved underground so that it would not trigger a formal complaint or legal challenge, yielding what Massey and Denton (1993, 96) called "discrimination with a smile." As discrimination moved out of sight during the 1970s and 1980s, however, an entirely new and much more visible institutional mechanism emerged to promote racial stratification in the United States: the prison industrial complex (Schlosser 1998).

Although the criminal justice system historically has functioned as a mechanism of social control imposed on African Americans, especially in the South, during the mid-1970s the system was radically transformed in ways that made it much more of a core "race-making" institution throughout the United States (Wacquant 2001). Just as slavery was succeeded by Jim Crow, the collapse of public support for principled racism in the 1960s and 1970s ushered in a new institutional configuration that facilitated the reproduction of racial inequality using mechanisms that were ostensibly "race-blind." In the past two decades, the prison system has become central to the collective stigmatization and subordination of African Americans (Wacquant 2000).

The outlawing of overt discrimination, the dismantling of Jim Crow, and the forced inclusion of blacks within the welfare state naturally made many whites feel uneasy, if not downright resentful, and their sense of alienation was heightened by the spread of urban riots and rising black militancy during the 1960s and early 1970s (Quadagno 1994; Skrentny 1996). The surge in racial conflict coincided with a broader increase in drug use and violence throughout American society; although both of these trends stemmed mainly from the passing of the baby boom through the delinquency-prone ages of fifteen to thirty, the rise in social disorder occurring against a backdrop of growing unemployment and declining real wages created a social milieu that was ripe for reaction against the liberalizing tendencies of the 1960s.

The most notable and far-reaching manifestation of this reaction was the shift of U.S. criminal justice away from its century-long focus on correction and rehabilitation to a new emphasis on retribution and punishment. This transformation was achieved through the deliberate racialization of crime and violence in public consciousness by political entrepreneurs who, by dramatizing urban violence and systematically pairing it with images of black criminality, were successful in mobilizing white racial fears to block progressive social change (Western 2006). Although the rate of black crime did not change, either absolutely or relative to whites, infractions committed by blacks were systematically targeted for more vigorous prosecution and much harsher punishment than before (Tonry 1996).

The racialization of criminal justice was led by Republicans who sought to use race as a "wedge issue" to pry apart the New Deal coalition (Massey 2005b). By manipulating stereotypes, reinforcing prejudices, and heightening racial fears, they sought to undermine popular support not only for civil rights initiatives among working- and middle-class whites but for other liberal policies as well. In the course of a generation, this strategy succeeded remarkably, transforming the "solid South" from a Democratic to a Republican bastion (Phillips 1969) and turning working-class whites into reliable Republican voters (Edsall and Edsall 1991).

The race-crime linkage debuted in 1964 when Republican presidential candidate Barry Goldwater decried "the growing menace in our country ... to personal safety, to life, to limb, and property" from "the license of the mob and of the jungle" (quoted in Western 2006, 59). His subtle use of language here exemplifies the Republican approach: linking crime to African Americans without explicitly doing so. In this case, the linkage was achieved symbolically by alluding to the "licentious" behavior of those in "the mob" (black rioters) and "the jungle" (the black ghetto). For whites upset at the rapid pace of racial change and the apparent breakdown of public order, this language resonated politically.

In 1964, however, the nation was not ready for a fully racialized politics, and Goldwater went down to defeat at the hands of Lyndon Johnson, who parlayed his landslide into enactment of the civil rights revolution. At the same time, Johnson also sought to deracialize the welfare state by declaring a new "war on poverty" that entailed "the maximum feasible participation" of the poor themselves. For a short time, Johnson's "Great Society" worked to transfer substantial power and resources to formerly excluded minorities in urban ghettos of the North and rural areas of the South. This success, of course, greatly antagonized working-class whites throughout the nation.

In response to this growing discontent, Governor George C.

Wallace of Alabama, a noted opponent of civil rights who once pledged "segregation forever," launched a third-party bid for the presidency in 1968 on an explicit "law and order" platform that played strongly upon white fears. At the same time, Senator Eugene McCarthy of Wisconsin launched an insurgency from the left in opposition to the Vietnam War. Faced with rebellions from both wings of his party, Johnson withdrew from the race in 1968, and Richard Nixon was elected president over Hubert Humphrey in a close three-way election in which Wallace captured five southern states.

Although he initially proceeded slowly in attempting to reverse the tide of civil rights, in his 1970 State of the Union speech President Nixon pointedly declared a new "war on crime" to combat "criminal elements which increasingly threaten our cities, our homes, and our lives" (quoted in Western 2006, 60). Few listeners could miss the sardonic allusion to Johnson's "war on poverty" or misunderstand Nixon's symbolic stance against urban rioters (those threatening our cities) and black criminals (those threatening our homes and lives). Blaming crime and disorder on the "permissive" liberal policies of the past, he led Republican efforts to build a new criminal justice system grounded in the politics of retribution.

Symbolically, this new focus on punishment and retribution took the form of support for the death penalty, which had been held unconstitutional by the "liberal" Supreme Court in 1972. By 1976, however, after the high court gave directions on how states could rewrite death penalty statutes to pass constitutional muster, thirty-nine states had passed legislation reinstating the death penalty (Banner 2002). Despite the symbolic importance of death penalty legislation, it is of little practical importance because of the relative infrequency of capital crimes. Of the 2.1 million people currently in prison or jail, only around 3,400 are on death row. Moreover, outside the South, executions are rare. Of the slightly more than 1,000 executions since 1967, more than 70 percent have been in states of the former Confederacy, with the vast majority of the condemned being black.

Despite evidence of systematic racial bias in the application of the death penalty (see U.S. General Accounting Office 1997), in practical terms incarceration has been of far greater importance as a mechanism of racial stratification (Western 2006). The increasing reliance of the criminal justice system on incarceration was achieved by specific legislative actions that eliminated judicial flexibility in sentencing, curtailed parole authority, established mandatory minimum sentences, and increased prison terms for repeat offenses. Between 1980 and 2000, the number of states enacting sentencing guidelines went from two to seventeen; the number abolishing or limiting parole went from seventeen to thirty-three; the number passing "three strikes" or similar legislation went from zero to twenty-four; and the number implementing "truth in sentencing" laws went from three to forty (Western 2006, 65). The end result, inevitably, was more people behind bars for longer periods of time.

That Republicans led this new "war on crime" is indicated by the fact that the strongest single predictor of imprisonment rates across states between 1980 and 2000 was a change from a Democratic to a Republican gubernatorial administration (Western 2006, 70). Imprisonment rates are also higher in states with Republican legislatures (Jacobs and Carmichael 2001), and nationally incarceration rates have grown more rapidly under Republican than under Democratic presidents (Jacobs and Helms 1996).

Richard Nixon's "war on crime" during the 1970s was followed by Ronald Reagan's "war on drugs" in the 1980s. In 1986 Reagan signed a national security directive that named drugs a threat to national security and authorized the military to cooperate with civilian authorities in prosecuting the newly declared "war" (Andreas 2000). Drug offenses that had formerly been left to the states to prosecute were now made against federal law, and mandatory minimum sentences were enacted for the newly federalized crimes (Western 2006). During the 1980s, severe penalties were enacted for nonviolent drug violations, and in the wake of the crack epidemic, possession or sale of that particular form of cocaine was singled out for much harsher punishment than for offenses involving its powdered counterpart (Tonry 1996). In a very real way, criminal possession of a controlled substance came to replace "vagrancy" as the statutory mechanism used most commonly by state authorities to regulate and control the behavior of poor African Americans (Dubber 2001).

In the wake of the twin wars on crime and drugs, infractions were more likely to result in arrests; arrests were more likely to result in imprisonment; imprisonment was likely to involve a long sentence; and long sentences were less likely to be shortened by parole. As a result, the U.S. prison population increased dramatically. Between 1970 and 2003, the number of people in state and federal penitentiaries rose from around 200,000 to 1.4 million. In the latter year, another 700,000 offenders were held in county jails, and 4.7 million people were on probation or parole, meaning that 6 percent of the U.S. adult male population was under criminal justice supervision (Western 2006, 3).

Growth in the number of prisoners far outstripped the rate of population growth generally, pushing rates of incarceration to new heights. Between 1980 and 2001, the rate of incarceration for violent crimes rose by a factor of 2.7, that for property crimes by 2.1, and that for drug crimes by 10.8 (Western 2006, 45). By the year 2001, the United States had the highest incarceration rate in the world, with 6.9 of every 1,000 people behind bars—5.4 times the rate of its closest competitor in the developed world (Western 2006). The only other countries to come close to the U.S. rate of incarceration were Russia at 6.3 per 1,000 and South Africa at 4.0 per 1,000.

This prison boom occurred not because people were committing more crimes—indeed, crime rates fell between 1980 and 2001—but because the crimes they committed were being treated differently. In Bruce Western's words (2006, 44), "at every stage of criminal processing, from policing, to the court hearing, criminal justice officials decide on the disposition of offenders and these effects on the scale of imprisonment far overshadow fluctuations in the level of crime." Moreover, as in all societies, the vast majority of crimes in the United States are committed by poor, young, socially unattached males, so that the shift from rehabilitation to retribution guaranteed a disproportionate effect on any social category fitting this demographic profile.

As one works through the categories of gender, age, race, and class, therefore, the weight of state punishment comes increasingly to bear on poor black males. Whereas only 0.7 percent of all Americans were behind bars in 2000, the figure was 2.1 percent for working-age adult males; among working-age males, the share behind bars was 1 percent for whites, but 7.9 percent for blacks. Among young black men of prime working age (twenty to forty years), the incarceration rate was 11.5 percent, but among those without a college degree it was 17 percent; among those without a high school degree, the share rose to one-third (Western 2006, 17).

Under the new regime, black-white disparities in imprisonment have come to exceed any other racial differential in American society. Whereas racial disparities in unemployment and infant mortality stand at roughly two to one, and the disparity in unwed childbearing is three to one, the differential with respect to imprisonment is eight to one. Indeed, according to Western (2006, 18), "among the most socially marginal men—African Americans in their twenties and thirties who had dropped out of high school—incarceration rates were nearly fifty times the national average." Young black men became more likely to go to prison or jail than to enter college, join the military, belong to a labor union, or go on welfare. The most common interaction between a black male and the state now occurs under the auspices of the criminal justice system.

A high risk of imprisonment at any point in time cumulates over the life course to very high lifetime probabilities of incarceration. Although "only" 11 to 12 percent of young black men may be in jail or prison at any given moment, among black men born between 1965 and 1969 the cumulative risk of incarceration by age thirty-five was 21 percent, and for those who were high school dropouts it was an astounding 59 percent (Western 2006). Thus, because of deliberate, racially encoded changes in public policy enacted after 1970, mass incarceration became a normative feature in the life of poor black communities. This state-directed insertion of criminal justice into the daily lives of poor African Americans has had profound consequences for the process of racial stratification, affecting in very powerful ways black employment, earnings, marriage, and health.

Invisible Inequality

At the aggregate level, the massive imprisonment of African Americans serves to obscure actual trends in wages and employment within the United States. This obfuscation occurs because people in jail and prison are excluded from the data sources used to compute income and unemployment rates from month to month and year to year, such as the Current Population Survey (CPS). Mass imprisonment thus renders America's most vulnerable citizens, quite literally, "invisible" to policymakers and the public (Western 2006, 85–130).

Fortunately, the decennial census includes prisoners among those enumerated, and in census years we can assess the effect that mass imprisonment has had on standard intercensal measures of work and wages. To determine what earnings and employment rates might look like if prisoners were routinely included, Western (2006) defined as jobless any person who was not employed or in the military and then computed jobless ratios with and without prisoners included in the base population. Using conventional definitions, he estimated that the jobless rate for young black males age twenty-two to thirty was 22.9 percent in 1980 and 23.7 percent in 2000. In other words, over two decades the level of joblessness among young black males appeared to change little.

This impression holds, however, only if we disregard black prisoners, because a growing fraction of the marginally employed found themselves incarcerated behind bars between the two dates. Whereas 19 percent of jobless black men were imprisoned in 1980, by 2000 the share was 35 percent. When we put these people back into the numerator and denominator of the jobless ratio, black joblessness is found not to have held steady but to have *increased* substantially from 1980 to 2000, going from 26.7 percent to 32.4 percent. In other words, by imprisoning a growing fraction of marginally employable black men during the last two decades, government policy artificially depressed the measured rate of unemployment for black males. Apparent stability in black male joblessness was entirely an artifact of the rising rate of black male incarceration.

The effect of imprisonment on conventional measures of male

joblessness is even greater among those lacking educational credentials. Among young black men without a high school degree, the rate of joblessness was 41 percent in 2000 according to conventional measures, but including imprisoned males in the calculation yields a jobless rate of 65 percent (Western 2006, 92). This pronounced effect occurs because fully half of young black men who were not working, in school, or in the military in the year 2000 were behind bars.

Given that black men are much more likely to drop out of high school and not go to college than white men, this discrepancy also carries important implications for the measurement of racial stratification itself. According to conventional measures, young, black, non-college-educated males were 2.5 times more likely to be jobless than comparable whites, but including prisoners in the calculation raises the differential to 2.9. A similar logic holds for the computation of black-white wage differentials. The conventional approach to measuring average black and white wages reveals a declining racial gap after 1985, suggesting progress toward racial equality in post–civil rights era earnings. But this computation does not take into account the selective imprisonment of low- versus high-wage workers over the period.

Roughly two-thirds of prison inmates were employed at the time of their incarceration, and at the time they entered prison these workers earned systematically lower wages than their non-incarcerated counterparts. After adjusting for the selective exclusion of these poorly paid workers from the labor force because of rising imprisonment, Western (2006, 100–1) found that the apparent improvement in black wages all but disappeared. Relative black wages rose in government statistics during the late 1980s and 1990s not because African American workers were earning higher wages relative to whites, but because those earning the lowest wages were systematically being removed from the labor force and put behind bars.

Double Stigmatization

Being of African ancestry historically has conferred a significant stigma on workers in the United States, yielding lower rates of pay and employment. In addition to whatever burdens African Americans must bear in job markets because of continued racial prejudice, a criminal record imposes a significant, *additional* social stigma, signaling to potential employers that a prospective employee is unreliable, undependable, dishonest, and perhaps even dangerous. At the micro level, therefore, not only does imprisonment remove marginal men from the labor market physically, but the stigma of a criminal record also makes it more difficult for them to find decent jobs once they are released (Western 2006).

One reason why this is so is that in many states a felony conviction disqualifies a person for employment in licensed occupations or in state and local government. Incarceration also undermines job prospects by eroding human and social capital and preventing young men from gaining work experience, learning new skills, and acquiring training. In addition, incarceration undermines mental and physical health, which are themselves important determinants of labor market success. Finally, spending long periods of time behind bars weakens ties to family and friends, attenuating the network connections that people customarily draw upon to find work.

For these reasons, Western (2006) hypothesized that ex-cons would have a harder time finding work upon release than comparably skilled workers without a criminal record and that when they did find a job, it was likely to offer systematically lower wages. In a simple tabulation of employment before and after imprisonment, Western found that annual weeks worked dropped from thirty-seven to twenty-three for whites and from thirty-five to twenty-one for blacks. Whereas the hourly wages earned by whites remained more or less the same before and after incarceration ($11.14 versus $11.80), black wages dropped by 10 percent, going from $10.25 to $9.25 per hour. Compared to white ex-cons, therefore, black ex-offenders returning to the labor market experienced double stigmatization: they were penalized for having a criminal record as well as for being black.

These conclusions from simple, uncontrolled comparisons hold up under more detailed statistical analysis. In his comprehensive regression analysis of nationally representative survey data from 1983 to 2000, Western (2006, 119) found that, net of a variety of control factors, incarceration reduced the number of weeks of employment among black males by 15.1 percent, lowered their wages by 12.4 percent, and depressed their annual income by 36.9 percent. Having a criminal record was also associated with more rapid job turnover and reduced tenure. Whereas African Americans without a criminal record averaged thirty-five weeks in their jobs, black ex-cons averaged just twenty-one in theirs (Western 2006, 124). Ex-offenders also received lower returns to work experience than those who had never been incarcerated. Whereas the average black worker without a criminal record enjoyed a 15 percent rise in wages between the ages of twenty-five and thirty-five, among black ex-cons the increase was just 5 percent.

As these analyses clearly show, incarceration carries a serious cost to the individual as well as society by lowering employment and wages among former prisoners compared to what they would have experienced had they never been incarcerated. Based on his analysis of observations of men during the period 1981 to 2000, Western (2006, 127) estimated that the average loss in lifetime income because of incarceration was $86,000 for black males, a total that was 42 percent below what they would have earned had they not been sent to prison.

Despite the robust findings and extensive statistical controls, however, Western's (2006) analyses are based on cross-sectional survey data and so are once again subject to the usual criticisms of bias from selectivity, simultaneity, and endogeneity. To overcome these objections, Pager (2003) systematically varied criminal record in her audit of entry-level jobs in Milwaukee and demonstrated not only the powerful negative effect of a criminal record but also a significant interaction between criminality and race. As already noted, employers expressed significantly less interest in black ex-cons than white ex-cons. In 95 percent of all cases, black ex-cons did not receive a callback, compared with only 82 percent for those who were white.

Thus, owing to discrimination on the basis of both race and criminal record, black former offenders are exceedingly unlikely to find a job, and even when they do achieve employment, they are unlikely to be paid very well. In their analysis of data from the Multi-

City Study of Urban Inequality, Harry Holzer, Stephen Raphael, and Michael Stoll (2004, 236) found that "employer willingness to hire former offenders is limited, even relative to other groups of disadvantaged workers (such as welfare recipients)." More than 60 percent of employers surveyed in Atlanta, Boston, Detroit, and Los Angeles said they definitely or probably would not be willing to hire ex-cons, and about one-third said they actually performed background checks (Holzer 1996).

Even among those employers who said they were willing to hire former offenders, moreover, the share who did so when given the opportunity was very small and was again significantly lower for blacks than whites (Pager and Quillian 2005). In addition, many small employers said they refuse to hire ex-offenders even though they do not carry out criminal background checks, suggesting to Holzer, Raphael, and Stoll (2004, 236) that "they may engage in statistical discrimination against a broader range of applicants, such as less educated young black men." Because such people are known to have higher rates of criminal conviction, employers steer clear of all those with these characteristics. Thus, mass incarceration may have contributed to an ancillary rise in statistical discrimination.

Family Values and Mass Imprisonment

Even as they emphasize "family values" as the moral bedrock of American society, conservative politicians have built a criminal justice system that systematically undermines marital stability and child well-being on a massive scale (Pattillo, Weiman, and Western 2004). According to prisoner surveys, 11 percent of incarcerated black men are married, and 70 percent have children. As a result, in the year 2000 more than one million black children had a father in prison or jail, representing 9 percent of all those under age eighteen (Western 2006). The criminal justice system has thus assumed a large and growing role within the African American family.

Marriage is perhaps the most basic social institution, and research has demonstrated its positive effects on men (Waite and Gallagher 2000) and children (McLanahan and Sandefur 1994). The prevalence of marriage in any population depends on the rate at which men enter into first marriages, the rate at which those marriages dissolve, the rate at which formerly married people enter into new unions, and the rate at which these new unions break up over time. At each stage in the process, incarceration has a significant negative effect.

Placing a man in prison obviously removes him from circulation and thus lowers the odds of marriage through physical separation. Imprisoned males are about 70 percent less likely to get married in the year they are incarcerated compared with their counterparts in the general population (Western 2006). Moreover, even after being released from prison, ex-offenders experience much lower odds of marriage than those without jail or prison experience. As with prospective employers, a criminal conviction signals to prospective spouses that a man is undependable, unreliable, and perhaps even dangerous (Edin, Nelson, and Paranal 2004). Likewise, just as job skills deteriorate in prison, so do a man's social skills in dealing with people—especially members of the opposite sex. The brutal conditions that pervade American prisons also have negative effects on mental and physical health that render ex-cons less attractive as mates (Collins 2004; Nurse 2004).

Controlling for a variety of background characteristics and selectivity into the population of married adults, Western (2006, 146) found that incarceration significantly reduced the odds of marriage among young black men. Whereas the typical black male experienced a 54 percent likelihood of marriage by age forty in the absence of a criminal record, those who had been incarcerated experienced only a 43 percent chance of marriage. Incarceration also increased the odds that a marriage would end in divorce. Indeed, few marriages survive a husband's incarceration, and even those that do experience a heightened risk of failure thereafter. However, because black divorce rates are higher than those of whites and imprisonment carries less stigma in the black community (where it is more common), the effect of imprisonment on divorce is greater among whites than among blacks. The typical white male evinced a 23 percent likelihood of divorce after six years of marriage in the absence of prison experience, but a 50 percent increase in risk if he had ever been imprisoned. In contrast, imprisonment increased the likelihood of divorce among black males only from 34 percent to 36 percent (Western 2006, 148).

Because the material interests of men and women are intertwined through the institution of marriage, the mass incarceration of black men inevitably has important consequences for the social and economic well-being of black women. By undermining marriage and increasing the risk of divorce, imprisonment lowers the odds that black women will enjoy support from a partner's income, and by lowering the employment and earnings of men after they are released, imprisonment reduces the income even of those black women who manage to buck the odds and remain married during and after a husband's incarceration.

Although black women may suffer economically from the mass imprisonment of black men, at least they are adults and have options to look out for themselves. Unfortunately, black children do not have such options and are far more vulnerable to the family disruption caused by male imprisonment. One year after the birth of a child, just 42 percent of formerly incarcerated black men were married or living with the mother, compared with 56 percent of those who had not been incarcerated (Western 2006, 152). For a typical unmarried black male, the likelihood of marrying the mother of his child within a year of the birth is reduced 21 percent by incarceration, and for those who were married at the time of the birth, the likelihood of separation is raised by 11 percent (Western 2006, 156). A father's imprisonment greatly increases the odds that a child will end up in the care of relatives, a foster family, or a government or private agency (Johnson and Waldfogel 2004).

Damaged Goods

A long period of confinement in a state or federal penitentiary, or even a relatively short stint in a county jail, is hardly a resort holiday. The brutal conditions that prevail in American correctional institutions have been well documented (Herivel and Wright 2003; Human Rights Watch 1991; Jacobson-Hardy 1998). Given high rates of gang activity, sexual predation, drug abuse, and violence within penal institutions, it is quite likely that the men leaving them will be quite different psychologically from the ones who went in. Exposure to sexual and physical violence, in particular, is likely to increase the risk of mental illness, susceptibility to violence, criminality, and sexual deviance (Macmillan 2001). In significant ways, men who spend time in American prisons are likely to return to communities and families as damaged goods (Collins 2004).

As a result, people living in communities with high proportions of ex-offenders experience much less collective efficacy and are much more suspicious than others, controlling for local poverty levels, crime rates, and a variety of personal characteristics (Lynch and Sabol 2004). Western's findings (2006, 159) suggest that there are good reasons for people to be apprehensive about the return of ex-offenders to their families and communities. Whereas the likelihood that a male non-offender will assault his pregnant partner is only 1 to 2 percent, the likelihood climbs significantly among ex-offenders, reaching 6 percent before pregnancy, 5 percent during pregnancy, and 9 percent after the birth.

The negative effect of imprisonment on domestic violence persists even after the introduction of controls for prior violent behavior and relationship quality, suggesting that the effect on violent behavior is attributable to imprisonment itself and not preexisting tendencies. Indeed, after controlling for prior history of violence and other factors, incarceration for a violent offense was found to increase the likelihood of domestic violence by 11 percent, incarceration for a drug offense increased it by 8 percent, and incarceration for other offenses raised it by 10 percent (Western 2006, 161).

In addition to heightening the risk of violence within black families, Johnson and Raphael (2005) show that mass incarceration has become a major vehicle for the transmission of HIV into the black community. Imprisonment increases the exposure of black men to homosexual activity and intravenous drug use, and the high concentration of HIV-positive men in prison (Hammett, Harmon, and Rhodes 2002), coupled with the tendency of prisoners to engage in high-risk behaviors (Krebs 2002; Swartz, Lurigio, and Weiner 2004), yields an extraordinarily high rate of HIV transmission, not only among offenders but later between offenders and non-offender partners after their release.

The high rate at which black men circulate through the prison system and the negative effect of imprisonment on the stability of unions dramatically increases the number of lifetime sexual partners and maximizes the number of concurrent or overlapping sexual relationships among black men and women (Adimora and Schoenbach 2005). As a result, rising rates of black male incarceration from 1982 to 2000 explain much of the widening racial differential in AIDS infection (Johnson and Raphael 2005). The spread of HIV-AIDS among African Americans stems far more from changes in sentencing than changes in risky behaviors or medical access among African Americans.

The New Racial Stratification

Racial inequality before the civil rights era was produced by a constellation of institutions and behaviors that were deeply embedded in American social practices and cultural conventions and extended well beyond the strictures of Jim Crow. Although legalized segregation in the South may have used state power to enforce the color line, racial stratification was also achieved by a popular, well-entrenched system of private discrimination that prevailed in the North as well as the South. In addition, as the federal government assumed a larger role in the political economy after the New Deal, the welfare state itself was racialized to exclude African Americans from the principal wealth- and income-producing engines of the postwar economy and leave them outside the social safety net it stitched together.

Although white support for the passage of laws to end Jim Crow was substantial outside the South and grew steadily through the 1960s and 1970s, there was much less support for efforts to deracialize the welfare state and dismantle the de facto system of discrimination. Once the civil rights movement achieved its goal of ending Jim Crow segregation and began to address other mechanisms of racial stratification, it met growing white resistance. Although whites ultimately came to accept racial equality in principle, they remained uncomfortable with its consequences in practice and were unsupportive of government efforts to enforce its application in American markets. This ambivalent stance led to a new alignment of race-making practices and institutions in the final decades of the twentieth century.

In terms of practice, overt racial discrimination largely ended, but discrimination itself did not disappear. Rather, now that naked racism is publicly condemned and discrimination is illegal, discriminatory practices have gone underground, becoming more subtle but remaining quite effective in perpetuating racial stratification. Likewise, although principled racism has waned and racist views are rarely voiced, substantial shares of whites continue to hold negative stereotypes about African Americans and unconsciously harbor negative racial sentiments that cause them to avoid contact with African Americans in families, schools, neighborhoods, churches, and other settings, yielding low levels of intermarriage and high levels of segregation between blacks and whites.

Since white Americans no longer see open discrimination around them, they believe it has been eliminated from U.S. markets, and since they no longer hear racist principles being espoused by respectable people, they believe that racial prejudice has receded, if not disappeared. They embrace the view that the United States has become a race-blind society and that state efforts to improve the welfare of African Americans violate the principle of racial neutrality. Hence, they oppose most federal programs and enforcement actions that have been proposed to close the gap between race-blind principles and racially stratified outcomes, which they attribute to nonracial causes.

Despite the reluctance of whites to accept the continuing reality of racism, however, there is abundant evidence—experimental as well as observational—that high levels of discrimination against African Americans persist in key U.S. markets. Quasi-experimental audit studies indicate that because of discrimination, blacks and whites do not achieve equal access to homes, credit, jobs, earnings, services, and consumer products. Much of this discrimination is indirect, occurring on the basis of traits and characteristics associated with race, such as place of residence, style of speech, naming conventions, and criminal convictions. The persistence of discrimination in U.S. markets translates directly into lower incomes, less housing wealth, poorer insurance coverage, and higher consumer prices.

In terms of institutions, two structural configurations are central to perpetuating black disadvantages in the post–civil rights era: the housing market and the criminal justice system. Studies consistently reveal institutionalized prejudice and discrimination in the real estate, banking, and insurance industries and have documented the surreptitious continuation of illegal practices such as redlining, steering, predatory lending, selective marketing, and linguistic profiling, as well as the web of lies, deceit, and subterfuge known as "discrimination with a smile." The rise of the prison industrial complex after 1970 did not occur in response to rising black crime but stemmed from a new punishment regime that increased the rate of prosecution, lengthened the sentences, and reduced the odds of parole for crimes committed by blacks. As a result of these institutional arrangements, the United States now displays the highest rate of incarceration and the highest levels of racial residential segregation in the world.

Both institutional configurations concentrate their effects on African Americans. A majority of urban black residents live under conditions of racial isolation that are so extreme that they satisfy the criteria for hypersegregation, and among black males rates of incarceration are such that a young black male without a high school degree has a 59 percent chance being imprisoned before his thirty-fifth birthday. The hypersegregation and mass incarceration of African Americans are central to the contemporary system of racial stratification because so many negative consequences follow from them.

High levels of racial segregation in housing lead axiomatically to other forms of separation characteristic of American apartheid: separate neighborhoods, separate schools, separate churches, separate stores, separate services, separate social networks, and separate jobs. Housing markets are critical to well-being because they distribute not only places to live but anything that is correlated with where one lives. Thus, housing markets distribute not just houses but also education, wealth, health, security, insurance, and social connections, and if African Americans are denied full access to housing markets, they are also denied access to these other benefits and resources (Massey and Denton 1993).

At the aggregate level, residential segregation is the structural feature of American society most responsible for the geographic concentration of poverty observed during the 1970s and 1980s. As inflation, unemployment, and economic restructuring drove up the rate of black poverty, the only possible outcome, given high levels of racial segregation, was a growing concentration of poverty in black neighborhoods (Massey and Fischer 2000). As the concentration of poverty rose, moreover, so did the spatial concentration of anything correlated with poverty—crime, violence, single-parenthood, joblessness, dependency, and addiction—and thus a remarkably disadvantaged social and economic environment was created for African Americans (Massey and Denton 1993). In addition to the disadvantages associated with individual and familial poverty, poor blacks are uniquely burdened with the disadvantages of very poor neighborhoods, which act independently to constrain socioeconomic mobility and undermine well-being (Massey, Gross, and Eggers 1991).

The concentration of poverty within black neighborhoods reinforces negative stereotypes of African Americans to make the system of segregation self-perpetuating. Studies clearly show that the avoidance of black neighbors by whites does not stem from the desire to live with other whites, perceived class differences from blacks, or other socioeconomic factors, but is determined mainly by the harboring of negative racial stereotypes. Thus, by concentrating poverty's negative correlates, segregation simultaneously makes them more salient to whites and more detrimental to blacks, and the resulting reinforcement of negative racial stereotypes perpetuates white resistance to integration, leading to the persistence of segregation.

One of the most important correlates of concentrated poverty is the geographic concentration of crime, which yields neighborhood environments characterized by high rates of violence and disorder that inflict high levels of stress on African Americans, thereby undermining their mental health, physical well-being, and cognitive skills through prolonged exposure to stress hormones such as cortisol (Massey 2004). Concentrated poverty also creates a dangerous milieu that compels young men to project a public reputation for violence as a means of self-protection (Massey 2001), thus enmeshing them in a self-perpetuating spiral of crime and deviance that dovetails with the rise of the prison industrial complex to fuel mass incarceration, which further hardens the lines of race and class to promote racial stratification.

The mass imprisonment of poor black males has accelerated the transmission of HIV-AIDS within the black community, not only to felons who are exposed to sexual predation and drug abuse while in prison but to the women in their sexual networks who are infected upon their release and the children to whom they give birth. For individual black men, a criminal record decisively lowers the odds of employment and reduces the level and growth of earnings among those who do manage somehow to find work. Imprisonment also reduces the likelihood that a black man will marry and increases the odds of separation and divorce among those who are married at the time of incarceration, while also increasing the odds of domestic violence after their release. At the aggregate level, therefore, the rise of the prison industrial complex contributes significantly to joblessness, depressed earnings, marital instability, unwed childbearing, dependency, and domestic violence in the black community.

In sum, not only did the civil rights legislation of the 1960s and 1970s fail to end racial stratification in the United States, but in some ways it gave birth to even more pernicious and intractable mechanisms of categorical inequality. Contemporary processes of discrimination are no less powerful in denying African Americans equal access to the nation's material, symbolic, and emotional resources, but they are less obvious and observable, allowing whites the luxury of "plausible deniability" and permitting self-serving rationalizations that "blame the victim." At the same time, a vastly more punitive criminal justice system has created an American gulag that exceeds anything the Soviets ever accomplished during the cold war and that systematically reduces the health, education, and welfare of African American citizens and denies even the most elemental of freedoms to a large and growing fraction of black men.

✥ CHAPTER 4 ✥

BUILDING A BETTER UNDERCLASS

African Americans are not the only disadvantaged minority group in the United States, of course. In the sweep of American history, many groups have become targets of prejudice and discrimination (Jacobson 1999; Perlmutter 1999). Successive waves of European immigrants and their descendants struggled long and hard to be accepted as "white" within American society (Brodkin 1999; Ignatiev 1996; Roediger 1991). Full "whiteness" was not attained socially by most southern and eastern Europeans until the 1970s (Alba 1990), and the process of "whitening" did not begin for groups such as the Chinese and Japanese until after the civil rights era (Daniels 1988).

As of the year 2000, however, intermarriage between European-origin groups had become extensive, and unions between whites and Asians of the second or third generation were common (Lee and Edmonston 2005). Among whites in the United States, ethnic ancestry had become a complex amalgam of European origins (Lieberson and Waters 1988; Waters 1990), and the number of Eurasians was expanding rapidly in places with a long history of Asian settlement, such as California (Williams-Leon 2002). The future of America would seem to be one in which various European and Asian ancestries are increasingly jumbled together in a way that makes categorical distinctions between them fade (Alba and Nee 2003; Edmonston, Lee, and Passel 2002). There is presently little conceptual framing or social boundary work going on to create social distinctions between Europeans and Asians in American society.

The erosion of categorical boundaries is less certain for the group that has now become the nation's largest minority—Latinos. A significant share of this population originates in the Caribbean, a region that once housed plantations reliant on African slave labor. As a result, many, if not most, Caribbean Hispanics are of mixed African and European origins, and a large fraction are African in appearance. Even though racially mixed Latinos may be accepted as "white" or placed in some intermediate racial category in their countries of origin (Graham 1990; Telles 2005; Wade 1997), in the United States they are generally perceived and treated as "blacks" by white Americans, who are socialized into dictates of the one-drop rule (Denton and Massey 1989).

Research has shown that black Hispanics face greater discrimination than white Hispanics in most U.S. markets (Allen, Telles, and Hunter 2000; Montalvo and Codina 2001; Yinger 1991). For example, darker-skinned Hispanics have been shown to earn lower wages (Darity and Mason 1998; Gomez 2000; Mason 2004; Rodriguez 1991; Telles and Murguia 1990), achieve less prestigious occupations (Espino and Franz 2002), inhabit poorer residential environments (Massey and Bitterman 1985; Relethford et al. 1983), suffer greater neighborhood segregation (Denton and Massey 1989), and generally experience more restricted life chances (Arce, Murguia, and Frisbie 1987; Duany 1998) compared with their lighter-skinned counterparts.

To the extent that Latinos from the Caribbean are successful in achieving acceptance as white Americans, like the southern and eastern Europeans before them they will probably avoid the categorical mechanisms of racial stratification that historically have undermined the status and well-being of Americans who trace their ancestry to Africa. Patrick Mason (2004) found, for example, that Latinos espousing a white racial identity earned higher wages and incomes than those who subscribed to a nonwhite identity. Likewise, Denton and Massey (1989) found that Latinos who identified themselves as white achieved greater residential integration than those who said they were black.

To the extent that racially mixed Hispanics are perceived by whites to be "black," however, they are likely to share the socioeconomic fate of African Americans (Duany 1998). Thus, Hispanics who say they are neither black nor white but espouse some racially mixed identity are treated more like blacks than whites in U.S. housing markets. Although their levels of segregation from non-Hispanic whites lie in between those of white and black Hispanics, indices of segregation for them are much closer to those observed at the black end of the continuum (Denton and Massey 1989). The segmentation of Hispanic socioeconomic outcomes on the basis of skin color yields a variegated pattern of integration that Alejandro Portes and Min Zhou (1993) have called "segmented assimilation." As Mason (2004, 817) concluded from his detailed research on the economic consequences of racial identity, "neither the abandonment of Spanish nor the abandonment of a specifically Hispanic racial self-identity is sufficient to overcome the penalties associated with having a dark complexion and non-European phenotype."

Whatever the future of Afro-Caribbean Latinos, they make up a relatively small share of all Hispanics in the United States. In the year 2000, for example, the three main Caribbean groups—Puerto Ricans, Cubans, and Dominicans—collectively amounted to just 15 percent of all Latinos in the United States (Guzman 2001). More relevant to the fate of Hispanics as a whole is how those from outside the Caribbean are perceived and treated. Among non-Caribbean Hispanics, the relevant racial mixture is not European and African, but European and Amerindian, a blend that people in the region generally label *mestizo*. In most of Latin America, the racial continuum runs not from white to black but from European to Native American.

According to the latest data (U.S. Bureau of the Census 2006), 8 percent of all Hispanics are from Central America and 5 percent are from South America, but by far the largest subgroup is Mexicans, who make up fully 66 percent of the entire Latino population. By themselves, Mexican Americans are easily the nation's second-largest minority group, with 28 million people, compared to 38 million African Americans. How Mexicans are perceived and treated by white Americans thus disproportionately affects the status and well-being of all Hispanics. Not only do Mexicans constitute two-thirds of the entire Latino population, but it is doubtful whether the average Anglo-American can distinguish between mestizos of Mexican, Guatemalan, Salvadoran, Peruvian, or Colombian origin. To the extent that boundary work and framing are carried out within American society to position Mexicans as a racialized "other," these processes are bound to have spillover effects on other Latinos.

The Historical Racialization of Mexicans

Mexicans are not only the second-largest minority group in the country but the second oldest; truth be told, their presence in what is now the United States predates that of African Americans. Santa Fe, New Mexico, for example, was founded in 1608, eleven years before the first African slaves arrived in Virginia in 1619. The first inhabitants of Santa Fe were not U.S. citizens, of course. That honor would not be bestowed upon them until 1848, when the Treaty of Guadalupe Hidalgo ended the Mexican-American War and ceded to the United States the present states of Texas, Arizona, New Mexico, and California, along with parts of Utah, Colorado, and Nevada. With its signing, some fifty thousand Mexicans suddenly became U.S. citizens (Jaffe, Cullen, and Boswell 1980); with the stroke of a pen, they were transformed from being a majority in their own country to a minority in an alien land (MacLachlan and Beezley 2003).

Manufacturing a Racial Other

The bulk of these new U.S. citizens lived in New Mexico and Texas, and the latter, being a slave state, quickly relegated Mexican Americans to the wrong side of the color line: they were not enslaved like African Americans, but they certainly were not accorded the rights and privileges of white Europeans (Gutierrez 1995). Through a variety of categorical mechanisms—some legal and some not so legal—Mexicans were systematically disenfranchised of their property and liberties and turned into landless laborers for white property and business owners (de León 1993; Zamora 1993). Although Mexicans were also disenfranchised and subordinated outside of Texas, the degree of subjugation elsewhere was not as severe (Gutierrez 1995).

In New Mexico, for example, the Hispanic population was larger in relative terms, more firmly established, and less mestizo. Indeed, many people did not even consider themselves to be Mexicans at all. At the time of the cession, Mexico had existed for only twenty-seven years as a nation, compared with three hundred years of Spanish colonial rule. Given that the Spanish and Pueblo Indian populations did not intermingle extensively, many New Mexicans considered themselves to be of Spanish origin and identified themselves as "Hispanos" rather than Mexicans (Jaffe et al. 1980).

The inhabitants of New Mexico were also more geographically isolated, and because they had fewer resources that could be readily exploited in a pre-industrial economy, in-migration by Anglo-Americans occurred slowly. As a result, New Mexico's Latinos were able to retain a greater hold on material resources and political power than in Texas (Beck 1969). Indeed, at the time the state constitution was ratified, it declared Spanish to be an official language along with English. Even today people of Hispanic origin constitute 42 percent of New Mexico's population, the largest share of any state.

In contrast to Texas and New Mexico, California and Arizona were both sparsely populated in 1848, and Arizona remained largely unsettled well into the twentieth century. Mexicans in California were quickly swamped, however, by the demographic tidal wave that began with the Gold Rush of 1849 (Cook and Borah 1979). Whereas just 14,000 people inhabited all of California in 1848, by 1852 the population had mushroomed to 224,000 through the in-migration of European-origin whites from the East. In contrast, Arizona's population remained under 10,000 until the 1870s and did not reach even 100,000 until 1900.

Nonetheless, wherever they were found, by the end of the nineteenth century Mexicans had been transformed socially and economically into a subordinate stratum of people subject to widespread discrimination and systematic exclusion (Grebler, Moore, and Guzman 1970). The degree to which Mexicans had been transmuted from masters of their own domain into a racialized source of cheap labor for whites is indicated by the Senate Dillingham Commission report of 1911, which described Mexicans as "notoriously indolent and unprogressive in all matters of education and culture" and doing dirty jobs fit only for "the lowest grade of nonassimilable native-born races," though their "usefulness is ... much impaired by [their] lack of ambition and [their] proneness to the constant use of intoxicating liquor" (U.S. Immigration Commission 1911, 59, 94, 110).

Of course, this process of racialization was not much different from that directed at southern and eastern Europeans at the time. The pecking order of the races perceived by Anglo-Americans was clearly revealed in the immigration quotas established by Congress in the early 1920s (Zolberg 2006). Whereas countries in northern and western Europe—Germany, Scandinavia, and the British Isles—got large numerical allocations, those in southern and eastern Europe were given tiny allotments, and Asians and Africans were banned entirely. Although Mexicans were viewed by lawmakers as even more racially deficient than Italians, Jews, and Poles, the number of Mexican immigrants in 1921 was small, and they were isolated geographically. Hence, they were not perceived as a threat to the nation. On the contrary, precisely because they were considered to be so inferior and "nonassimilable" by the Dillingham Commission, legislators believed that Mexican migrants would not seek to remain north of the border (Zolberg 2006). As a result, Congress did not bother to assign an immigration quota to Mexico—or to any other country in the Western Hemisphere—when it passed the National Origins Quota Acts in the early 1920s.

Expanding an Exploitable Class

The roughly 50,000 Mexicans absorbed into the United States in 1848 expanded mainly through natural increase until the twentieth century. Although fertility rates were high, so were levels of mortality, and the rate of demographic expansion was modest. As of 1900, the Mexican-origin population of the United States numbered only around 150,000, and in that year just 237 Mexicans arrived as immigrants. Although racism against Mexicans was real and ongoing, their small numbers and geographic isolation meant that categorical mechanisms of inequality established to ensure their subordinate status had little effect on inequality within the nation as a whole. Mexicans did not even enter the consciousness of most white Americans as a meaningful social group.

This status quo was upset in 1907. In that year the United States and Japan concluded a "Gentlemen's Agreement" under which Japanese authorities agreed to prevent the departure of their citizens for the United States, in return for which the United States agreed not to visit upon Japan the indignity of banning them from entering (Zolberg 2006). This action caused a serious disruption of western labor markets, for after the Chinese Exclusion Act of 1882, Japanese immigrants had come to constitute the backbone of the region's unskilled workforce. From the viewpoint of white westerners, however, the problem with Japanese workers was not that they were inferior but that they proved to be *too* industrious (Kitano 1969). Rather than remaining content as agricultural laborers, gardeners, or menial service workers, they saved their money and pooled resources within families to purchase farms, start businesses, and enter services where they competed with whites (Petersen 1971).

Angered by the rise of the Japanese above their assigned station in the local racial hierarchy, state legislatures throughout the West passed a series of harsh laws that made no pretense of being anything other than overt mechanisms of exploitation and exclusion directed against people of Japanese origin (Maki, Kitano, and Berthold 1999). After prevailing upon Congress to prohibit Japanese immigrants from naturalizing to U.S. citizenship, for example, state legislatures banned property ownership by foreign citizens, restricted their civil liberties, segregated them spatially, ostracized them socially, and systematically excluded them from desirable occupations (Daniels 1988).

The curtailment of labor migration from Japan may have eliminated unwanted competition from Asian immigrants, but it also created a serious labor shortage. In response, western employers looked southward and began to recruit Mexicans, first to work on the railroads, then in mines and farm fields, and finally in factories (Cardoso 1980; Durand and Arias 2000). As the Dillingham Commission put it, "The Mexican immigration may increase for some time as this race offers a source of labor to substitute for the Asiatics in the most undesirable seasonal occupations." Indeed, the commission continued, "in the two southern California districts where the force of field workers is predominantly Mexican, the Mexican is preferred to the Japanese. He is alleged to be more tractable and to be a better workman in one case. In the other he is said to be a quicker and better workman than the Japanese" (U.S. Commission on Immigration 1911, 50, 110).

Figure 4.1 shows trends in Mexican migration to the United States between 1900 and 1930, focusing on three categories of movers: legal immigrants, temporary workers, and illegal migrants. Temporary workers were those who crossed the border legally for short-term labor in the United States, mostly in agriculture, and illegal migrants were those who entered the country without authorization. Although the number of illegal migrants is unknown, the volume of the inflow is very roughly indicated by the annual number of apprehensions.

As can be seen, few Mexicans entered the United States before the Gentlemen's Agreement with Japan, but thereafter the flow of legal immigrants accelerated rapidly, from near-zero in 1907 to 16,000 in 1909. Emigration was given an additional boost by the outbreak of the Mexican Revolution in 1910, but after a short surge, legal immigration declined as the revolt degenerated into a violent civil war (Hart 1987). With the outbreak of the First World War in 1914, however, U.S. employers were cut off from supplies of immigrant labor in Europe, and as demand for American products grew, employers increased their recruitment of workers from south of the border (Cardoso 1980). When the United States finally entered the First World War in 1917, labor demand spiked and worker shortages became chronic as white factory workers were mobilized for military duty.

In response, the U.S. government established an official labor recruitment program to assist growers in the Southwest (Morales 1982; Reisler 1976), and factory owners throughout the Midwest re-

Figure 4.1   Mexican Migration to the United States, 1900 to 1930

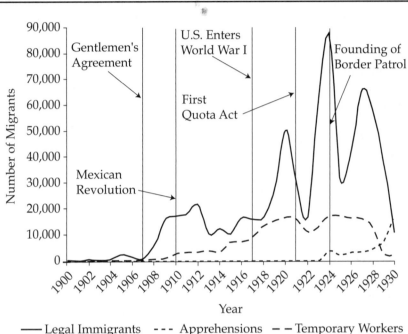

Source: U.S. Immigration and Naturalization Service.

doubled their private recruitment efforts (Durand and Arias 2000). The number of contract workers entering the United States grew to 17,000 in 1920, and legal immigration reached an unprecedented 51,000 persons. American insecurities about all things foreign came to a head during the recession that followed the war, and the red scare of 1918 to 1921 was accompanied by a wave of anti-immigrant hysteria. Congress passed the first quota law in 1921 to curtail immigration from southern and eastern Europe and enacted an even stricter version in 1924. During this period, both legal immigration and contract migration by Mexicans fell, reaching lows in 1922 of 18,000 and 12,000, respectively. But economic recovery led to the sustained economic boom known as the Roaring Twenties, and given the new restrictions on European immigration and steadily tightening labor markets, recruitment of Mexicans soon resumed. Legal immigration surged again to peak at 88,000 in 1924, and the entry of contract laborers climbed to 18,000.

Until the 1920s, the Mexico-U.S. border was little more than a line on a map (Massey, Durand, and Malone 2002). The border existed mostly in people's imaginations and was largely unmarked in physical space. Residents of border communities moved back and forth at will for work, shopping, and socializing. Many families were of mixed citizenship, depending on which side of the line they happened to be born. In response to growing immigration from Mexico, however, in 1924 Congress created the U.S. Border Patrol, and for the first time the border with Mexico became a tangible reality.

The creation of the Border Patrol brought into existence a new category of Mexican in the United States—the illegal migrant. During its first year of operation, the U.S. Border Patrol apprehended around 4,600 Mexicans attempting to enter the country without documents, despite the fact that the agency had just 450 officers to patrol the entire two-thousand-mile frontier (Massey, Durand, and Malone 2002). Legal entries rebounded in the middle part of the decade, however, to reach 68,000 documented immigrants and 17,000 contract workers in 1927. As these two streams declined in the late 1920s, illegal immigration correspondingly rose, with apprehensions reaching 18,000 in 1930.

The 1920s were critical to the formation of the Mexican American community. Proportionate to population, more people emigrated from Mexico during the 1920s than at any time before or since, laying the foundations for the large Mexican barrios of Los Angeles and Chicago (Cardoso 1980; Durand and Arias 2000; Massey, Durand, and Malone 2002). These two metropolitan areas continue to house the largest Mexican populations of the United States (Fischer and Tienda 2006). From the Gentlemen's Agreement in 1907 to the end of 1929, the number of Mexican-born persons in the United States more than quadrupled, going from 178,000 to 739,000 in a little over two decades and making Mexicans a visible minority in cities throughout the Southwest, Midwest, and Pacific regions (Durand and Arias 2000).

Unneeded Workers, Unwanted Race

With the crash of the American stock market in 1929, however, the surge in Mexican immigration ended as quickly as it had begun. In keeping with precepts laid out by the Dillingham Commission, Mexicans were considered expendable as workers and unassimilable as citizens, and in an era of rising austerity, whites framed them as taking jobs that rightfully belonged to "real" Americans and burdening taxpayers with relief payments that rewarded their natural "indolence" (Hoffman 1974). After 1929, federal authorities, in cooperation with state and local officials, organized a series of deportation campaigns that, over the course of a few years, cut the Mexican population of the United States in half (Jaffe et al. 1980). During the period 1929 to 1937, some 458,000 Mexicans were arrested and expelled from the United States without due process, including many native-born children who were U.S. citizens. Thousands more, facing a social climate of rising hostility and poor economic prospects, decided to return home "voluntarily" (Hoffman 1974).

By 1940, only 377,000 Mexican immigrants remained in the country (Jaffe et al. 1980). With agricultural jobs increasingly going to "Okies" and other internal refugees from the Dust Bowl, those Mexicans who remained were pushed to the margins of society, segregated in dilapidated barrios where they attended segregated schools and received inferior services (Grebler, Moore, and Guzman 1970). In these enclaves, Mexicans were transformed from aspiring immigrants into a self-conscious domestic minority, and increasingly they called themselves not Mexicans but Chicanos (Gutierrez 1995; Sanchez 1995).

The degree to which Mexicans were racialized during this period is indicated by the fact that in 1930 the U.S. Census Bureau, for the first and only time in its history, enumerated Mexicans as a separate race, alongside blacks (Bean and Tienda 1987). In Texas, of course, Mexicans were subject to the same violence and intimidation as African Americans. From 1848 to 1928, nearly six hundred Mexicans were lynched by white mobs, with peaks of violence corresponding to periods of Anglo-American expansion, economic com-

123

petition, and diplomatic tensions with Mexico (Carrigan and Webb 2003). Although Mexicans were lynched throughout the Southwest, the practice was heavily concentrated in Texas, and nearly half of all extralegal executions occurred in that state (Carrigan 2004). During the era of Jim Crow, white Texans made few distinctions between "niggers" and "spics" when it came to racial violence.

Officially Disposable Workers

With the entry of the United States into the Second World War, however, American industry once again mobilized and full employment resumed. In combination with renewed military conscription, the war created serious labor shortages, especially in the Southwest. In response, federal authorities forgot about the deportations and quietly turned southward to negotiate a binational treaty for the "temporary" importation of farmworkers from Mexico, who became known as *braceros*. The resulting "Bracero Program" was operated by the U.S. Departments of State, Labor, and Justice in cooperation with the Mexican government, and in September 1942, the first braceros arrived for agricultural work in Stockton, California (Calavita 1992).

The Bracero Program was instrumental in restarting a migratory flow that had been dormant for more than a decade. Figure 4.2 shows trends in Mexican migration from 1940 to 1965. In the years leading up to 1942, Mexican immigration to the United States was virtually nil, and although labor flows were revived by the Bracero Program, the number of contract workers remained rather small throughout the war. From 1942 through 1945, a *total* of only 168,000 braceros were recruited into the United States. Within urban areas, the children of earlier Mexican immigrants took advantage of the return to full employment and moved upwards economically, working at unionized jobs in war industries and translating their newfound affluence into a flashy style known as *pachuco*, whose emblem was a baggy ensemble known as the "zoot suit" (Mazón 1984).

As with the Japanese earlier in the century, white Californians re-

Figure 4.2   Mexican Migration to the United States, 1940 to 1965

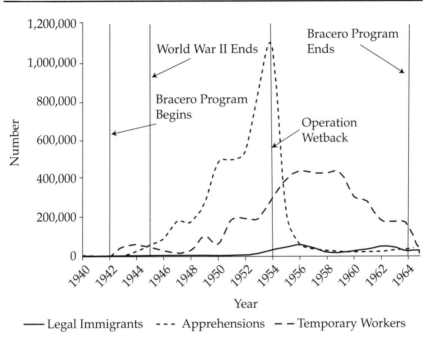

Source: U.S. Immigration and Naturalization Service.

sented racial inferiors rising above their assigned station, and in the charged atmosphere of wartime Los Angeles, anti-Mexican rioting broke out. On June 3, 1943, a group of servicemen on leave complained that they had been assaulted by a gang of pachucos wearing zoot suits (Obregón Pagán 2003). In response, an angry mob of white soldiers and civilians headed into the Mexican barrio of East Los Angeles, where they attacked all males wearing zoot suits, beating them severely while ripping off the offensive garments and burning them on the spot.

Rather than protecting U.S. citizens of Mexican origin, the Los Angeles police swept into the barrio and arrested hundreds of already beat-up pachucos for "disturbing the peace"; several of them died later in jail for want of medical treatment. Although nine white sailors were arrested over the next few days, eight were released without charge, and one was let go after paying a small fine. The attacks on Mexicans ceased only when military authorities declared Los Angeles off-limits to service personnel. For Mexican Americans, however, a strong message had been sent: even in progressive California, people of Mexican origin were not going to be accepted as equals, no matter where they were born, how much they earned, or how stylishly they dressed (Mazón 1984).

Although the Bracero Program was originally envisioned as a "temporary" wartime measure, the booming postwar economy perpetuated growers' fears of a labor shortage, and under pressure from the Texas and California congressional delegations, the House and Senate joined together to extend the program on a year-to-year basis through the late 1940s. Despite the extensions, however, the number of bracero visas remained insufficient to meet rising grower demand, and so employers increasingly took matters into their own hands by recruiting illegal migrants directly, especially after 1950, when reinstatement of the draft during the Korean War markedly tightened U.S. labor markets. As Mexicans crossed the border in larger numbers on their way to farms and fields where they knew they would be hired, the annual number of apprehensions rose from around 7,000 in 1942 to reach 544,000 in 1952.

With the end of the Korean War, a brief economic recession combined with another surge of antiforeign hysteria during the McCarthy era to make illegal migration a hot political issue. In 1953–54, the U.S. Immigration and Naturalization Service (INS) responded to the rising clamor by launching "Operation Wetback" (Calavita 1992). In cooperation with state and local authorities, the INS militarized the Mexico-U.S. border and organized a mass arrest of Mexicans—or more accurately, Mexican-looking people. During 1954 the number of Mexicans apprehended by the INS swelled to over one million for the first time in U.S. history.

A key difference compared with the deportation campaign of the 1930s, however, was that this time around Congress simultaneously acted to expand the number of temporary work visas, roughly doubling the annual number of braceros admitted. From 1955 through 1959, between 400,000 and 450,000 braceros were annually imported into the United States. Legal immigration also surged, going from 9,600 in 1952 to 65,000 in 1956 before leveling off (Massey, Durand, and Malone 2002). It was this increase in access to legal avenues for entry, more than stepped-up border enforcement, that reduced illegal migration to a trickle during the late 1950s. From a figure of 1.1 million in 1954, the number of apprehensions fell in 1959 to just 30,000, where it remained well into the 1960s. For a time, Americans seemed content in having a disposable workforce that seasonally traveled to the United States for difficult and demanding work but regularly returned to Mexico once that work was done.

Unofficially Disposable Workers

In the wake of Operation Wetback and the expansion of the Bracero Program, illegal immigration may have disappeared as a political issue, but as the civil rights movement picked up steam, immigration became controversial in a different way. In addition to overturning Jim Crow and banning discrimination from U.S. markets, civil rights activists sought to purge the nation's immigration system of its racist legacy. As a result, during the 1960s both the Bracero Program and the national-origins quotas came under attack. The Bracero Program was viewed by civil rights advocates as a corrupt, coercive, and exploitive labor system, roughly on a par with black sharecropping in the South. The national-origins quotas were perceived as insulting and discriminatory by the children and grandchildren of Italian and Polish immigrants, who were now voting citizens and included powerful congressmen such as Peter Rodino and Dan Rostenkowski.

The last hurrah of the quotas came in the 1950s. On the eve of Operation Wetback, Congress reaffirmed its support for discriminatory limits by passing the Immigration and Nationality Act over President Truman's veto. Also known as the McCarran-Walter Act, the legislation reauthorized strict limits on southern and eastern European immigration, set aside a token number of visas for Asians, and continued the outright ban on entry by Africans.

The Bracero Program was the first to collapse under the weight of the civil rights onslaught. Under intense pressure from religious groups, unions, and civil rights organizations, Congress downsized the Bracero Program in the early 1960s—reducing the annual number of work visas from 438,000 in 1959 to 178,000 in 1964—before voting in the following year to end the program altogether. In the same year, 1965, Congress passed amendments to the Immigration and Nationality Act that finally abolished discriminatory national-origins quotas and lifted the ban on immigration from Asia and Africa. Instead of racist quotas, the new legislation set a neutral cap of 20,000 immigrant visas per year for each country outside the Western Hemisphere. These visas were allocated to people using a "preference system" that took into account national employment needs and humanitarian needs for family reunification (Zolberg 2006).

Although the 1965 immigration act was viewed as a landmark achievement by the civil rights movement, it also launched a new trend of restrictive immigration policies toward Mexico in particular and toward Latin America in general. Specifically, the amendments imposed the first-ever numerical limits—120,000 visas per year—on immigration from the Western Hemisphere. Subsequent amendments passed in 1976, 1978, and 1980 successively put nations in the Western Hemisphere under the 20,000-per-country visa limit, then abolished separate hemispheric quotas, and finally established a single worldwide ceiling that was reduced to just 270,000 visas. Whereas in 1965 Mexicans seeking to become U.S. citizens faced no numerical limit, by 1980 they found themselves pitted against aspiring immigrants from all over the world in a fierce competition for scarce visas.

Together with the termination of the Bracero Program, these actions dramatically restricted the possibilities for legal entry and virtually guaranteed a rise in undocumented migration. The effect of closing legal avenues of entry is immediately obvious in figure 4.3. Whereas 480,000 Mexicans entered the United States each year as

Figure 4.3   Mexican Migration to the United States, 1965 to 2005

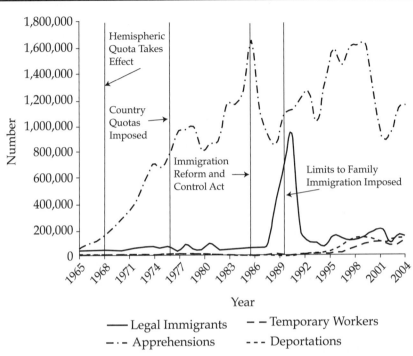

Sources: U.S. Immigration and Naturalization Service; U.S. Department of Homeland Security.

braceros or legal immigrants during the late 1950s, the total inflow of Mexicans through legal channels fell to just 62,000 per year from 1965 to 1985—13 percent of its former level. The gap between the demand for visas on the part of employers and workers and the paltry number offered by the government was increasingly made up through undocumented migration, and annual apprehensions along the border climbed steadily from 55,000 in 1965 to 1.6 million in 1985.

In essence, the shift in U.S. immigration policy after 1965 transformed Mexican migration from a de jure guest-worker program based on the circulation of braceros into a de facto guest-worker program based on the circulation of undocumented migrants (Durand and Massey 2003). Until 1985, this flow remained overwhelmingly circular; it was composed primarily of young men moving back and forth for seasonal work in agriculture, construction, manufacturing, and services. According to estimates by Massey and Singer (1995), from 1965 through 1985, 85 percent of undocumented entries were offset by departures, and among those migrating illegally during this period, three-quarters were men (Massey, Durand, and Malone 2002). Although the number of unauthorized Mexicans present in the country increased over time, the net annual increment to the population was small compared with the size of the gross inflow, averaging only 150,000 persons per year (Passel and Woodrow 1987; Warren and Passel 1987).

Under the unofficial temporary worker program that prevailed between 1965 and 1985, Mexicans remained disposable as workers and unwanted as citizens, as in the Bracero Program, but labor flows were regulated informally as a by-product of border enforcement rather than under the terms of a formal binational agreement. Although the presence of undocumented Mexicans in the United States was technically illegal, until the mid-1980s the consequences of this illegality were relatively benign for migrants as well as the nation. The size and budget of the Border Patrol rose modestly each year to keep pace with a gradual increase in the underlying volume of undocumented migration, and the probability of apprehending an undocumented border crosser remained constant at 33 percent (Espenshade 1994; Massey, Durand, and Malone 2002; Massey and Singer 1995).

During the 1970s and 1980s, crossing the border without authorization became a ritualized game of "cat and mouse" between migrants and Border Patrol agents (Kossoudji 1992). Migrants came to understand that they could take whatever aggressive actions they wished to avoid apprehension, but that once caught they were expected to cease all resistance. If they did so, they would simply be taken into custody, asked to sign a voluntary departure order, and then sent back across the border, whereupon both the arresting officer and the migrant knew the migrant would soon try to cross again, yielding a scripted encounter that Josiah Heyman (1995) called the "voluntary departure complex" and Thomas Espenshade

(1990) labeled a "repeated trials model" of border entry. Whatever it was called, the encounter between migrants and agents along the border became an institutionalized social script that informally regulated the migration of Mexican labor (Singer and Massey 1998; Massey, Durand, and Malone 2002).

Given a 33 percent chance of being caught on any attempt at border crossing, the cumulative odds of getting caught are very high over successive attempts. Given a base likelihood of one in three, the probability of successfully entering after two attempts is 55 percent, 70 percent after three, 80 percent after four, and 86 percent after five. Moreover, the odds of apprehension are lowered by hiring a border smuggler, whose fees before 1990 averaged $300, and the accumulation of personal border-crossing experience and know-how could reduce those odds still further (Singer and Massey 1998). Nearly all undocumented migrants ultimately gained entry, and once in the United States the probability of apprehension was exceedingly low. Undocumented migrants were basically free to seek jobs at established destinations, and employers had no fear of hiring them because doing so was legal under prevailing law.

At this time, the terms of undocumented employment were negotiated directly between migrants and employers, and the latter did not discriminate on the basis of legal status. Although undocumented migrants earned lower wages on average than their legal counterparts, the lower pay reflected their more limited work experience in the United States, shorter job tenures, and weaker English-language skills. When these factors were controlled in wage regressions, the negative effect of illegal status disappeared (Chiswick 1984; Dávila, Pagán, and Grau 1998; Donato, Durand, and Massey 1992b; Massey 1987; Phillips and Massey 1999).

Thus, the political economy of Mexican migration before 1985 was such that an undocumented migrant could reasonably expect to arrive at the border and achieve entry after a few tries, at small personal risk and with a modest financial investment. He could then proceed without hindrance to a known destination area, where he would be offered a job that in short order would pay off the smuggling fees and trip costs and allow him to begin sending money home. Starting wages were modest, but illegal migrants made as much as anyone else with the same characteristics, and if a migrant worked hard, gained fluency in English, and accumulated experience in the U.S. labor market, he could expect to earn more. Moreover, if he proved valuable to an employer, he might be sponsored for permanent legal status, opening up an even larger world of opportunities (Borjas and Tienda 1993; Massey, Alarcón, et al. 1987; Tienda and Singer 1995).

At the aggregate level, immigration had mostly positive, though modest, effects on the wages and employment of native workers; among those few segments of the domestic workforce where negative effects could be observed, their size was tiny and insignificant (Bean, Lowell, and Taylor 1988; Borjas 1984, 1987; Borjas and Tienda 1987). By encouraging circulation rather than settlement, moreover, the illegality of the migrants allowed Americans to extract the labor of Mexicans as workers but avoid their costs as people. Once again, Americans had found a formula to create disposable workers.

The New Politics of Demonization

The rise of undocumented migration after 1965 was accompanied by new demonization of Mexicans. They and other Latin American immigrants were increasingly framed as threats to the nation's security, workers, culture, and way of life. Leo Chavez (2001) studied U.S. magazine covers devoted to immigration between 1965 and 2000 and classified them as affirmative, alarmist, or neutral in their portrayal of immigrants. Covers coded as "affirmative" used text and images to celebrate immigration; "alarmist" covers used text and images to convey problems, fears, or dangers associated with immigration; and "neutral" covers were accompanied by articles that offered balanced and factual coverage of immigration issues that was neither affirmative nor alarmist.

Chavez found that alarmist themes overwhelmingly predominated in coverage of immigration after 1965, characterizing two-thirds of all covers devoted to the topic from 1965 through 1999, compared with just 9 percent classifiable as neutral and 19 percent as affirmative. In addition, most of the affirmative covers were ritualized celebrations of immigration timed to coincide with the

Fourth of July. Some 68 percent of all affirmative covers appeared during the month of July. In general, the frequency of alarmist covers increased markedly over time: 18 percent of the alarmist covers appeared in the 1970s, 38 percent were published in the 1980s, and 45 percent appeared in the 1990s. Upsurges in alarmist text and imagery also coincided with recessionary periods in the United States (Chavez 2001, 21–24).

Not only did immigration-related images tend to be alarmist, but they were also selective with respect to their portrayal of the race, ethnicity, and gender of immigrants. As part of his analysis, Chavez (2001) coded the characteristics of people shown on immigration-related magazine covers; table 4.1 summarizes his data, showing the distribution of immigrants and non-immigrants depicted in photos and illustrations by gender, race, and ethnicity. For purposes of comparison, the first two columns present the corresponding distributions among immigrants who actually entered the United States during the 1990s and for the U.S. population as a whole in 2000.

In general, immigration-related magazine covers overrepresent males and nonwhites compared to their actual frequency among arriving immigrants. Whereas in reality a majority of immigrants are female, in magazine cover photos 79 percent of those depicted were male, as were 73 percent of those shown in cover illustrations. Moreover, although immigrants from Europe made up 15 percent of the total who arrived in the 1990s, none of the cover illustrations showed whites, and just 10 percent of the cover photographs did so. In contrast, whereas immigrants from Africa and the Caribbean jointly constituted only 15 percent of all immigrants, 23 percent of the cover photos and 46 percent of the cover illustrations depicted people of black or African ancestry; similarly, whereas Asians made up 31 percent of arriving immigrants, they constituted 40 percent of the people shown on cover photos. Finally, 37 percent of immigrants were Latin Americans, but they made up 45 percent of cover illustrations (Chavez 2001, 32–33).

In contrast to immigrants, the depiction of U.S. natives on magazine covers understated the proportion of blacks in the American population. Whereas 13 percent of all Americans were black in

Table 4.1   Distribution of People Depicted on Magazine Covers, by Race, Ethnicity, and Gender, Compared to Distribution Among Immigrants and U.S. Population

Variable and Distribution	Actual Data		Cover Photos		Cover Illustrations	
	Immigrants, 1990s	U.S. Total, 2000	Immigrants	Non-immigrants	Immigrants	Non-immigrants
National origin, race, ethnicity						
European/white	15%	69%	10%	71%	0%	69%
Asian	31	4	40	12	9	0
Afro-Caribbean/black	15	13	23	2	46	2
Latin American/Hispanic	37	13	26	1	45	25
Gender						
Male	55	51	79	70	73	100

Sources: Office of Immigration Statistics, U.S. Department of Homeland Security; U.S. Bureau of the Census; Chavez (2001).

2000, the relative number of black faces depicted among non-immigrants on magazine covers was just 2 percent, in both photographs and illustrations. Likewise, Hispanics appeared in just 1 percent of photographs of non-immigrants compared with their 13 percent share of the U.S. population, and Asians were represented in none of the illustrations of non-immigrants, though they are 4 percent of the population. In short, magazine covers were structured to overstate the nonwhite origins of immigrants while understating the nonwhiteness of Americans. The words printed in the texts that accompanied the images generally reinforced the sense of alarm and urgency communicated by the pictures (Chavez 2001). In time-honored fashion, editors made heavy use of marine metaphors, depicting immigration as a "tidal wave" that was "flooding" the United States and threatening to "inundate" its culture.

During the 1970s and 1980s, however, a new metaphor appeared with growing frequency as immigrants and immigration were framed increasingly in martial terms. The Mexico-U.S. border was portrayed as a "battleground" that was "under attack" from "alien invaders" who constituted a "time bomb" waiting to explode and destroy American culture and values. In this militarized portrayal, Border Patrol officers became "defenders" who were "outgunned" as they tried to "hold the line" against attacking "hordes" (Andreas 2000; Dunn 1996). Whether the metaphorical language was martial or marine, however, it always portrayed immigration from Mexico as a "crisis."

Going back to the earliest days of the republic, politicians have found it convenient to demonize immigrants during periods of social upheaval and economic insecurity (Higham 1955); during the 1980s the symbolic portrayal of immigrants as a threat reached new heights (Zolberg 2006). Ronald Reagan, in particular, framed immigration as a question of "national security" and linked it to his ongoing prosecution of the Cold War. As a result of communist insurgencies in Central America, he predicted "a tidal wave of refugees—and this time they'll be 'feet people' and not boat people—swarming into our country seeking safe haven from communist repression to the south" (*Washington Post*, June 21, 1983). In a 1986 speech, he reminded Americans that "terrorists and subversives are just two days' driving time from [the border crossing at] Harlingen, Texas" (quoted in Kamen 1990), and his 1987 Task Force on Terrorism reported that immigrants constituted a potential fifth column in the United States because extremists would "feed on the anger and frustration of recent Central and South American immigrants who will not realize their own version of the American dream" (quoted in Dunn 1996).

From Unofficial to Underground

The labeling of immigration as a national security threat, the symbolic portrayal of the Mexico-U.S. border as a defensive bulwark, and the demonization of Latinos as subversives reached a crescendo in the middle 1980s (Massey, Durand, and Malone 2002). The year 1986 was pivotal. Late in that year Congress passed the Immigration Reform and Control Act (IRCA), which contained three far-reaching provisions that drastically reshaped the political economy of migration and transformed the position of Mexicans in the United States (Durand, Massey, and Parrado 1999). First, IRCA sharply increased funding for border enforcement, initiating an unprecedented expansion in the Border Patrol that continued unabated for two decades. Second, it authorized two legalization programs: one for long-term residents who had been in the country for at least five years and another for short-term agricultural workers. Finally, it criminalized the hiring of undocumented workers and applied sanctions against employers who knowingly did so.

After 1986, the size and budget of the Border Patrol grew rapidly in a way that was completely disconnected from the underlying volume of migration (Durand, Massey, and Malone 2002). Whereas in 1986 the agency had 3,700 officers and an annual budget of $151 million, by 2002 it had grown to 6,200 officers with a budget of $1.6 billion, and it had become the largest arms-bearing branch of government save the military itself (Andreas 2000; Nevins 2001). The budget of the Border Patrol's parent agency, the Immigration and Naturalization Service, itself went from $474 million to $6.2 billion as it came to operate a growing network of prisons—a new "American gulag" as part of the larger prison industrial complex—where inhumane treatment and prisoner abuse became routine (Dow 2004).

Despite vast expenditures on border enforcement, the rate of illegal entry remained virtually constant before and after IRCA's passage (Donato, Durand, and Massey 1992a; Massey, Donato, and Liang 1990). According to data from the Mexican Migration Project, the overall probability of taking a first undocumented trip has fluctuated narrowly around 1 percent for the past twenty-five years, and the probability of taking an additional trip actually fell slightly, going from 14 percent to 8 percent per year. Moreover, even as IRCA sought to shut down the flow of Mexican workers through unilateral police actions along the border, it temporarily expanded avenues for legal immigration through its two legalization programs, which authorized immigrants who could document five years of U.S. residence or demonstrate agricultural labor in the United States during 1985–86 to apply for temporary protected status. Once registered, immigrants could then "adjust status" to become permanent resident aliens by demonstrating facility in English and a knowledge of American history (Fuchs 1990). Some 2.3 million Mexicans applied for temporary protected status between 1987 and 1989, and 95 percent ultimately became legal permanent residents and eligible for citizenship.

Despite expectations that IRCA would slow Mexican immigration, by 1990 it was clear that the legislation was not working. Although border apprehensions fell between 1987 and 1989, by 1990 they were rising again, increasing 26 percent over the prior year. Moreover, it turned out that the 2.2 million Mexicans legalized under IRCA had numerous relatives in Mexico, including spouses and children who now qualified for legal entry under the preference system and other relatives who used their tie to a legalized immigrant to facilitate an undocumented trip (Massey and Espinosa 1997). With both legal and illegal migration growing, Congress passed another major revision of U.S. immigration law in 1990. In addition to authorizing funds for 1,000 additional Border Patrol officers, tightening employer sanctions, streamlining deportation procedures, and increasing penalties for immigration violations, the new legislation also attempted to impose new limits on family migration.

Congress perceived a need for these limits because a growing fraction of immigrants were entering through categories *not* subject to numerical limitation—as spouses, sons, daughters, and parents of U.S. citizens. Of the 1.5 million legal immigrants admitted to the United States in 1990, for example, fewer than 20 percent were subject to numerical limitation. The 1990 Immigration Act sought to limit the entry of family members to 480,000 visas per year and to cap total immigration at 675,000 per year.

Under the terms of the legislation, immediate relatives of citizens could still enter the United States without numerical restriction, but rather than entering *in addition to* those admitted under numerically restricted family categories (mostly spouses and minor children of legal resident aliens), in the future they would be *subtracted from* the next year's family quota. Although pro-immigrant lawmakers opposed the caps, they were unable to block them; they were, however, able to insert language that made the caps "pierceable," in that no more than 226,000 visas could be subtracted from the family quota in any year. In practice, the 1990 act permanently deleted these visas from numerically limited family categories, further lengthening already long waiting times for resident aliens seeking to sponsor the entry of their dependents.

As shown in figure 4.3, IRCA's effect on migration during the years 1986 through 1992 was dramatic. With the bill's passage, millions of undocumented migrants who had formerly circulated back and forth across the border remained in the United States to apply for legalization. As a result, the number of apprehensions plummeted from 1.7 million in 1986 to 866,000 in 1989. The fact that the cessation of border crossing by 2.3 million applicants for temporary protected status produced a drop of 800,000 apprehensions is consistent with an apprehension rate of 33 percent.

The adjustment of millions of former illegal migrants to permanent resident status led to a huge surge in legal immigration between 1989 and 1993, peaking at nearly one million in 1991. After the wave of newly legalized immigrants had passed, however, immigration levels from Mexico did not return to the status quo ante. Whereas legal Mexican immigration averaged 59,000 in the four years preceding IRCA, afterward it averaged 163,000 per year as newly legalized immigrants took advantage of the family reunification provisions to sponsor the entry of relatives. At the same time, guest-worker recruitment quietly resumed under the auspices of the H2 visa program. Between 1977 and 1985, temporary labor migration from Mexico averaged just 4,300 persons annually; afterward it rose steadily to reach 170,000 in 2005.

Despite the increase in temporary labor migration and the expansion in the number of permanent residents through legalization, the general thrust of U.S. immigration policy after 1986 was restrictive, as indicated by the rising tide of forced removals. From a figure of just 11,000 in 1985, the annual number of Mexicans arrested in the interior of the United States and deported across the border grew steadily to reach 150,000 in 2005, the largest number since the deportation campaigns of the Great Depression.

The rising tide of restrictionist policies created new incentives for Mexicans who had attained legal status to go one step further and become U.S. citizens. As just noted, though IRCA's legalization had increased the number of resident aliens seeking to sponsor the entry of spouses and children, the 1990 act subtracted 226,000 visas from the available pool. By taking out American citizenship, newly legalized immigrants could instantly make their spouses and minor children eligible for unrestricted entry. They also acquired the right to sponsor the entry of their parents, older and married children, and siblings.

Congress further enhanced the incentive to naturalize in 1996 when it passed the Illegal Immigration Reform and Immigrant Responsibility Act, which called upon states to limit public assistance to *legal* immigrants and increased the income threshold required for families to sponsor the entry of relatives. In the same year, Congress passed the Personal Responsibility and Work Opportunity Reconciliation Act, which prohibited *legal* immigrants from receiving food stamps and Supplemental Security Income (SSI) and banned them from means-tested social programs for five years after admission. It also gave states new flexibility to set eligibility rules and affirmed their right to exclude legal immigrants if they chose to do so.

Immigrants were naturally alarmed at their loss of social benefits and grew worried that more restrictions were on the way. In just ten years, Congress had completely transformed the cost-benefit calculus of naturalization for Mexicans. On the one hand, IRCA pushed legalizing immigrants toward citizenship by requiring them to learn English, history, and civics, something not usually required of new permanent resident aliens. On the other hand, the 1990 act restricted the ability of resident aliens to sponsor the entry of spouses and children, and the 1996 legislation curtailed their access to public services. The response to these altered incentives was predictable: an unprecedented surge in naturalization. Between 1990 and 2002, a record 1.3 million Mexicans were admitted to U.S. citizenship—twice the number who had naturalized over the previous one hundred years!

In the end, the militarization of the border, IRCA's massive legalization, and the ensuing boom in naturalization ruptured the institutionalized pattern of circular migration that had prevailed before 1986 (Massey, Durand, and Malone 2002). Whereas the probability that a Mexican would initiate undocumented migration remained constant in the years following IRCA and the probability of taking an additional U.S. trip fell slightly, the likelihood of returning to Mexico once entry had been achieved plummeted after 1986. The new enforcement regime tripled the rate of death at the border and quadrupled smuggling costs (Massey, Durand, and Malone 2002), and in response to these new costs and risks, undocumented migrants did the rational thing—they minimized border crossing.

Rather than deciding not to leave for the United States in the first place, however, undocumented migrants instead chose to stay longer once they had run the gauntlet at the border and successfully made it into the country (Durand and Massey 2003). The probability of returning to Mexico within twelve months of entry declined from an average of 45 percent before IRCA to just 25 percent by the year 2000 (Massey 2005d). Put another way, the probability of remaining in the United States as an undocumented migrant rose from 39 percent in 1986 to 80 percent ten years later (Riosmena 2004).

As male workers remained longer north of the border, they increasingly sought to bring in their wives and children. As a result, the share of women among undocumented migrants rose from 26 percent before IRCA to 34 percent afterward, and the share of nonworking dependents increased from 12 percent to 20 percent (Massey, Durand, and Malone 2002). Moreover, as legal resident aliens increasingly took up U.S. citizenship, the probability of return migration fell among legal immigrants as well, going from 15 percent before IRCA to 5 percent afterward (Massey, Durand, and Malone 2002).

The falling rate of out-migration and the steady rate of in-migration combined to increase the rate of net undocumented migration and cause an unprecedented acceleration in the number of Mexicans living north of the border. In essence, restrictive U.S. immigration and border policies backfired. Instead of reducing the net annual inflow of Mexican migrants, these policies doubled it. The dramatic effect on undocumented population growth is indicated by figure 4.4, which uses indirect estimates from Woodrow-Lafield (1998) and Hoefer, Rytina, and Campbell (2006) to show changes in the number of undocumented Mexicans living in the United States from 1965 to 2005 (using an approach adapted from Massey and Bartley 2005).

As can be seen, the size of the undocumented population grew slowly but steadily from the end of the Bracero Program in 1965 until 1982, when the onset of an economic crisis in Mexico caused a short-term upsurge in growth and then a return to trend from 1983 through 1986. During the ten years preceding IRCA's passage, the undocumented Mexican population grew by an annual average of 180,000 persons. The massive legalization of the early 1990s moved several million people from the undocumented to the documented population, cutting it from a peak of 4.4 million in 1993 to 2.7 million in 1996. When growth resumed, however, it was under a new demographic regime characterized by lower rates of return migration that no longer offset the rate of in-migration as before, yielding an increase in the annual net inflow to 378,000 per year.

Figure 4.4   Growth of the Undocumented Mexican Population of
the United States, 1965 to 2005

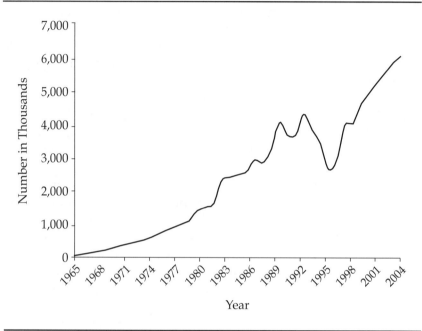

Sources: Woodrow-Lafield (1998); Hoeffer, Rytina, and Campbell (2006).

Thus, U.S. immigration and border policies transformed Mexican immigration from a circular flow of male workers into a settled population of families. By the year 2005, the total number of undocumented Mexicans present north of the border had reached 6.1 million, and the total number of foreign-born Mexicans had climbed to 11 million. These figures imply that one of every ten people born in Mexico now lives in the United States, and 55 percent are present in illegal status. At the same time, immigrants now constitute a growing fraction of all Mexican Americans, roughly 40 percent as of 2005, and the large number of undocumented among them means that midway in the first decade of the twenty-first century, more than half of all Mexican-born persons—and more than one-fifth of all persons of Mexican origin—lack any social, political, or economic rights in the United States. Mexicans are now more exploitable than at any time since the 1850s.

In addition, compared with the period before 1985, Mexican Americans face a much more hostile and daunting economic environment, largely because of IRCA's criminalization of undocumented hiring. This provision obviously did not stop undocumented migration by removing the "magnet" of U.S. jobs, as its proponents had hoped. It did, however, transform the structure of the U.S. labor market in ways that were detrimental to the economic well-being not only of undocumented migrants but of legal immigrants and U.S. citizens as well (Massey, Durand, and Malone 2002).

Congress, of course, *sought* to induce employers to discriminate against Mexicans on the basis of legal status, and in this sense the legislation was successful. Whereas before 1986 legal and illegal immigrants earned similar wages once human capital characteristics were controlled, afterward a significant gap opened up in the wages of documented and undocumented migrants (Donato and Massey 1993). According to estimates by Phillips and Massey (1999), in the wake of IRCA, illegal migrants came to earn 25 percent less than their legal counterparts after controlling for differences in background characteristics.

The post-IRCA labor market was also characterized by falling returns to human capital regardless of legal status. Greater education, job experience, and English-language ability no longer brought rewards to workers, documented or undocumented. Rather, wages were increasingly dependent on social capital—ties to people with U.S. migratory experience. Rather than *what* workers knew, the key determinant of economic success became *who* they knew. As Aguilera and Massey (2003) discovered, social capital, instead of leading directly to higher wages, affected earnings indirectly by increasing access to formal-sector employment, which in turn led to higher wages. Without social connections leading to jobs in the formal economy, Mexican immigrants were increasingly trapped in lousy jobs that offered few possibilities for earnings growth or economic mobility.

In addition to its intended effect of promoting discrimination against undocumented migrants, however, IRCA also had the spillover effect of promoting discrimination against Hispanics in general, as its critics had feared (U.S. General Accounting Office 1990). Given that the vast majority of undocumented migrants are Latin American, an easy way for employers to reduce the risk of violating IRCA's sanctions is simply not to hire anyone who "looks Hispanic," and this is apparently what many bosses did after 1986 (Lowell, Teachman, and Jing 1995). Among those migrants who did manage to get hired in the wake of IRCA, moreover, wages were much lower than before, suggesting that employers engaged in wage discrimination to compensate themselves for the perceived risk of hiring foreigners (Cobb-Clark, Shiells, and Lowell 1995; Fry, Lowell, and Haghighat 1995; Lowell and Jing 1994; Sorensen and Bean 1994).

A final consequence of IRCA was a radical transformation in the hiring process. Whereas before IRCA most employers hired undocumented workers themselves, afterward they shifted to a pattern of *indirect hiring* through subcontractors. Under a subcontracting arrangement, a U.S. citizen or resident alien contractually agrees with an employer to provide a specific number of workers for a certain period of time to undertake a defined task at a fixed rate of pay per worker. Since the workers are technically not employees of the firm but of the subcontractor, the employer escapes liability under the law. In return for providing this legal buffer, the subcontractor retains a portion of the workers' wages as income.

Such arrangements quickly became standard in industries with high turnover rates and significant numbers of immigrant workers, such as agriculture, construction, gardening, and custodial services (Durand 1997; Martin 1996; Martin and Taylor 1991; Taylor 1996; Taylor, Martin, and Fix 1997; Taylor and Thilmany 1993). As indirect hiring became the norm, moreover, it was imposed on *all workers* regardless of legal status. If a citizen or legal resident wished to get a job in agriculture or construction, he or she had to work through a subcontractor and forfeit a share of wages in return for the opportunity to work. In this way, a perverse consequence of IRCA's employer sanctions was to lower the wages and working conditions not only of undocumented migrants but of legal immigrants and U.S. citizens as well (Durand and Massey 2003).

Under labor subcontracting, moreover, there are few returns to experience, English-language ability, education, or job tenure, thus explaining the falling returns to human capital and the rising importance of formal-sector employment as paths to economic mobility. By eradicating the routes to higher earnings that had prevailed before 1986, IRCA not only undermined the wages paid to undocumented migrants but had a greater effect on the wages of legal immigrants: as the real value of wages earned by undocumented migrants fell by 12 percent from 1986 to 1996, the real value of wages earned by documented migrants fell by 29 percent, and along with lower wages came greater informality, with migrants experiencing longer hours and more payments in cash (Massey, Durand, and Malone 2002).

In sum, IRCA's employer sanctions radically restructured the market for unskilled labor in the United States, increasing discrimination on the basis of legal status, exacerbating discrimination on the basis of ethnicity, and pushing employers toward labor subcontracting as the principal hiring mechanism. Moreover, as IRCA's provisions were raising the penalties for being illegal, Hispanic, and unskilled in the U.S. economy, its militarization of the border backfired and acted forcefully to increase the relative number of people in these categories (Massey and Bartley 2005). In other words, as the rules of the political economy were being rewritten to become more exploitive, the number of people in exploitable categories expanded, with predictable results.

After 1986, analysts began to detect stronger and more negative influences of immigration on the economic standing of natives. Whereas studies based on the 1980 census (before employer sanctions) had shown positive or tiny negative effects of immigration on the wages and employment rates of domestic workers, those based on the 1990 and 2000 censuses (after employer sanctions) found larger and more negative effects, particularly on unskilled workers and minorities (Borjas, Freeman, and Katz 1992, 1996; Borjas 1993, 1994, 1997, 1999). The political economy of the United

States had become dramatically less favorable to working men and women, whether immigrant or native.

Postmodern Racialization

Rather than blaming the deterioration of Mexican wages and negative labor market effects on structural changes in the political economy, however, conservative economists such as George Borjas (1995) attributed the trend to a "declining quality of immigrants," singling out Mexicans in a way that would be familiar to members of the Dillingham Commission. Although the demonization of Latino immigrants as "invaders" and "terrorists" slackened somewhat during the economic boom of the 1990s, these framings returned with a vengeance after September 11, 2001, both inside and outside of academia.

Within the academy, intellectuals such as the Harvard political scientist Samuel P. Huntington (2004) offered a reprise of the Dillingham Commission's assertions about the unassimilability of Latin American immigrants:

> The persistent inflow of Hispanic immigrants threatens to divide the United States into two peoples, two cultures, and two languages. Unlike past immigrant groups, Mexicans and other Latinos have not assimilated into mainstream U.S. culture, forming instead their own political and linguistic enclaves— from Los Angeles to Miami—and rejecting the Anglo-Protestant values that built the American dream. The United States ignores this challenge at its peril.

Outside of the ivory tower, the former Nixon speechwriter and conservative pundit Patrick Buchanan (2006) warned of an "Aztlan Plot" fomented by Mexican conspirators to recapture lands lost under the Treaty of Guadalupe Hidalgo, thus effecting a "reconquista" of the American Southwest. Comparing Mexicans to the barbarians invading ancient Rome, he referred to "the Third World invasion and conquest of America" as a "state of emergency." In an

146

interview with *Time* magazine, he warned: "If we do not get control of our borders and stop this greatest invasion in history, I see the dissolution of the U.S. and the loss of the American southwest—culturally and linguistically, if not politically—to Mexico. It could become a part of Mexico in the way that Kosovo is now a part of Albania" (August 28, 2006, 6).

Even more hyperbole was forthcoming from Chris Simcox of the Minutemen Civil Defense Corps, a vigilante group he founded to patrol the Mexico-U.S. border. On the organization's website, he rhetorically asks, "Are terrorists exploiting our porous borders?" and then supplies the following answer: "We know drug dealers, gang bangers and way too many criminal foreign nationals are creating havoc in our communities and threatening our public safety."

The legal foundations for the criminalization not just of undocumented hiring but of undocumented migrants themselves were laid by the 1996 Antiterrorism and Effective Death Penalty Act, which gave the federal government new police powers for the "expedited exclusion" of any alien who had *ever* crossed the border without documents (no matter what his or her current legal status) or who had *ever* committed a felony (no matter how long ago). These provisions—coming on the heels of a decade of draconian drug laws and three-strikes legislation—instantly rendered deportable thousands of legal resident aliens, many of whom had entered as infants and spent their entire lives in the United States.

The law also delegated to the State Department absolute authority to designate any organization as "terrorist," thereby making all members of groups so designated immediately excludable and deportable. It also narrowed the grounds for asylum and added alien smuggling to the list of crimes covered by the RICO (racketeer-influenced corrupt organizations) statute, while severely limiting the possibilities for judicial review of deportations. According to the Washington University law professor Stephen H. Legomsky (2000, 1616), this legislation constitutes "the most ferocious assault on the judicial review of immigration decisions" ever launched "by creating new removal courts that allow secret procedures to be used to remove suspected alien terrorists; by shifting the authority to make 'expedited removals' to immigration inspectors at ports of entry;

and by setting unprecedented limits on judicial review of immigration decisions."

The events of September 11 thus occurred against a background of rising animus toward immigrants and a growing assault on their civil liberties and social rights. In response to the terrorist attacks, Congress on October 26, 2001, passed the USA PATRIOT Act, which granted the executive branch expansive new powers to deport, without a hearing or any presentation of evidence, all aliens—legal and illegal—that the attorney general had "reason to believe" might commit, further, or facilitate acts of terrorism. For the first time since the Alien and Sedition Acts of 1798, Congress voted to permit the arrest, imprisonment, and deportation of noncitizens upon the orders of the attorney general without judicial review.

Over the course of U.S. history, attacks on immigrants have waxed and waned. What distinguishes the current wave of anti-immigrant hysteria from its predecessors is not its demonizing of foreigners or its harsh treatment of noncitizens per se, but its use of the fear of foreigners to launch a broader assault on the civil liberties not just of immigrants but of all Americans, for the PATRIOT Act also permits unprecedented surveillance and incarceration of U.S. citizens, again at the discretion of the executive branch and without review. As Aristide Zolberg (2006, 450) notes, "While the challenges posed by international migration are real and warrant a worldwide reconsideration of prevailing regimes, the resurgence of nativist responses constitutes a more immediate threat to liberal democracy than immigration itself." It is no coincidence that the only U.S. citizen now held in indefinite detention without charge and without a hearing is a dark-skinned Latino, Jose Padilla.

All of the boundary work being done by academics, pundits, and politicians to frame Latin American immigrants as a threat and categorize them socially as undesirable has affected public opinion, turning it steadily against Latinos. According to polls conducted by the Pew Charitable Trusts, as late as 2000 only 38 percent of Americans agreed that "immigrants today are a burden on our country because they take our jobs, housing, and health care." Five years later, the percentage had risen to 44 percent, and as the drumbeat of anti-immigrant rhetoric reached a crescendo in 2006 it became a majority viewpoint at 52 percent. In keeping with this shift, the percentage of Americans who rated immigration as a moderately big or very big national problem rose from 69 percent in 2002 to 74 percent in 2006 (Kohut and Suro 2006).

As of the year 2006, almost half of all Americans (48 percent) opined that "newcomers from other countries threaten traditional American values and customs," and 54 percent said that the United States needed to be "protected against foreign influence." Not surprisingly, given these views, 49 percent said they believed that "immigrants keep to themselves and do not try to fit in"; 56 percent said immigrants "don't pay their fair share of taxes"; 58 percent believed that immigrants "do not learn English in a reasonable amount of time"; and 60 percent of those who had heard of the Minutemen approved of their activities. Given the hysteria surrounding immigration and border control, it is perhaps unsurprising that Americans also drastically overestimate the relative number of immigrants present in the country. Although the true percentage of immigrants in the United States stands at 12 percent, some 53 percent of poll respondents thought that it was 25 percent or greater (Kohut and Suro 2006).

Recent studies by Tiane Lee and Susan Fiske (2006) applied the stereotype content model to various immigrant groups. Based on respondent and subject ratings, they plotted the position of different groups in the two-dimensional space defined by the intersection of warmth and competence; the results of this exercise are reproduced in figure 4.5. As expected, the social space generally occupied by esteemed in-group members (high warmth, high competence) includes groups such as Canadians, Europeans, documented immigrants, and third-generation immigrants. Likewise, the space generally occupied by envied out-groups (high competence, low warmth) is occupied by classic middlemen minorities such as the Koreans, Chinese, Japanese, and Asians generally. Eastern Europeans, first-generation immigrants, Russians, Germans, French, and Middle Eastern immigrants occupy a middle position of moderate warmth and moderate competence.

Note, however, which groups occupy the space of low warmth and low competence that corresponds to the most despised out-

Figure 4.5   Stereotype Content Model Applied to Immigrants

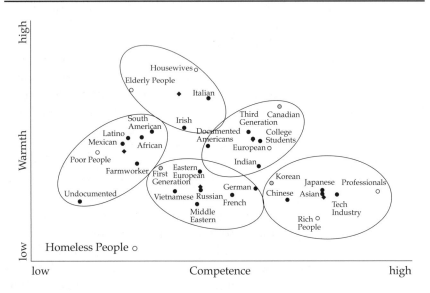

Source: Lee and Fiske (2006). Reprinted with permission from Elsevier.

groups: South Americans, Latinos, Mexicans, farmworkers, and Africans. The most despised immigrant group of all is undocumented migrants, who rate lowest of all on both warmth and competence, such that they approach the portion of the graph usually reserved only for the most detested and socially stigmatized groups, such as criminals and drug dealers. In societal terms, this is dangerous territory, since it implies that undocumented migrants are not perceived as fully human at the most fundamental neural level of cognition, thus opening a door to the harshest, most exploitive, and cruelest treatment that human beings are capable of inflicting on one another.

Categorical Stratification After 9/11

Just as the criminal justice system has emerged as a new and powerful institution in promoting categorical inequality between blacks

and whites, the U.S. immigration system has assumed a new centrality in the exploitation and exclusion of Latinos. The implementation of employer sanctions increased discrimination against Hispanics in U.S. labor markets, lowering their wages, depressing the
returns to human capital, and closing off long-established pathways of upward mobility. At the same time, IRCA promoted a
wholesale shift to subcontracting in the unskilled labor market. The
militarization of the Mexico-U.S. border, meanwhile, raised the rate
of undocumented population growth to increase the number of
people in exploitable, powerless categories. Finally, as private discrimination increased and larger shares of the population were being exploited economically, Congress increased the social penalties
for being poor, Hispanic, foreign, and undocumented, cutting even
legal immigrants off from public services for which they had previ-
ously qualified.

As a result of these deliberate policy actions, the political economy facing Hispanics is now vastly harsher and more punitive
than the one prevailing before 1986. Historically, Hispanics occupied a middle position between blacks and whites in the American
stratification system, but with the restructuring of the political
economy of immigration in the late 1980s and early 1990s, the relative standing of Hispanics declined and they came to replace
African Americans at the bottom of the class hierarchy. Figure 4.6
illustrates the change by showing the ratio of minority to white income for blacks and Hispanics from 1972 to 2002.

The bottom two lines show income ratios for Hispanic and black
men. In the early 1970s, the average black male earned roughly 60
percent of what the average white male earned, while Hispanic
males earned 70 percent of the white male level. These relative income ratios prevailed through the early 1980s, but in the middle of
that decade IRCA transformed the structure of the low-wage labor
market, and the bargaining position of Hispanic men deteriorated.
From 1983 to 1986, the ratio of Hispanic to white income fell from
.70 to .60, where it hovered until 1991, and then dropped below .60
for the first time ever. At about the same time, black male incomes
began rising relative to those of white males, and in 1993 the income ratio crossed over the Hispanic-white ratio. From that point

151

Figure 4.6   Hispanic and Black Personal Income as a Ratio of
White Income

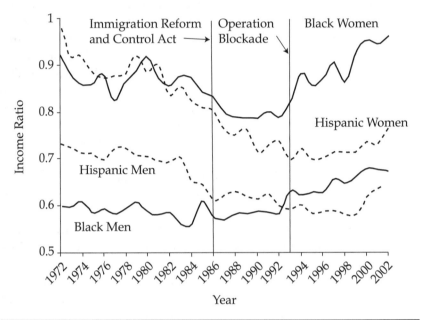

Source: U.S. Bureau of the Census.

onward, Hispanics replaced blacks at the bottom of the male earnings hierarchy.

The top two lines show trends in the relative earnings of Hispanic and black women to reveal a similar switching of positions,
one that occurred even earlier than among minority men. In 1972
Hispanic women earned the same income as white women, while
black women earned 92 percent of what their white counterparts
earned. During the 1970s and 1980s, however, the earnings of
women in both minority groups deteriorated relative to those of
white women, but the decline was more rapid among Hispanic
women. In 1981 the two lines crossed, and from then on Hispanic
women replaced black women at the bottom of the female earnings
hierarchy.

Figure 4.7   Ratio of Hispanic to Black Poverty Rates

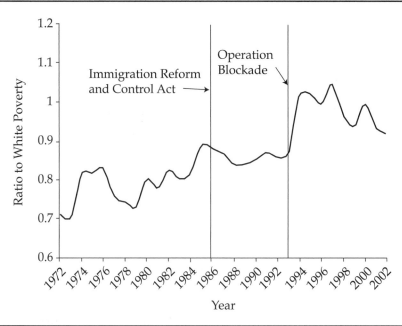

Source: U.S. Bureau of the Census.

Despite this early crossover, however, the Hispanic-white and black-white income ratios remained quite close to one another until IRCA passed in 1986. After this date, the deterioration in black female income slowed down, and then in the early 1990s it reversed and began to move upward. In contrast, the deterioration in Hispanic women's earnings accelerated, and the two income ratios began to pull apart at a rapid pace, yielding a widening gap. From 1987 to 2002, the ratio of black female income to white female income rose from .80 to .96, while the income ratio for Hispanic females fell from .80 to .70 before coming back up to end the decade at .77.

The shifting fortunes of Hispanics and African Americans in the U.S. labor market are also clearly reflected in American poverty statistics. Historically, rates of Hispanic poverty were far below those of blacks, but over the course of the 1980s and 1990s the differential disappeared, and the two groups ended the twentieth century at rough parity in terms of material deprivation. Figure 4.7 shows the ratio of Hispanic to black poverty from 1972 to 2002. Through the 1970s and early 1980s, Hispanic poverty fluctuated at 70 to 80 percent of the black level, but during the late 1980s and early 1990s Hispanic poverty rates rose and came to range between 80 and 90 percent of black rates. With the increase in settlement by undocumented migrants and the shift to family migration following the border buildup that began with Operation Blockade in El Paso, Hispanic rates of poverty came to equal or exceed those of blacks, and the ratio pushed above 1.0 for the first time since poverty statistics had been collected.

The deterioration in the labor market position of Hispanics relative to blacks has been accompanied by a parallel shift in housing markets: the 2000 Housing Discrimination Study revealed a significant increase in discrimination against Hispanics. Whereas in 1989 Hispanics were 19 percent *less likely* than blacks to experience adverse treatment in America's rental markets, in 2000 they were 8 percent *more likely* to suffer discrimination. Moreover, although the incidence of discriminatory treatment fell for both groups in the sales market, the decline for Hispanics was much smaller. As a result, whereas blacks in 1989 were twice as likely as Hispanics to experience discrimination in home sales, by 2000 Hispanics were 18 percent *more likely* than blacks to experience it (Turner, Ross, et al. 2002). Consistent with these data, in their audit of rental housing in the San Francisco Bay Area, Thomas Purnell, William Idsardi, and John Baugh (1999) documented extensive "linguistic profiling" that excluded speakers of Chicano English as well as speakers of black English from access to housing.

As discrimination against Latinos in housing markets increased, so did levels of Hispanic residential segregation. While the overall level of black segregation fell by ten points over the past decade and black neighborhood isolation dropped by twelve points, Hispanic segregation rose by six points and isolation increased by ten points (Charles 2003), and whereas Hispanics did not satisfy the criteria for hypersegregation in any metropolitan areas in 1980 or

1990, by 2000 both New York and Los Angeles had earned the dubious distinction of becoming hypersegregated for Latino residents (Wilkes and Iceland 2004).

In the social realm, researchers have also documented the "chilling effect" of the 1996 immigration and welfare legislation on the use of public services by immigrants (Fix and Zimmermann 2004; Zimmermann and Fix 1998). Among undocumented migrants, the use of social services, always quite low, fell even further, so that after 1996 fewer than 5 percent reported receiving food stamps, welfare, or unemployment insurance while in the United States, and just 7 percent reported putting their children in public schools. More surprising was the decline in services consumed by legal immigrants. After 1996, usage rates for welfare, unemployment insurance, and food stamps all fell sharply to 10 percent or less (Donato, Massey, and Wagner 2006), and according to estimates by George Borjas (2004), every 10 percent cut in the fraction of the public on public assistance raises the relative number of food-insecure households by five percentage points.

It thus seems that in 1996 Congress sent a clear signal to legal as well as illegal immigrants that they were unwelcome in what remained of the American welfare state, and that both sets of immigrants got the message loud and clear. In addition to restricting the eligibility of legal immigrants for federal means-tested benefits, however, Congress in 1996 also raised the income threshold required to obtain an affidavit of support. With this document, which is required of all persons seeking to sponsor the legal entry of a family member, a household must prove that it has enough resources to support the immigrant should he or she become indigent. Congress, of course, sought to curtail family immigration, but rather than standing by and allowing the government to declare them ineligible to bring in relatives, immigrant households fought back by sending more family members into the workforce to bolster collective earnings so they could meet the higher income threshold. After 1996, older children in Mexican families increasingly dropped out of school and went to work, thus depressing already low levels of education among Latino children and permanently undermining their economic prospects (Donato, Massey, and Wagner 2006).

Although Hispanics have not been swept into the prison industrial complex to the same extent as African Americans, they nonetheless constitute a sizable share of inmates that is disproportionate to their share of the U.S. population. Around 5 percent of Hispanic males age twenty to forty were in prison or jail in 2000, compared with 12 percent of blacks and just 2 percent of whites (Western 2006). Moreover, in the spring of 2006 the U.S. House of Representatives passed legislation sponsored by Republican congressman James Sensenbrenner to make "unlawful presence" in the United States a felony. It defined unlawful presence so broadly that almost every immigration violation, no matter how minor, technical, or unintentional, became a federal crime subject to imprisonment and deportation. If this act passes the Senate to become law, it will render 12 million people instantly subject to incarceration and represent the largest expansion of the prison industrial complex ever, potentially tripling the size of America's prison population, already the largest on earth.

In *American Apartheid* (Massey and Denton 1993, 182–83), Nancy Denton and I offered a blueprint of how to build an underclass:

> To begin, choose a minority group whose members are somehow identifiably different from the majority. Once the group has been selected, the next step in creating an underclass is to confine its members to a small number of continuous residential areas and then to impose on them stringent barriers to residential mobility.... Once a group's segregation in society has been ensured, the next step in building an underclass is to drive up its rate of poverty.... The interaction of poverty and segregation acts to concentrate a variety of deleterious social and economic characteristics.... Through prolonged exposure to life in a racially isolated and intensely poor neighborhood, poverty will quite likely be passed to children in the next generation. When this point is reached, a well-functioning and efficient structure for the construction and maintenance of an urban underclass will have been created.

The evidence reviewed in this chapter suggests that U.S. policies are moving Mexican Americans steadily away from their middle position in the economic hierarchy and toward formation as an underclass. Segregation levels are rising, discrimination is increasing, poverty is deepening, educational levels are stagnating, and the social safety net has been deliberately poked full of holes to allow immigrants to fall through. Whether or not Mexicans become a new urban underclass remains to be seen, but it is already clear that after occupying a middle socioeconomic position between whites and blacks for generations, the economic fortunes of Mexicans have now fallen to levels at or below those of African Americans.

In one critical way, moreover, Mexicans are much worse off than black Americans. Whatever discriminatory barriers African Americans still face, they at least have the legal right to live and work in the United States. In contrast, one-fifth of all Mexican Americans lack any legal claim on American society because they are present without authorization, and this fraction is rising rapidly. If the share of Latinos in undocumented status continues to rise, the resulting underclass will be even "better" than the one that emerged in black inner cities during the 1980s. Not only will its members be exploited and excluded, but they will be outside the law itself, deportable at a moment's notice and perhaps even at serious risk of incarceration for the felonious crime of living and working in the United States without permission.

❧ CHAPTER 5 ❧

REMAKING THE POLITICAL ECONOMY

The prior two chapters have described categorical processes that operate in the United States to perpetuate ethnic and racial inequalities. Although whites no longer espouse racist beliefs in principle, they remain distinctly uncomfortable with African Americans in practice and continue to harbor antiblack stereotypes and engage in subtle forms of discrimination, both conscious and unconscious, that deny blacks equal access to markets for housing, credit, capital, insurance, jobs, services, and consumer goods. They also support a racialized criminal justice system that systematically undercuts black employment, income, family stability, and health. Meanwhile, the framing of Latinos as a threat to the nation's social, economic, and political security has intensified prejudice and discrimination against them and fostered support for immigration policies that have increased the number of Mexicans living north of the border in statuses conferring limited social, economic, and political rights.

These racialized mechanisms of stratification do not operate in isolation, of course, but interact with other, class-based processes that generate inequality between people on the basis of income and wealth. There are major differences between processes of class and racial stratification, however, especially in the United States, which lacks a strong tradition of class formation and identity (Hochschild 1995; Kluegel and Smith 1986). Whereas racial stratification is achieved by singling out entire classes of people—presently African Americans and Mexicans—for invidious treatment within or exclusion from markets, class stratification is achieved more by

158

incorporating class bias into the structure of the market itself—specifying the rules and parameters of competition in ways that favor the haves over the have-nots.

Thus, class stratification in the United States is more subtle and less obvious than racial or ethnic stratification. Indeed, most working- and middle-class Americans do not even perceive it to be occurring (Achen and Bartels 2006; Bartels 2005a; Lamont 2000). Nonetheless, the restructuring of the U.S. political economy over the past several decades to generate asymmetries in market power has given producers, owners, and managers the upper hand over consumers, workers, and employees. Under these circumstances, there is little need for overt discrimination and explicit exclusion on the basis of class. Markets have been rigged systematically to produce outcomes favoring the elite. There is no need for overt exclusionary mechanisms when lower-class citizens simply cannot afford to occupy the same social and economic spaces as the rich.

The Political Economy of Poverty

During the 1930s, the New Deal created a political economy that worked to the benefit of the middle and lower classes at the expense of the wealthy. Markets were regulated in the public interest to moderate their excesses and avoid failures. A system of social insurance was created to protect ordinary citizens from the vicissitudes of the economic cycle, the misfortunes of life, and dependency in old age. To fund these expanded state responsibilities, a progressive tax system was created, and its net effect was to redistribute income and wealth away from the rich toward the middle and lower classes. Lyndon Johnson's Great Society took the New Deal a step further by seeking to eliminate racism from the welfare state that Roosevelt had created.

The wealthy had long opposed these redistributive policies, of course, but until the 1960s they gained little traction politically. As long as the South remained solidly Democratic and allied with northern workers, northeastern liberals, and western progressives, conservatives could do little more than chip away at the edges of the

New Deal. More than any other factor, it was the decision to enfranchise African Americans and include them under the protections of the welfare state that broke apart the New Deal coalition and led to a political realignment that restructured the American political economy in favor of the rich and powerful (Edsall and Edsall 1991; Lemann 1991; Massey 2005b; Phillips 1969; Quadagno 1994).

The passage of the Civil Rights Act of 1964 began the process of realignment. In one stroke it ended the South's traditional support for populist economic policies and transformed the former Confederacy from a Democratic to a Republican bastion. According to Bill Moyers, a close aide to President Lyndon Johnson:

> The night that the Civil Rights Act of 1964 was passed, I found him in the bedroom, exceedingly depressed. The headline of the bulldog edition of the *Washington Post* said, "Johnson Signs Civil Rights Act." The airwaves were full of discussions about how unprecedented this was and historic, and yet he was depressed. I asked him why. He said, "I think we've just delivered the South to the Republican Party for the rest of my life, and yours." (quoted in Gittinger and Fisher 2004)

Blue-collar voters in the North likewise began to abandon the Democratic coalition in 1968, when passage of the Fair Housing Act threatened to integrate schools and neighborhoods (Massey and Denton 1993) and affirmative action programs began to force blacks into white unions (Skrentny 1996). As northern blue-collar workers and southern Democrats increasingly sided with economic conservatives (Phillips 1969), and as the Republican Party turned rightward after being taken over by southerners (Lind 2002), the wealthy finally began to make serious headway in reversing the tide of the New Deal.

Racing to De-unionize

Despite the rise of unions under the New Deal, the labor movement never achieved the same level of prominence in the United States that it did in other industrial democracies (Western 1997). Owing to the decentralized political economy of the United States, collective bargaining took place on a firm-by-firm basis rather than across industries, unemployment programs were run by fifty states rather than the unions themselves, and labor was never able to establish its own political party. These peculiarities of the American system limited the size and influence of unions in the United States compared to other industrialized nations. Whereas unionization levels in 1985 were above 80 percent in Belgium, Finland, and Sweden, in the United States the level stood at just 18 percent (Western 1997).

The decentralized nature of the American political economy and the barriers to union organization that follow from it are in no small way attributable to the unique role of race in shaping the politics and policies of the United States. The U.S. Constitution's granting to states of all powers not specifically allocated to the federal government stemmed from the need, unique among nations that would become industrial powers, to bind slaveholders and freeholders into a common political union. In writing the U.S. Constitution, southerners were determined to create a weak national government that would not be able to end slavery and impose a system of free labor on the states. The resulting fragmentation of power between states and the federal government limited the legal tools available to promote unionization compared with other industrial nations.

Even at the height of the New Deal, when southern Democrats supported progressive, pro-union policies they did so only as long as the policies did not threaten the racial status quo; as a result, sectors of the labor market with significant black employment had to be excluded from coverage in major pieces of labor legislation (Katznelson 2005). Because of these wholesale exclusions, levels of unionization reached their natural limit much earlier than in Europe, weakening the power of workers in collective bargaining.

The heyday of union power and influence was the period 1935 to 1946. After the Second World War, however, northern-based unions began to achieve unexpected success in organizing black textile and service workers in the South, and southern congressional representatives came to fear that unionization would fuel demands for civil rights (Katznelson 2005). In response, for the first time since Roosevelt's election, populist southern Democrats deserted labor and joined with pro-business Republicans in the North to roll back the National Labor Relations Act and attenuate enforcement of the Fair Labor Standards Act. Although President Harry Truman denounced the legislation as a "slave labor bill," with southern support it passed over his veto (Katznelson 2005, 67–68).

The 1947 Taft-Hartley Act represented the first breach in the walls of the New Deal and was a harbinger of things to come. It prohibited requiring union membership and dues paying as a condition of employment and outlawed secondary labor actions, banning boycotts, strikes, and picketing against firms that were not engaged in a labor dispute but did business with one that was. It also gave federal authorities new power to issue injunctions *against* collective labor actions and *to impose* an eighty-day "cooling-off period" whenever a strike was deemed to "imperil national health or safety." The legislation also curtailed federal authority to investigate and prosecute unfair labor practices and authorized employers to file suit against unions for monetary damages incurred during stoppages that were later determined to be unlawful under the act (Katznelson 2005, 53–64).

In 1959 the Landrum-Griffin Act further tightened prohibitions on secondary labor actions and gave employers another tool in the fight against unionization by permitting non-union members to vote in certification and decertification elections. Employers could thus hire scab workers to replace those on strike and then have the scabs vote as employees to decertify the union that originally called the strike (Azari-Rad, Philips, and Prus 2005). Together, the Taft-Hartley and Landrum-Griffin Acts took an increasing toll on the labor movement beginning in the 1960s, especially as manufacturing began to decline.

Figure 5.1 shows the rate of union membership in the United States expressed as a percentage of all non-agricultural workers between 1900 and 2004. Aside from a brief surge at the end of the progressive era in 1920–21, unions achieved little success in penetrating the U.S. workforce until passage of the National Labor

Figure 5.1   Level of Unionization in the United States, 1900 to 2004

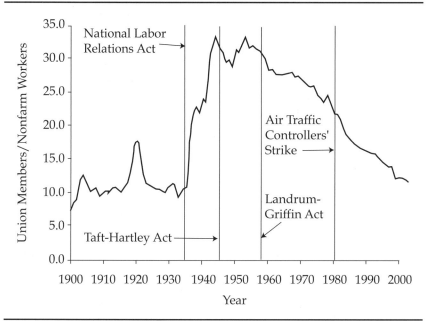

Source: Carter et al. (2006).

Relations Act in 1935, whereupon union membership surged, more than tripling from around 10 percent of workers in 1935 to one-third of all workers just ten years later.

With the passage of the Taft-Hartley Act in 1949, however, union membership ceased growing and then began to decline after 1959 when Landrum-Griffin further strengthened the hand of employers. From a peak rate of 33 percent in 1954, unionization fell to 23 percent by 1980, at which time Ronald Reagan was elected to the presidency. His first year in office proved to be pivotal. In 1981 the union representing air traffic controllers voted to go on strike for better working conditions and improved safety requirements. Invoking Taft-Hartley, President Reagan declared the strike illegal and promised to fire all those who did not return to work within two days (Pels 1995). He brought in replacement air traffic controllers from the military, and although flights were disrupted and air traffic reduced, the union was broken and 85 percent of its members lost their jobs. An important message had been sent: the resurgent Republicans were willing to use all of the tools available from Taft-Hartley and Landrum-Griffin to prevent public-sector unionization, one of the few pathways left for union expansion. After 1980, the pace of de-unionization accelerated, and by 2004 only 11.8 percent of all American workers were union members, the lowest level since 1933.

As union power waned, so did the frequency and success of labor actions. Figure 5.2 shows frequencies of work stoppages and successful certification elections from 1936 to 2000. Each series is expressed as a fraction of its 1946 value to place trends on the same scale. In many ways, the year before passage of the Taft-Hartley Act can be considered the high point of the labor movement in the United States. Despite year-to-year volatility, the overall trend in labor actions has been steadily downward since then, with the exception of a brief period in the late 1960s and early 1970s during the Vietnam War. After Reagan's breaking of the air traffic controllers' union, the frequency of strikes plummeted to near zero.

Over the same period, the frequency of successful certification elections steadily dropped. Whereas in the four years prior to the air traffic controllers' strike of 1981 an average of 8,600 union certification elections were held each year, by the late 1990s the number had fallen to around 3,400; as the number of union elections fell, so did the success rate. Until 1946, unions routinely won 86 percent of their certification elections. From peak success rates above 80 percent in the 1940s, the rate fell to a nadir during the Reagan administration, when unions won just 40 percent of certification votes.

Falling levels of unionization translate directly into lower worker earnings. Holding constant a variety of job and worker characteristics, studies indicate that union jobs pay around 15 percent more than non-union jobs (Card 1996; Freeman and Medoff 1984; Kuhn and Sweetman 1998; Robinson 1989). As rates of unionization have declined, average wages have been pulled down as the

Figure 5.2   Relative Frequency of Strikes and Successful Union
              Elections, 1936 to 2000

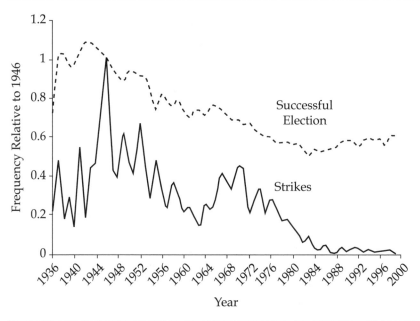

Source: Carter et al. (2006).
Note: 1946 = 1.

share of workers enjoying this earnings premium declines as well.
In addition, with unionization no longer viewed as a credible threat
by employers, they have little incentive to pay workers higher
wages as an inducement *not* to form a union. Studies reveal that in
the past the threat of unionization served to boost the wages of all
workers, even those who were not union members (Corneo and
Lucifora 1997; Freeman and Medoff 1984; Leicht 1989; Neumark
and Wachter 1995), including even midlevel managers (Rosenfeld,
forthcoming).

As a result, over time there has been a strong positive relationship in the United States between the frequency of strikes and the

wages earned by workers (Ashenfelter and Johnson 1969; Ashenfelter, Johnson, and Pencavel 1972; Kalleberg, Wallace, and Raffalovich 1984). The breaking of the air traffic controllers' union in 1981 effectively ended employers' perception of unionization as a threat and led to a "complete decoupling of the wage-strike relationship" (Rosenfeld 2006). At the dawn of the new millennium, unions were no longer a significant institutional player in determining the wages and employment conditions for workers in the United States.

Minimizing the Minimum

Specific policy decisions made by Congress and the president in 1947, 1959, and 1981 to weaken labor's bargaining position thus had their desired effect. Without the collective power of unions behind them, workers moved out of the middle of the income distribution and downward toward its lower reaches. Benefits also disappeared as wages fell steadily toward the legal minimum, a benchmark that itself came under increasing attack from conservatives. As figure 5.3 shows, through its actions and inactions Congress progressively reduced the real value of the minimum wage to the lowest level seen since the great wage compression of the 1940s (Goldin and Margo 1992).

The golden age of the progressive political economy was 1948 to 1968, when in real terms the minimum wage steadily rose from $3.50 an hour to a peak of $9.20 at the height of the Great Society. As inflation increased during the late 1960s and early 1970s, however, Congress declined to adjust the minimum wage for changes in the cost of living, and in real terms its value fell sharply, reaching $7.20 during the Nixon administration before stabilizing in the Ford and Carter years. With the accession of Ronald Reagan to the presidency after 1980, the minimum wage resumed its race toward the bottom, reaching a value of just $5.40 in 1989. After fluctuating around $6.00 per hour during the Clinton years, the wage declined once again under President George W. Bush to end at $5.30 in 2005, the lowest level since Taft-Hartley passed in 1949.

Using government data compiled by Courtland Smith (2006),

Figure 5.3   Real Value of the U.S. Minimum Wage (2002
              Dollars), 1938 to 2004

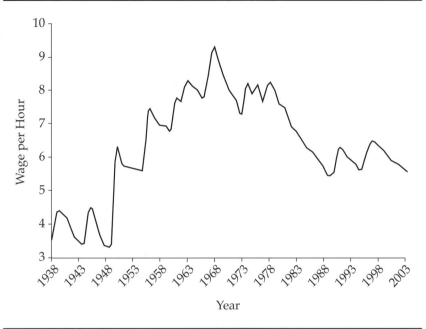

Source: U.S. Bureau of Labor Statistics.

figure 5.4 illustrates the effect of these wage reductions on the welfare of families supported by low-wage workers.[1] Specifically, it computes how much income would be earned working full-time (38.5 hours per week) for a full calendar year (52 weeks) and expressing the result as a share of the official poverty level for a family of four. As can be seen, never in the course of the past fifty years has the official minimum wage been sufficient to lift a family with one breadwinner out of poverty, although during the height of Johnson's Great Society it came close. In 1968 a minimum-wage worker employed full-time generated annual earnings equal to 93 percent of the federal poverty limit.

The figure has been labeled to show Republican versus Democratic administrations. After the 1960s, Republican administrations

Figure 5.4   Earnings for a Full-Time Minimum-Wage Job as a
              Share of Poverty Earnings for a Family of Four

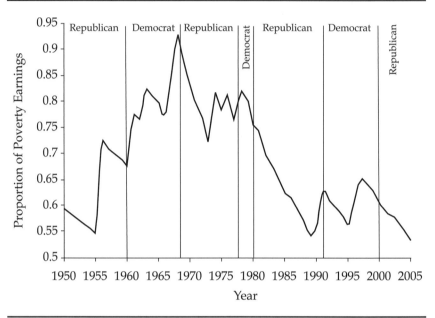

Sources: U.S. Bureau of Labor Statistics; U.S. Bureau of the Census,
Statistical Abstract of the United States.

were very clearly associated with falling minimum wages, whereas
Democratic administrations were associated with steady, fluctuating, or rising minimum wages. A well-controlled and more comprehensive analysis by Larry Bartels (2004) showed that Republican presidents indeed produce greater income growth for rich than
poor families and that rising inequality is reliably associated over
time with Republican administrations. By minimizing the minimum wage, Congress by the year 2005 guaranteed that the poorest
workers in America would make no more than 53 percent of the
federal poverty rate even if they worked full-time. In other words,
even two full-time workers employed at the minimum wage would
earn barely enough money to keep a family of four above the
poverty threshold of $19,800 per year.

Frayed Safety Nets

Although declining rates of unionization and a falling minimum wage may have lowered the wages of workers after the 1960s, in a sense they were the lucky ones, for despite their reduced earning capacities, at least they had jobs. In recent years, as the earnings of workers have stagnated in response to legislated changes in the U.S. political economy, the safety nets erected by the New Deal to catch those who fall out of the labor market were cut back through reductions in funding and coverage. Figure 5.5 shows per capita spending on unemployment insurance from 1970 through 2000. During the early 1970s, unemployment benefits steadily rose based on momentum carried over from Lyndon Johnson's Great Society, going from $4,900 per unemployed worker in 1970 to $12,000 per unemployed worker in 1973. During Nixon's second term (completed by Gerald R. Ford), benefits were cut back further before they stabilized at $8,000 per unemployed worker during the first half of the Carter administration. As inflation eroded the value of unemployment benefits during the late 1970s and early 1980s, real spending on unemployment benefits plummeted. With the exception of a brief period during 1993–94, spending on unemployment has remained below $4,000 per unemployed worker since the early 1980s.

Financial aid to unemployed Americans has thus been cut back to around one-third of its peak level in the early 1970s. However, unemployment insurance payments are time-limited, and once eligibility is used up, families must fall back on other forms of relief. Figure 5.6 shows real per capita spending on social services for the poor from 1930 to 1995 in constant dollars.[2] From virtually nothing before 1932, the Roosevelt administration increased spending on the poor to around 10 cents per capita by 1940. Although expenditures on behalf of the poor fell during the Second World War, they rebounded after 1945, and funding remained at around 10 cents per capita during the Eisenhower administration.

During Lyndon Johnson's war on poverty, spending on social services for the poor soared, and the legislation he enacted carried this acceleration in spending well into the Nixon administration.

Figure 5.5   Spending on Unemployment Benefits per
               Unemployed Worker

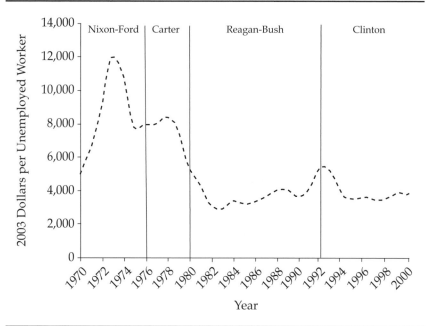

Source: U.S. Bureau of the Census, *Statistical Abstract of the United States*.

From a per capita level of around 12 cents in 1960, spending on antipoverty programs more than tripled to peak at 30 cents in 1972 before falling precipitously during Nixon's second term. The free fall in poverty-related social services was checked early in the Carter administration but then resumed during the inflation of the late 1970s as Congress failed to make adjustments to transfers to reflect the rising cost of living. Throughout the presidencies of Ronald Reagan and George H. W. Bush, antipoverty spending remained flat at only slightly above the level it had been on the eve of the Great Society, a level that persisted through the early years of the Clinton administration.

Thus, in terms of social spending on the poor, by the early 1990s it was as if Johnson's war on poverty had never happened. Even

Figure 5.6   Per Capita Public Spending on Social Services for the
              Poor, 1930 to 1995

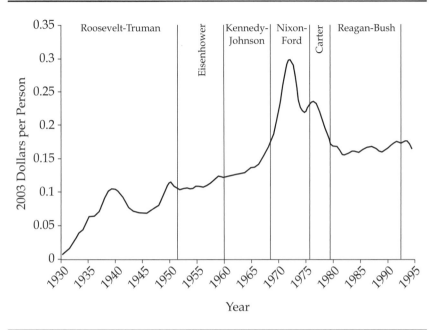

Source: Carter et al. (2006).

this reduced level of spending on the poor was too much, however, for congressional conservatives, who in 1996 succeeded in passing the Personal Responsibility and Work Opportunity Reconciliation Act (PRWORA), essentially forcing mothers of dependent children off of welfare rolls and into the labor force by ending the entitlement to open-ended income transfers. Aid to Families with Dependent Children (AFDC) was replaced by a new program called Temporary Assistance for Needy Families (TANF), which gave mothers only two years of assistance before requiring them to work. According to the terms of the legislation, 25 percent of all families were supposed to leave the welfare rolls by 1997, with 50 percent expected to be working by 2002.

As indicated by figure 5.7, which depicts the percentage of poor

Figure 5.7   Poor Families Receiving AFDC or TANF, 1960 to 2005

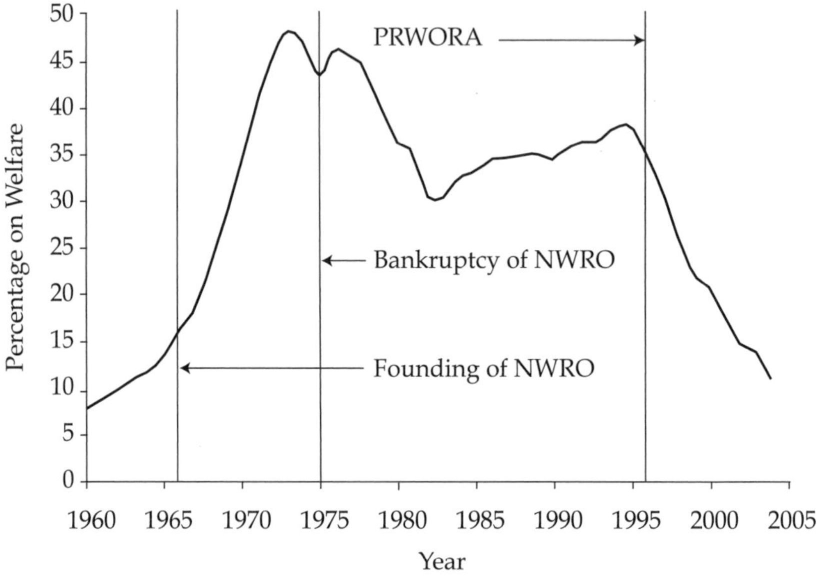

Sources: Carter et al. (2006); U.S. Bureau of the Census.

families receiving AFDC or TANF benefits by year, the effect of the new law on welfare use was sudden and dramatic. Historically the rate of welfare use in the United States had been low because Congress wrote the Social Security Act to exclude black workers and delegate to states the right to determine eligibility. Given the over-representation of African Americans among the poor and the disproportionate location of all poor families in southern states with stringent eligibility requirements and low payments, only a tiny fraction of the poor actually received welfare before the 1960s. Indeed, until 1965 the share of poor families receiving income transfers ranged only from 10 to15 percent.

The passage of civil rights laws and other federal reforms during the Great Society made it more difficult for states to deny relief to poor families, and in 1966 the National Welfare Rights Organization (NWRO) was formed to organize poor minority women, get them to apply for AFDC, and go to court if necessary to force reluctant state officials to honor entitlements (Katz 1986). At its peak, the NWRO had thirty thousand members, mostly poor, black women with dependent children (Roach and Roach 1978), and the organization's militant tactics indeed overcame the administrative deterrents to enrollment (Piven and Cloward 1977).

As a result, the number of women on welfare increased dramatically after 1965. Figure 5.7 shows that the share of poor persons supported by AFDC jumped from 15 percent in 1966 to 48 percent in 1973. As Richard Nixon scaled back the war on poverty and reduced federal funding for antipoverty organizations such as the NWRO, the movement experienced financial difficulties, and in 1975 it was forced into bankruptcy (Abramovitz 2000). In the wake of the NWRO's collapse, the share of poor women receiving AFDC fell to 30 percent in 1982 before leveling off and slowly rising back up to 36 percent in 1995.

Although the demise of the NWRO brought about a decline in the rate of welfare usage, the situation did not return to the status quo ante. The welfare rights movement had raised awareness of entitlements among poor women, and welfare use remained at more than twice its pre-1965 level. Ironically, however, the very success of the NWRO laid the foundations for the ultimate demise of AFDC as a program, for after 1965 welfare came to be irrevocably associated in the public mind with poor, African American women, who were portrayed in political rhetoric and the media as undeserving, irresponsible "welfare queens" who bore children out of wedlock to increase the size of AFDC payments and prosper at the expense of overburdened taxpayers (Neubeck and Cazenave 2001). Through such racialized portrayals, the public came to overestimate the cost of the welfare system and the representation of black women within it, and AFDC and related entitlements thus became increasingly unpopular with white voters (Gilens 1999, 2003).

Having gained control of both houses of Congress in 1994, Republicans were able to translate this public animus against welfare

Figure 5.8   Real per Capita Spending on Food Stamps, 1970 to 2002

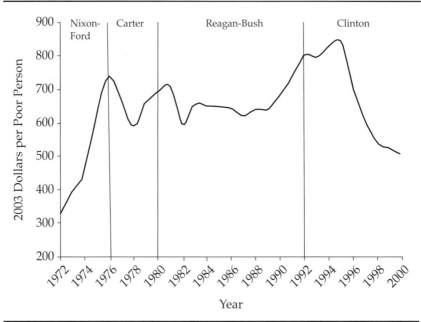

Year

Source: U.S. Bureau of the Census, *Statistical Abstract of the United States.*

into legislation. The 1996 Personal Responsibility and Work Opportunity Reconciliation Act was a self-proclaimed effort to "end welfare as we know it," and as is obvious from figure 5.7, the effect on usage rates was immediate and profound. From a figure of 36 percent in 1996, the share of poor families receiving federal income transfers fell sharply to just 10 percent in 2004, a level of welfare utilization last observed in 1963. Along with the decline in welfare receipt came a drop in spending for other entitlements that were tied to it, such as food stamps. As shown in figure 5.8, real expenditures for food stamps fell dramatically as the new welfare policy pushed women off of welfare and into ineligibility for food stamps. Whereas federal spending on food stamps had totaled $840 per poor person on the eve of welfare reform, by 2000 the figure had fallen to just $500, about the same amount spent right after the program's founding in 1973. The decline in welfare receipt and income transfers did not stem from a drop in the rate of poverty, but from the systematic shifting of poor women away from public supports. In essence, poverty was privatized as poor mothers were forced into the labor force and made to bear the full cost of their meager lives.

The foregoing trends are emblematic of broader shifts throughout the American political economy that have undercut the income supports available to families at the lower end of the class hierarchy (Scholz and Levine 2001). Since the 1970s, the only forms of social spending that have reliably increased in real terms are those associated with the elderly. While spending on Medicare and old-age survivor's insurance steadily increased, funding for Supplemental Security Income, low-income housing, early childhood education, food supplements for women and infants, and school lunch programs remained flat (Scholz and Levine 2001). The only antipoverty funding that increased in real terms was that for Medicaid, which did not stem from rising state generosity toward the poor but more from the mandatory provision of emergency and stopgap medical services to the rising number of Americans who lacked health insurance.

Downsizing the Employer of Last Resort

For poor minorities, the public sector historically has served as an employer of last resort, and federal employment has been particularly important as an anchor for the black middle class (Landry 1987). For this and other reasons, a long-cherished dream of conservatives has been to shrink the size of the federal government to the point where, in the words of the Republican strategist Grover Norquist, it could be "drowned in the bathtub" (Massey 2005b). Figure 5.9 shows the number of nondefense federal employees per thousand persons in the U.S. population. In relative terms, the high-water mark of federal employment came during Lyndon Johnson's war on poverty, when the number of federal workers per thousand rose from 8.5 to 9.5. The number then declined during the

Figure 5.9   Nondefense Government Workers per 1,000
               Population

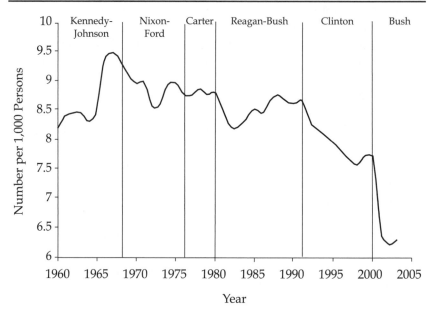

Sources: Carter et al. (2006); U.S. Bureau of the Census, *Statistical Abstract of the United States.*

Nixon and Ford administrations and stabilized at 8.8 workers per thousand under President Jimmy Carter.

The decline in federal employment resumed during the first Reagan administration, but then recovered somewhat before experiencing a sustained decline over the course of the two Clinton administrations. The election of George Bush in 2000, however, brought an unprecedented assault on federal employment: the number of federal workers per thousand fell to a record low of 6.2 within two years of his assuming office, the fastest drop in federal employment in American history. In relative terms, the federal government is now smaller than at any point since 1940, reflecting its reduced capacity for managing and regulating the U.S. political economy.

The New Debtors

Falling rates of unionization, a declining minimum wage, reduced welfare coverage, falling income transfers, and declining federal employment have placed families in the lower portion of the income distribution in very precarious circumstances. Living so close to the edge of financial solvency on a daily basis, Americans are increasingly vulnerable to negative income shocks caused by illness or injury, the loss of a job, a reduction in hours worked, or some other family emergency. For the rising share of Americans who lack health insurance, in particular, a visit to a hospital or clinic can quickly overwhelm household finances to create an acute financial crisis.

When money coming into a family budget cannot cover current spending, in the absence of government transfers the only way to make ends meet is through private borrowing, and in recent years Americans have accumulated unprecedented levels of debt, most commonly by running up balances on credit cards in a desperate effort to make it from one month to the next. Contrary to popular belief, most families become mired in consumer debt not because of frivolous shopping sprees but in response to economic shocks beyond their control—usually family emergencies that force them into a downward spiral of debt and borrowing (Manning 2000; Sullivan, Warren, and Westbrook 2000; Warren and Tyagi 2003).

Figure 5.10 shows trends in per capita consumer debt from 1945 to 2005. Through the mid-1970s, per capita consumer debt rose at a steady pace of around 10 cents per year in real terms, going from around 40 cents in 1945 to $3.40 in 1975. With high rates of inflation and interest in the late 1970s and early 1980s, however, consumer borrowing slowed, but then accelerated once again in the late 1980s. After a lull in the early 1990s, borrowing grew at an unprecedented and breakneck pace after 1993, increasing by around 25 cents per year through the year 2005, when per capita consumer debt approached a record level of $8.00 per person, or $2.3 billion in the aggregate.

Much of this debt is held in revolving credit card accounts whose interest rates have steadily risen in real terms as the total amount owed has increased, generating immense profits for banks. Figure

Figure 5.10   Per Capita Consumer Debt, 1945 to 2005

Source: U.S. Federal Reserve.

5.11 plots the average interest rate charged on credit cards com-pared with the interest rate prevailing in the rest of the economy. As can be seen, the gap between the two series was relatively narrow during the 1970s, averaging only 4.4 percentage points. Over the course of the 1980s and 1990s, however, the gap steadily widened, earning credit card lenders, in real terms, more money per dollar loaned. During the period 2000 to 2005, the gap between the inter-est rate on credit cards and the prevailing rate averaged 8.2 percent-age points.

The rising mountain of consumer debt is not without risks to banks, of course, despite high interest rates and record profits, for if the debt becomes too burdensome to sustain, some credit card holders simply walk away from their obligations by declaring bankruptcy. Historically, bankruptcy laws in the United States were

Figure 5.11 Interest on Credit Card Debt Versus Overall Interest
Rates, 1975 to 2005

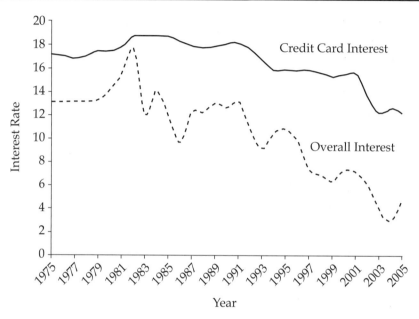

Source: U.S. Federal Reserve.

relatively lenient with consumers who borrowed over their heads, allowing them to go to court and wipe away most of their obligations to begin their financial lives afresh. For bankers left with the unredeemable loans, however, this act represented an "abuse" of the bankruptcy system, and at their behest, Congress in 2005 passed the Bankruptcy Abuse Prevention and Consumer Protection Act.

The new law placed barriers on the road to bankruptcy and forced struggling consumers to pay down more of their accumulated debt. After 2005, debtors were obligated to undergo "credit counseling" in a government-approved program before being allowed even to file for bankruptcy, and then once a filing had been made, they had to pay all back taxes before being allowed to proceed. The new law eliminated automatic stays in eviction proceedings, license suspensions, divorce proceedings, and child support cases, and for the first time it applied a means test to filers. After 2005, those debtors whose monthly income fell above the median in their state had to continue making payments to creditors based on a strict expenses-to-income formula (Henry 2006). Henceforth, families who got into financial trouble by accumulating large debts would have a much harder time starting over, no matter what the reason for their insolvency. The country may not yet have returned to debtors' prisons, but the new law clearly moves it in the direction of indentured servitude.

The Political Economy of Affluence

As the political economy of poverty has become steadily more unforgiving over the past several decades, the political economy of affluence has moved in the opposite direction. As political leaders rewrote the rules of the American market to reduce the bargaining power of labor, lower the minimum wage, curtail social safety nets, limit transfer payments, constrict public employment, and make debt more expensive to acquire and difficult to escape, they also rewrote the rules of the economic game to make life easier for the affluent by reducing their financial obligations in support of the public good. This restructuring was achieved mainly by dismantling the system of progressive taxation that had been created during the New Deal and shifting the tax burden from rich to poor.

Shifting the Tax Burden

The federal income tax was first authorized in 1913 by the Sixteenth Amendment to the U.S. Constitution. Figure 5.12 summarizes the history of federal income taxation by showing the top rate on regular income and the overall rate on capital gains (profits realized from the sale of assets). Initially, the top tax rate was set at 7 percent, and there was no differentiation between earned income and capital gains. When the United States entered the First World War, top tax rates climbed dramatically, going to 15 percent in 1916, to 67

Figure 5.12   Top Marginal Tax Rates and Capital Gains Tax
Rates, 1913 to 2005

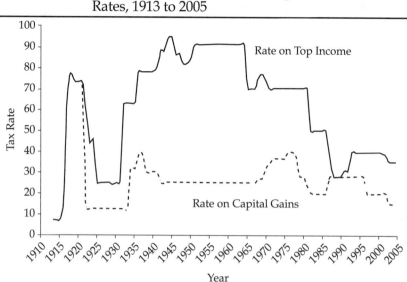

Sources: Carter et al. (2006); U.S. Bureau of the Census, *Statistical Abstract of the United States.*

percent in 1917, and reaching 77 percent in 1918, again with no differentiation between capital gains and regular income. The end of the war brought a slight reduction in taxes, with the top rate falling to 73 percent until 1922, when a Republican administration and Congress lowered the top rate to 58 percent before easing it steadily downward to 44 percent in 1923 and 25 percent in 1924, where it remained until the election of Franklin Roosevelt in 1932. At the same time, beginning in 1922, Congress also differentiated capital gains from regular income, reducing the rate of tax on gains from the sale of assets such as stocks and bonds to just 12.5 percent.

The advent of the New Deal revolutionized American tax policy by introducing a progressive system that taxed additional income at steadily higher rates as earnings rose. From 1932 through 1935, the wealthiest Americans paid 63 percent on regular income over $1 million, and the tax on capital gains rose from 12.5 percent to

31.5 percent. During the remainder of the 1930s, the top tax rate rose to 78 percent, and the tax on capital gains increased briefly to 39 percent before falling back to 30 percent in the last years of the decade. In the political economy of the New Deal, in other words, those with the most resources were expected to shoulder the lion's share of payments toward the collective good.

Although the capital gains tax fell to 25 percent beginning in 1942, the top tax on income went to 94 percent during 1944 and 1945 to finance the war effort. Beginning in 1951 and continuing through 1964, the top tax rate stabilized at 91 percent, and the rate on capital gains held steady at 25 percent. A tax cut in 1965 reduced the top rate to 70 percent, but President Johnson soon found that he had to raise taxes upward to finance the Vietnam War. From 1968 to 1970, the top tax rate rose briefly to 77 percent before falling back to 70 percent again in 1971. In the end, the war was financed more by an increase in the capital gains tax, which rose steadily to peak at 40 percent in the late 1970s before being scaled back to 20 percent.

Ronald Reagan was elected in 1980 on a campaign pledge of cutting taxes, which he proceeded to do with alacrity upon assuming office. Over the course of his presidency, the top tax rate was more than halved, and by the time he left office the top rate for both income and capital gains both stood at just 28 percent, the lowest point since Roosevelt was first elected. In 1991 his successor, George H. W. Bush, famously broke his pledge of "read my lips— no new taxes" and raised the top tax rate from 28 percent to 31 percent. Although modest in size, this increase was enough to cost him the election; the wealthy fared even worse, however, under Bush's successor, Bill Clinton, who raised the top rate to 39.6 percent. Vowing not to repeat the mistake of his father, George W. Bush entered the White House with a firm commitment to cut taxes: the top rate was reduced to 35 percent and the rate on capital gains to just 15 percent, with more cuts proposed for the future.

Clearly, since 1980 taxes paid by the wealthiest Americans have been substantially reduced. The data in figure 5.12 are incomplete, however, because they refer only to income taxes and exclude payroll taxes, which constitute a large share of the burden for most Americans. The two principal payroll taxes are Social Security (6.2

percent of earned income) and Medicare (1.45 percent). Moreover, whereas the Medicare tax applies to all earned income, the Social Security tax applies only up to an income ceiling that in 2005 stood at $90,000. Earnings over this amount are not subject to the 6.2 percent Social Security tax, which means that the burden of supporting Social Security falls disproportionately on poor and middle-income families.

In terms of Social Security, the greater the income above $90,000, the lower the average tax rate, which is the relative share of income that people contribute given payroll taxes and whatever progressivity is built into income taxes. Figure 5.13 shows average tax rates estimated for households at three levels of income from 1965 to 2005 (expressed in constant 2005 dollars): $20,000 (roughly the poverty level for a family of four), $200,000 (an affluent household), and $2 million (a wealthy household). Despite some fluctuations, the progressivity built into the tax system during the New Deal persisted through 1980 as wealthy taxpayers consistently paid around two-thirds of their income in taxes compared with 30 to 40 percent among affluent families and 10 to 20 percent among poor families. By design, those with the most income at their disposal contributed more to the common good than others.

This progressivity largely evaporated during the Reagan and Bush years, with the average tax rate for wealthy households going from 67 percent to 28 percent in just eight years. Given an income of $2 million, this shift yielded tax savings of around $780,000 *per year*. Although affluent households saw their average tax rate drop as well, the change was considerably more modest, going from 41 percent in 1980 to 29 percent in 1988. The poor, meanwhile, saw their tax burden *rise* under President Reagan, with the average rate after 1986 going from 16 percent to 23 percent.

With respect to net after-tax income, therefore, the changes introduced under Reagan dramatically increased the take-home pay of the wealthy, modestly increased that of the affluent, and actually lowered that of the poor. Despite the political price he paid in the 1992 election, moreover, George H. W. Bush's tax cut had little real effect on the average tax rate of the wealthy, which rose only slightly. It was Bill Clinton who restored a modicum of progressiv-

Figure 5.13   Average Tax Rates for Households Earning $20,000, $200,000, and $2 Million per Year

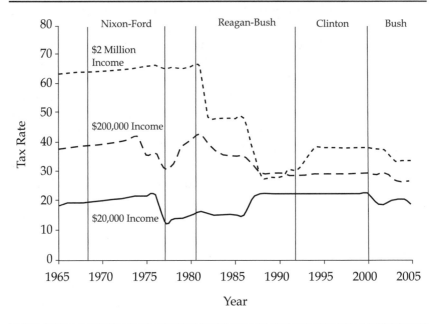

Source: Author's calculations.

ity to the system, raising the average tax rate to nearly 40 percent for wealthy households while leaving the rates paid by affluent and poor household about the same.

Most recently, George W. Bush's tax cuts reduced the average rate for all three classes, but progressivity was substantially reduced compared to the Clinton years, and the burden of paying for government was shifted downward in the income distribution. As of 2005, poor households paid 20 percent of their income in taxes, affluent households paid 27 percent, and wealthy households paid 34 percent—not quite the bonanza for the rich achieved at the end of the second Reagan administration, but a far cry from the progressive taxation that prevailed from 1932 to 1980 under arrangements set by the New Deal.

Not only have taxes for the wealthy been dramatically reduced since 1980, but federal enforcement efforts have shifted away from their historical focus on the rich (who make most of the money, pay most of the taxes, and therefore have the greatest incentive to cheat) as IRS auditing efforts have been redirected toward the poor. Whereas 11.4 percent of taxpayers with incomes over $100,000 were audited in 1988, only 1.2 percent of such people were audited in 1999. In contrast, the percentage of audits done to taxpayers with incomes under $25,000 *rose* slightly, going from 1.0 percent to 1.4 percent over the same period (Phillips 2002, 327). At the end of the twentieth century, in other words, a household with an income barely above the federal poverty level was more likely to be audited for tax compliance than an affluent household earning more than twice the median income.

Different from You and Me

As F. Scott Fitzgerald famously observed, "The very rich are different from you and me." Indeed, as the foregoing sections indicate, the political economy of the United States was quite radically transformed in recent decades to benefit the rich at the expense of the poor and middle classes. The egalitarian capitalism that prevailed from 1935 to 1975 was replaced by a stratified political economy characterized by an unprogressive tax structure, regressive tax enforcement, and a shrunken state that is no longer capable of regulating the American political economy in the public interest. The minimum wage has fallen to its lowest level in decades, access to federal income transfers has been curtailed, and millions of families have been forced into debt at usurious rates as their legal ability to escape financial liabilities has been restricted by legislative fiat.

How have policies that so obviously benefit the few been implemented and ratified in an electoral system ostensibly controlled by the many? An obvious answer is that money talks and politicians listen, or in the infamous words of Pennsylvania congressman Michael "Ozzie" Meyers, videotaped by the FBI as he took a $50,000 bribe, "Money talks and bullshit walks." In the contemporary political economy of the United States, wealthy donors provide politicians with the money they need to get elected and re-elected, and in return these donors receive access and a sympathetic hearing for their concerns. The poor and their "bullshit," meanwhile, are shown the door.

Something in the neighborhood of $3 billion was spent on electoral campaigns during the year 2000 (Public Campaign 2003). In the 2002 elections, less than one-tenth of 1 percent of all Americans accounted for 83 percent of all campaign funds expended (Ivins and Dubose 2003). Among donors to congressional elections in 1996, one study found that 20 percent had incomes of $500,000 or more, 26 percent had incomes of $250,000 to $500,000, and 35 percent had incomes of $100,000 to $250,000, but only 5 percent had incomes under $50,000 (Phillips 2002). If Congressman Meyers is right—and he would know—then it is hardly surprising that policies enacted by politicians favor the class interests of those whose financial largesse is responsible for their continuation in public office.

When Martin Gilens (2005) used national surveys administered between 1981 and 2002 to determine the policy preferences for poor, middle-class, and affluent voters, he found that on issues where preferences differed by class, legislative outcomes were strongly associated with the preferences of the affluent, had a weak relationship to those of the middle class, and bore no relationship at all to the opinions of the poor. Likewise, in his analysis of roll-call votes in the U.S. Senate, Bartels (2005b) found that senators were significantly more responsive to the views of affluent constituents than to those of the middle class and that the political views of the poor had no effect at all on voting patterns. He also found that Republican senators were more than twice as responsive as Democrats to the political views of affluent constituents.

These well-controlled statistical analyses are backed up by circumstantial evidence compiled by Common Cause (2003). During the 2000 presidential campaign, George W. Bush cultivated a wealthy elite of large donors he called the "Bush Pioneers." Of those participating in this donor network, 242 people raised at least $100,000, and another 310 contributed sizable amounts of cash without reaching the $100,000 threshold (Massey 2005b, 134).

When Common Cause examined the amounts given and the treatment received by Bush's Pioneers, it found that donors reaped a bonanza of special favors from the administration once it entered office, including privileged access to leases on federal property, favorable terms for the exploitation of federally owned resources, the easing of EPA restrictions, favorable rulings by government regulators, veto power over regulatory actions they objected to, specifically targeted tax breaks, subsidies for selected production and manufacturing, and access to no-bid federal contracts (see Massey 2005b, 135).

Rather than honoring the ideal of "one person one vote," the political system of the United States has increasingly shifted to a de facto policy of "one dollar one vote." The rise of television as the principal instrument of political communication, along with the deregulation of the mass media, has dramatically inflated the cost of running for public office, leading elected officials to spend ever-larger portions of their time raising money for media ads. Political organization on the ground has become less important for winning elections than access to television time on the air, and to get access to the cash they need politicians have increasingly turned to a narrow class of wealthy individuals and corporations.

Although the concentration of wealth and income has clearly played an important role in shifting the political economy rightward in recent years, the influence of money by itself does not account for the change, for as America has grown more unequal economically, it has also become more polarized politically. Over the past several decades, Democrats and Republicans have increasingly split along ideological lines that have little to do with economic equity, differing fundamentally on issues such as sexuality, religion, feminism, patriotism, and, as always in the United States, race. It is the ability of these cultural concerns consistently to trump economic self-interest that has prompted liberals such as Thomas Frank and Paul Krugman to ask plaintively, "What's the Matter with Kansas?" (Frank 2004) and to lament the nation's "Great Unraveling" (Krugman 2003).

Over the course of the twentieth century, ideological polarization and income inequality have moved hand-in-glove. Both fell beginning in the 1930s, bottomed out in the 1960s, and rose again after the middle 1970s. Nolan McCarty, Keith Poole, and Howard Rosenthal (2006) used detailed data on congressional voting behavior to derive a quantitative measure of political polarization between the parties. On a year-to-year basis from 1947 to 2003, they found a very strong temporal correlation of 0.94 between the Gini index for income inequality and the index of political polarization.

Over the longer term, from 1913 to 2000, the correlation between ideological polarization and the share of income earned by the top 1 percent of the population was 0.78 (McCarty, Poole, and Rosenthal 2006). Figure 5.14 reproduces the graph in McCarty et al. (2006) to show the timing of trends in income inequality and ideological polarization over the twentieth century. It is clear from the figure that from 1930 until around 1960, declines in ideological polarization *preceded* declines in economic inequality. Republicans grew more liberal and increasingly supported redistributive policies that reduced inequalities with respect to income while voting for programs that mitigated the concentration of wealth.

During the 1960s, however, something happened to reverse this pattern. Income inequality and political polarization both reached low levels; when somewhere in the middle of the decade a structural shift occurred, the two trend lines crossed. Polarization turned upward decisively beginning in 1969, followed by income inequality around 1979. After 1969, increases in political polarization *preceded* increases in income inequality, turning the historical pattern on its head. The obvious explanation for the "structural shift" of the 1960s was the definitive turn of the Democratic Party toward civil rights.

As soon as the Democratic Party committed itself to dismantling Jim Crow in the South, combating de facto segregation in the North, and deracializing New Deal programs throughout the nation, southern and blue-collar support for the New Deal's populist economic agenda evaporated. Southerners bolted the Democratic Party to push the Republican Party rightward and engaged in a systematic ideological campaign to reverse the progressive policies of the 1930s. According to McCarty and his colleagues (2006), the relationship between income inequality and political polarization

Figure 5.14   Indices of Income Inequality and Political
               Polarization Developed by McCarty, Poole, and
               Rosenthal (2006)

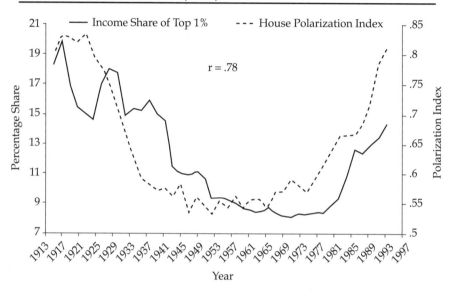

Source: Piketty and Saez (2001), figure 1.2. Reprinted with permission from MIT Press.

represents a complex choreography, a "dance of ideology and un-equal riches" in which polarization inhibits support for redistribution, which produces greater inequality, which feeds more polarization, which generates even more inequality.

They argue that the power of this choreography has been exacerbated by an increase in the number of poor people without political rights who cannot vote and thus cannot exert political pressure from the bottom in support of redistributive policies. They point to the post-1965 revival of immigration and note that the correlation between the percentage foreign-born and political polarization is 0.92. The current potential for polarization and inequality is even greater than they suppose, however, for they do not take into account the huge increase in the share of immigrants who are not only foreign (and therefore cannot vote) but also undocumented (and therefore have no rights at all). Political polarization also follows directly from the mass incarceration of black men (Pattillo, Weiman, and Western 2004).

With respect to voting, all but three states practice some form of felon disenfranchisement. Aside from Maine, Utah, and Vermont, all states and the District of Columbia prohibit prisoners from voting during their period of incarceration. In addition, twenty-nine states forbid convicts on probation from voting; thirty-two prohibit convicts on parole from voting; and fifteen ban ex-felons from voting even after they have served their time (Sentencing Project 2006). The rising share of ex-cons in the black population has thus significantly reduced the number of poor people eligible to vote (Uggen and Manza 2004).

Felon disenfranchisement also opens the door to broader processes of political exclusion. In 1999, for example, the Florida Department of Elections awarded a $2.3 million no-bid contract to a Republican-controlled firm known as Database Technologies to purge voter rolls of unauthorized voters—namely, convicted felons—in preparation for the 2000 election (Palast 2002). Through a skillful manipulation of programming algorithms, the firm was able to purge from the voter list any *black* voter who might *conceivably* have been convicted of a felony, no matter how shaky the computerized evidence, while *not purging any white voters* unless a variety of more stringent criteria were met. Although the firm was required by contract to verify manually any decision to strike a voter from the list, the mandated verifications were never done (Palast 2002).

As a result of the firm's work, 57,000 voters were removed from the registration list to prevent them from voting in the 2000 election. Some 54 percent of those on the list were minorities and thus were likely to be Democratic voters, and at least 90 percent of the names included on the "scrub list" were not in fact felons and were thus inappropriately purged from the voter rolls and denied the right to vote (Palast 2002). Given that George Bush won Florida by a few hundred votes to take the presidency, it is virtually certain that voter fraud enabled by felon disenfranchisement cost Al Gore the presidency. Likewise, it was the systematic suppression of black voters in Ohio in 2004 that reelected the most conservative president in modern American history (Kennedy 2006; Miller 2005).

The growth of a large population of undocumented Latinos can be expected to further fuel political polarization and promote income inequality. In the run-up to the 2006 elections, for example, Republicans in battleground states worked assiduously to enact stricter voting laws that required government-issued identification and proof of citizenship to register and vote (Purnick 2006). Given that these forms of documentation are not accessible to many poor Americans, the net effect will be a further disenfranchisement of the disadvantaged, native as well as foreign.

The New Ecology of Inequality

Over the past forty years, the foregoing categorical mechanisms of class stratification have combined with those grounded in race and ethnicity to produce rising levels of inequality and turn the United States into the most unequal society in the developed world (Brandolini and Smeeding, forthcoming; Smeeding 2005, 2006). This increase in inequality has come at a considerable cost to most Americans. Whereas indices of social well-being—life expectancy, access to housing, nutrition, education, child well-being, crime, drug use, and so on—improved in lockstep with increasing GDP through 1970, afterward trends in social and economic well-being departed from one another at an increasing rate (Miringoff and Miringoff 1999). As the United States got richer after 1970, increases in wealth were no longer translated into greater social well-being for most Americans.

If social conditions have deteriorated throughout the United States, why has the decline not affected the lives of the wealthy and affluent so as to make them more amenable to remedial action? The answer is that over the past several decades the economic elite has increasingly separated itself from the rest of American society in social, cultural, and geographic terms, thereby insulating itself from the negative consequences of rising inequality. Americans have come to inhabit a postmodern political economy characterized by fragmented markets, segregated geography, segmented social or-

191

ganization, and a differentiated culture (Harvey 1991), yielding a mosaic of distinct societal niches whose inhabitants are similar to one another but different from those around them, a phenomenon that Michael Weiss (1988, 2000) called the "clustering of America."

Spatial Separation

Although racial and ethnic segregation have been a characteristic feature of the American social geography for centuries, after 1970 the United States came to experience a new kind of segregation on the basis of class (Fischer et al. 2004; Massey 1996; Massey and Eggers 1990, 1993). Using calculations by Massey and Fischer (2003), figure 5.15 shows the degree of residential segregation between affluent and poor families in the nation's fifty largest metropolitan areas from 1970 to 2000. Segregation is measured using the well-known index of dissimilarity (Massey and Denton 1988), which varies from zero (no segregation) to one (total segregation).

Following Smith (1988) and Massey and Eggers (1990), I have designated families earning incomes below the federal poverty line for a family of four as poor and those earning incomes more than four times the poverty level as affluent.

As the figure shows, class segregation increased sharply between 1970 and 1990, with residential dissimilarity between poor and affluent households rising from .287 to .430, an increase of 50 percent in twenty years. Class segregation moderated somewhat during the economic boom of the 1990s, with income dissimilarity dropping to .373 owing to the rise in real wages at the bottom of the occupational hierarchy and a decline in overall income inequality. This modest decline was not enough, however, to offset the substantial increase in class segregation from 1970 to 1990, so that the degree of geographic separation between rich and poor still remained roughly one-third above the 1970 level.

If the distribution of income becomes more unequal and class segregation simultaneously rises, then the only outcome that is demographically possible is an increase in the geographic concentration of affluence and poverty (Massey and Fischer 2000). The spa-

Figure 5.15   Income Segregation in Large Metropolitan Areas
of the United States, 1970 to 2000

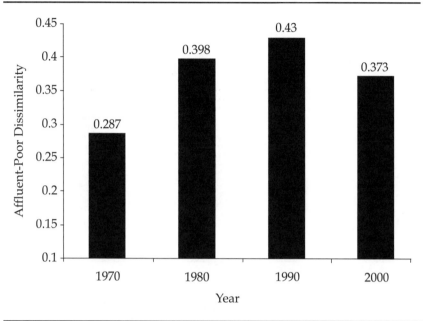

Source: Massey and Fischer (2003).

tial concentration of advantage and deprivation is best measured using the P* isolation index, which yields the proportion of poor or affluent families in the neighborhood of the average poor or affluent person (Massey and Denton 1988; Massey and Eggers 1990). Figure 5.16 shows trends in the concentration of poverty using P* indices computed for 1970 through 2000, and figure 5.17 does the same for the concentration of affluence.

At all points in time over the past thirty years, affluence has been more concentrated spatially than poverty. In other words, those with money are more likely to live in homogenously affluent environments than are those without money to live in homogenously poor environments. Geographic concentration increased at both

Figure 5.16   Concentration of Poverty in Large U.S.
Metropolitan Areas, 1970 to 2000

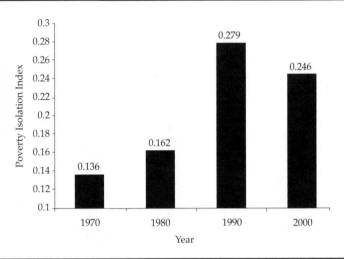

Source: Massey and Fischer (2003).

Figure 5.17   Concentration of Affluence in Large U.S.
Metropolitan Areas, 1970 to 2000

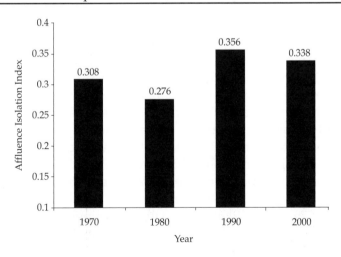

Source: Massey and Fischer (2003).

194

ends of the income distribution between 1970 and 1990 and then fell back slightly by 2000. Over the entire period, however, there was a net increase in both indices. Concentrated affluence rose by 10 percent between 1970 and 2000 to end the century at .338, whereas concentrated poverty rose by 80 percent to end the century at .246.

At the dawn of the new millennium, therefore, the typical affluent family in metropolitan America lived in a neighborhood that was about one-third affluent, and the average poor family lived in a neighborhood that was one-quarter poor. As the nation polarized economically during the last third of the twentieth century, it also polarized spatially, with the greatest change being a marked increase in the geographic concentration of poverty. As poverty became more concentrated spatially, of course, so did everything associated with it: crime, violence, disorder, substance abuse, welfare dependency, poor health, and lagging educational achievement. In other words, the negative externalities associated with rising income inequality were increasingly concentrated in areas inhabited mainly by poor people—places where few affluent citizens ever set foot, much less lived. The end result was the emergence of a new geography of inequality—a categorical segmentation of America's social geography that gave rise to a new set of self-reinforcing political, educational, social, economic, and cultural mechanisms that hardened the lines of class stratification and deepened inequality in the United States.

Political Mechanisms

The spatial segregation of rich and poor families has great potential for stratification through political means. To the extent that the boundaries of governmental and administrative units can be arranged to approximate the geographic contours of concentrated affluence and poverty, and to the degree that taxes and service delivery can be shifted down the administrative hierarchy, then the potential for reifying class advantages and disadvantages is maximized (Massey 1996, 2005a). Once poverty and affluence become geographically concentrated in different parts of the social geography, the affluent acquire the ability to separate themselves politically from the poor by judiciously drawing administrative lines. If they can create separate governmental districts that encompass concentrations of poverty, and if they can force these poor districts to supply and pay for their own services, then the affluent can insulate themselves from the negative consequences of poverty while avoiding financial responsibility for ameliorating it (Orfield 2002).

In contemporary America, the political isolation of the poor is accomplished by the segmentation of metropolitan regions into a patchwork of separate municipalities (Dreier, Mollenkopf, and Swanstrom 2001). The Chicago metropolitan area, for example, contains 1,458 local governments, that of Boston has 1,000, and that of Philadelphia 877 (Altshuler et al. 1999, 23). The concentration of affluence in certain favored suburbs yields high real estate values that allow the affluent to tax themselves at low rates while offering generous, even lavish municipal services to residents. The concentration of poverty in central cities and older suburbs, in contrast, generates a high demand for services but yields low property values, thereby requiring higher tax rates to support inferior services.

The end result is a vicious cycle whereby taxes are raised in relatively poor municipalities to maintain deficient services, driving out families of means, which lowers property values further, causing more tax increases and additional middle-class flight, which further exacerbates the concentration of poverty (Dreier et al. 1999). Under an ecological regime of concentrated affluence and poverty, efforts to decentralize government and shift the financing and provision of public services to lower administrative levels offer a remarkably efficient mechanism for enhancing the social and economic well-being of the rich at the expense of the poor.

Educational Mechanisms

One primary mechanism by which class position becomes institutionalized in the new ecology of inequality is through the school system. Education is one of the most important resources exchanged on global markets, and in recent years workers with college and postgraduate degrees have seen their earnings rise, while high school graduates and dropouts have seen their wages fall. Access to high-quality education has thus become a crucial factor that determines one's position in the post-industrial stratification system.

Because America's current ecological structure concentrates the best-prepared students in areas of resource abundance while gathering the least-prepared in areas of resource scarcity, it reinforces class inequities to promote a more rigid stratification system. Students from low-income families with poorly educated parents, little experience reading books, and multiple social problems end up in schools with the fewest resources to help them learn, while students from affluent families with well-educated parents, extensive experience with books and reading, and few social problems attend well-funded schools that are in the best position to promote learning, a configuration precisely opposite that required to maximize human capital formation and promote equality. In other words, the spatial concentration of affluence and poverty in rich and poor school districts raises the odds that affluent children will receive a superior education and that poor children will get inferior schooling, virtually guaranteeing the intergenerational transmission of class position.

On top of these advantages, affluent Americans benefit from an insidious form of affirmative action that is not well understood outside of the elite itself. Although public attention has focused on minority affirmative action, in reality American colleges and universities support three major affirmative action initiatives: one for minorities, one for athletes, and one for the children of alumni (Massey and Mooney, forthcoming). The latter program, commonly known as "legacy admissions," reinforces the class position of affluent families by granting the children of well-educated, high-earning graduates of elite institutions a significantly greater chance of gaining admittance to the same institutions—a bonus that is conferred *in addition to* whatever advantages these children accrue from their affluent upbringing.

A survey conducted by Hunter M. Breland and his colleagues (1995) found that affirmative action for alumni children is practiced widely at both public and private institutions. Indeed, Daniel

Golden (2003) found that 23 percent of freshmen enrolled at Notre Dame were alumni children, compared with 14 percent at the University of Pennsylvania, 13 percent at Harvard, 11 percent at Princeton, and 11 percent at the University of Virginia. These seemingly modest percentages under 15 percent belie the fact that alumni children constitute a small share of all applicants to selective schools. When one controls for the number of applicants, the children of alumni exhibit exceptionally high admission rates. According to William Bowen and Derek Bok (1998), legacies had a two-to-one admissions advantage over nonlegacies. Cameron Howell and Sarah Turner (2004) found a similar advantage at the University of Virginia, where just 32 percent of regular applicants were admitted compared with 57 percent of the children of alumni.

The preferential boost given to alumni children appears to be greatest at private institutions. In the University of Pennsylvania's class of 2008, for example, legacies accounted for 4.6 percent of applicants but made up 11.2 percent of admissions; whereas the overall admission rate at Penn was 21 percent, it was 51 percent for the children of alumni, yielding an advantage of 2.4-to-1 (University of Pennsylvania 2005). In their study of three private research universities, Thomas Espenshade, Chang Chung, and Joan Walling (2004) found that 50 percent of legacies were admitted compared with only 25 percent overall.

The foregoing statistics can be misleading, however, because they do not take into account the scholarly qualifications of different sets of applicants. Although in raw terms, legacies may enjoy a two-to-one admissions advantage, the children of alumni may also be better qualified than the average applicant. The only comprehensive study to control for academic qualifications is that of Espenshade and his colleagues (2004), who used special tabulations of admissions data to estimate models predicting the likelihood of admission controlling for sex, citizenship, SAT score, and high school GPA, along with race, athletic recruitment, and legacy status. Other things equal, they found that being the child of an alumnus translated into an admissions bonus of around 160 SAT points, tipping the odds of admission very strongly in their favor.

Economic Mechanisms

Once an ecological order of concentrated affluence and poverty has emerged and a political order has been created such that poor and affluent families are located in separate administrative districts, then private economic interests inevitably come into play in ways that reinforce the ecology of inequality. Producers of goods and services naturally seek to maximize profits and therefore selectively locate offices and factories in municipalities where taxes are low, public services are good, and risks are minimal. Retailers likewise seek out zones where buying power is concentrated and the costs and risks of doing business are modest. Affluent households also selectively settle in communities where services are good, taxes are affordable, and safety is ensured.

The adjustment of private behaviors and expectations to fit existing social structures is what Charles Tilly (1998) calls *adaptation*, and over time processes of adaptation lock in and institutionalize patterns of inequality. Consider the Philadelphia metropolitan area. If there were no separately incorporated suburbs and just a single municipal government responsible for taxes and services, then these factors would not loom large as factors in household decisionmaking. Families would decide where to live using other criteria—distance to work, style of housing, access to transportation, nearness to family, for example. There would be sorting among households by income, life cycle, and ethnicity, of course, but selective migration and settlement would not be shaped by radically different structures of taxation and service provision in different segments of the urban environment. All households in the metropolitan area would pay the same taxes and get the same services whether they lived near the center or at the fringe.

As already mentioned, however, the Philadelphia metropolitan area has 877 units of local government, two of which correspond to the City and County of Philadelphia, whose boundaries have been coterminous since 1854. In 2000 the city housed a population in which 23 percent of families were poor and 18 percent spoke a foreign language at home, compared with statewide figures of 11 percent and 8 percent. To provide municipal and human services to this relatively disadvantaged population, the City of Philadelphia collects a lot of taxes, imposing a tax on wages earned in the city, a tax for the "privilege" of doing business in the city, a tax on net profits earned in the city, a tax on dividend and interest earned by city residents, plus the usual taxes assessed on real estate. Despite these heavy taxes, public services in the City of Philadelphia are insufficient to meet the demand and are often mediocre; some, notably education, are decidedly substandard.

In contrast, tax rates in most of the 875 surrounding municipalities are lower, and the range and quality of services better. No other municipality in the Philadelphia metropolitan area has a city wage tax, and most lack the deadly combination of business privilege and net profit taxes. Given this pattern of metropolitan fragmentation, over time families have "voted with their feet" based on their ability to pay. The poor have increasingly been trapped in the central city while the middle class has selectively moved to the suburbs, thus hardening and reinforcing the lines of class advantage and disadvantage.

From the viewpoint of the business executive, the most favorable political organization for a post-industrial metropolis is to have municipal boundaries drawn to encompass as closely as possible the outline of specific office parks, shopping malls, or factory districts. Then the owners of these enterprises can tax themselves at very low rates to satisfy their minimal needs for public services (or pay for them privately) while forcing other municipalities to pay for the health, education, electricity, water, sewer, fire protection, and police services of the people who work in their offices, stores, and factories.

Often business and political interests collude to produce just such an ecology. In Los Angeles, for example, there is an eighteen-mile-long, worm-shaped municipality known as the City of Industry. Incorporated in 1958, it meanders through Los Angeles County and includes just 680 residents, many of them residents of a mental hospital. Despite its small population, however, the City of Industry houses 2,100 factories, warehouses, and shopping centers in addition to a luxury golf course and resort hotel (Davis 1998). The original mayor of the City of Industry served for forty years until passing the job on to his son, who, like his father, served at the pleasure of the business elite, the city's true "citizens." The costs of educating, housing, and protecting workers in the City of Industry fall on nearby suburbs, many of which are rather poor and heavily Latino. Under this spatial configuration, employers are able to extract labor from workers without contributing anything to their maintenance as human beings. Similar ecological structures are observed in other U.S. metropolitan areas (Davis 1998; Dreier, Mollenkopf, and Swanstrom 2001; Orfield 2002).

The imitation of this categorical form of inequality across metropolitan areas, which institutionalizes processes of stratification and makes them durable, is what Tilly (1998) calls *emulation*. Like business interests, affluent households also attempt to isolate themselves within enclaves that systematically exclude the poor and their social problems, even though they court the poor to serve as their child care workers, housecleaners, gardeners, garbage haulers, and municipal employees. Poor people are welcome as workers, but not as residents. Sometimes this exclusion is achieved through political means, as when a municipality adopts zoning restrictions, lot size requirements, density limitations, and construction standards that preclude the construction of housing for low- to moderate-income families.

Given the demand for low-level service workers in the community, it might be quite profitable for a developer to purchase a large lot and erect an apartment building that offered workers low rents and easy access to jobs in the surrounding affluent community. But in exclusive residential areas, developers are prevented from doing so by zoning restrictions, which thus force workers to commute from more distant neighborhoods and to bear high transportation costs. The resulting ecology of inequality does not reflect the operation of the market but rather the operation of categorical mechanisms of exploitation and opportunity hoarding.

Despite the ubiquity of political mechanisms, the process of exclusion is increasingly occurring under private auspices. As social problems proliferate in areas of concentrated poverty, more and more developers have offered affluent consumers "gated communities" to protect themselves from the negative fallout of rising inequality; these exclusive enclaves not only exclude the unwanted poor through invisible mechanisms such as lot sizes and density requirements but more concretely through physical barriers such as walls, fences, and gates manned by uniformed private security officers. Long a fixture in cities of the developing world (Montgomery et al. 2003), gated communities have become increasingly common in developed countries (Dreier, Mollenkopf, and Swanstrom 2001; Webster, Glaze, and Frantz 2002).

Social Mechanisms

Whatever their material circumstances, people always spend time and energy building social networks from which they derive emotional satisfaction and reap material and symbolic rewards. At the low end of the income distribution, people lack the income necessary for full use of postmodern technologies such as computers, the Internet, email, and jet travel. As a result, they interact most intensively with other people in their immediate surroundings, and thus their social networks connect them socially to a rather restricted set of people who themselves lack access to the full range of resources available from the global economy. In this way, the class disadvantages of the poor are socially compounded and their "underclass" identity is solidified to perpetuate poverty across the generations (Castells 1997). Not only do the poor lack material resources themselves, but because of the growing concentration of poverty, their personal and extended networks are also dominated increasingly by people who lack resources.

At the other end of the continuum, people with high incomes live and work in residential and occupational settings with others of similar education, social status, and income. Not only do they possess the income to gain ready access to computers, the Internet, and various modalities of transportation and communication, but given their likely membership in transnational networks and organizations, they are in a position to use these technologies to maintain interpersonal connections across a variety of social and geographic settings, thereby maximizing both the quantity and quality of their information and opportunities. They are well connected to many people at home and abroad who command formidable social, economic, and cultural resources, and these connections reinforce their identity as members of a privileged "overclass" and transmit multiple advantages across the generations (Castells 1996).

Social networks are important to people at both the top and the bottom of the socioeconomic hierarchy, though in radically different ways. Social networks serve quite different functions in areas of concentrated poverty and affluence. Although people in all circumstances turn to those they know to gain emotional satisfaction, material support, and symbolic rewards, what differs by class is the degree to which their network connections possess capital—financial, social, cultural, and physical—to share.

In areas of concentrated poverty, social networks serve more to ensure individual survival than to promote upward mobility (Lomnitz 1975; Stack 1974). Poor people living in poor neighborhoods cultivate ties of kinship, friendship, and acquaintance and then draw on these during times of social crisis and economic stress to get by and make it to the next day. Network members provide support as part of a strategy of generalized reciprocity, because they know that given their precarious material circumstances, they are quite likely to need assistance themselves at some point in the future. Social networks thus operate as a means of redistributing uncontrollable economic shocks and diversifying the risks across time and space.

Under these circumstances, network members who do manage to accumulate a small cushion of emotional, material, and symbolic resources are at constant risk of having their meager surplus disappear in response to the incessant demands from friends, relatives, and acquaintances in desperate need of assistance. Under conditions of concentrated deprivation, therefore, networks function as a mechanism of social leveling and undermine the odds of individual advancement. The greater the concentration of poverty, the more this fact holds true, and to the extent that marginal economic status coincides with single-parenthood and fragmented families, the mobility-limiting effects of networks are further reinforced. Unstable households and transient pair bonding limit the possibilities for income pooling and risk diversification within households, making it more likely that during times of crisis people will be forced to fall back on extended networks.

Precisely the opposite circumstances prevail among people who are fortunate enough to live in areas of concentrated affluence. For them, networks operate to consolidate a privileged class position and enable them to accumulate even more emotional, material, and symbolic resources (Lomnitz and Pérez-Lizaur 1987; Mills 1956). Once again people within social networks provide support as part of a strategy of generalized reciprocity, but instead of using their relationships to ensure survival, which is already secured, they are manipulated to accumulate further social and economic advantages. The affluent grant assistance to friends, relatives, and associates as part of an emotional exchange that brings satisfaction to all parties but that also provides access to tangible material and symbolic benefits. A favor granted to an acquaintance pursuing an economic opportunity may be repaid at a later time and place when the grantor is pursuing his or her own opportunity. Rather than serving to redistribute income and diversify risks, therefore, conditions of concentrated privilege yield social networks that provide significant social, cultural, and financial capital, and once again, the greater the concentration of affluence, the greater the utility of networks in accumulating additional resources.

Cultural Mechanisms

The spatial concentration of people with similar traits also gives rise to distinct subcultures, each corresponding to a specific ecological niche defined by the intersection of social, economic, and demographic characteristics and reflecting the circumstances and perceptions of the people who live within it (Fischer 1975, 1995). As already noted, the concentration of poverty also concentrates any trait correlated with poverty. As the density of poor people rises in a residential area, so does the density of joblessness, crime, family dissolution, substance abuse, disease, and violence. In such a setting, not only do the poor have to grapple with the manifold problems stemming from their own lack of income, but they must also confront the social fallout that stems from living in an environment where most of their neighbors are also poor. The concentration of affluence, in contrast, yields a social environment that is opposite in virtually every respect: already privileged people are surrounded by low levels of joblessness, crime, family dissolution, substance abuse, disease, and violence.

The way people grapple with the circumstances of their daily lives is through culture. They innovate attitudes, beliefs, values, and behaviors and tailor them to the conditions they encounter, constructing conceptual schemas and behavioral scripts that routinize commonly repeated thoughts and actions (Fiske 2004). Culture is not a fixed and invariant attribute of a group that replicates itself unchangingly over time, but a dynamic repertoire of patterned concepts, sentiments, and behaviors that develop in response to environmental conditions and change over time as those conditions change (Kuper 1999).

In the new ecology of inequality, therefore, the behavioral and conceptual repertoires of the poor and the affluent increasingly diverge from one another to yield distinct and often opposing subcultures. Among those at the low end of the income distribution, the spatial concentration of poverty creates a harsh and destructive environment that perpetuates values, attitudes, and behaviors that, while adaptive within a niche of intense poverty, are injurious to society at large and destructive of the poor themselves. At the upper end of the ecological order, a contrasting subculture of privilege emerges from the spatial niche of concentrated affluence to confer additional advantages on the rich, thereby consolidating their social and economic dominance of society.

Perhaps no consequence of concentrated poverty is as destructive as the proliferation of crime and violence. Because criminal behavior is strongly associated with income deprivation, the geographic concentration of poverty necessarily yields a concentration of crime, delinquency, and violence in poor neighborhoods (Massey, Condran, and Denton 1987). According to estimates developed for Philadelphia, each point increase in the neighborhood poverty rate raises the major crime rate by 0.8 points (Massey 2001).

In Columbus, Ohio, the crime rate for neighborhoods with a poverty rate under 20 percent is just 7 per 1,000, but in neighborhoods where the poverty rate is 40 percent or higher, it is 23 per 1,000 (Krivo and Peterson 1996). Other things equal, a resident of the latter neighborhood experiences three times the likelihood of criminal victimization than a resident of the former neighborhood. Clearly, the greater the concentration of poverty in one's neighborhood, the greater the chances of becoming a victim of crime or violence.

How do the poor adapt culturally to an environment where violence is endemic and the risk of victimization great? At the behavior level, a logical adaptation is to become violent oneself. In his ethnographic fieldwork, Elijah Anderson (1994, 1999) has discovered that by adopting a threatening demeanor, cultivating a reputation for the use of force, and backing up that reputation with selective violence, residents of low-income neighborhoods—especially males—deter potential criminals and increase the odds of survival. In a social world characterized by rampant violence, an obsessive concern with respect becomes an important adaptive strategy (Bourgois 2003) in much the same way it does for people in herding and horticultural societies.

Given the concentration of poverty, therefore, some poor people are sure to adopt violent attitudes and behavior as survival strategies (Massey 2001). As more people adopt more violent strategies for self-preservation, the average level of violence within poor neighborhoods rises, leading others to adopt still more violent behavior. As the average level of violence rises over time, more people adopt increasingly violent strategies to protect themselves from the growing threat of victimization, yielding a self-perpetuating upward spiral of violence.

The fundamental need to adapt to conditions of endemic violence that are structurally imbedded leads to the emergence of a "code of the streets" that encourages and promotes the use of force (Anderson 1999). Asking residents of poor neighborhoods to choose a less violent path or to "just say no" to the temptation of violence is absurd, given the threatening character of the ecological niche in which they live. To survive in such areas, one must learn, and to a significant extent internalize, the code of violence described by Anderson, and in this way aggression is passed from person to person in a self-feeding, escalating fashion.

High rates of violence within neighborhoods give rise to a particular cultural style characterized by a reluctance to intervene publicly for the common good, a belief in one's inability to influence one's social environment, and a fatalistic acceptance of social disorder and decline. Whereas people living in areas of concentrated affluence expect people they encounter to be civil, to treat them with respect, and to be responsible, trustworthy human beings, those who reside in areas of concentrated poverty cannot make these assumptions. As a result, they are very guarded in their public behavior and cautious in their attitudes, and poor neighborhoods come to lack a sense of "collective efficacy." The absence of this intangible social resource contributes to the escalation of social disorder and decline by lowering the degree of public vigilance and limiting the willingness of residents to assume responsibility for conditions in the public sphere (Sampson, Morenoff, and Earls 1999; Sampson, Raudenbush, and Earls 1997).

The contrasting ecologies of affluence and poverty also breed opposing peer subcultures. As the concentration of affluence grows, the children of the privileged increasingly socialize with other children of well-educated and successful parents. Knowledge of what one does to prepare for college and an appreciation of the connection between schooling and socioeconomic success are widespread in the schools of the affluent. Students arrive in the classroom well prepared and ready to learn. School officials need only build on this base of knowledge and motivation by using their ample resources to hire well-informed guidance counselors and enthusiastic, talented teachers.

The children of the poor, meanwhile, attend schools with children from other poor families, who themselves are beset by multiple difficulties stemming from a lack of income. Their parents are poorly educated and lack adequate knowledge about how to prepare for college, and children do not fully appreciate the connection between education and later success. Supervision and monitoring of students is difficult because so many come from single-parent families, and schools are in a poor position to make up for this deficit because of funding limitations. Students arrive in the classroom poorly prepared, and neither dispirited guidance counselors nor overworked and underpaid teachers expect much from the students.

Within such settings, an alternative status system is likely to develop. Under circumstances where it is difficult to succeed according to conventional standards, the usual criteria of success are often inverted to create an oppositional identity (Ogbu 1978, 1991). Children formulate oppositional identities to preserve self-esteem when expectations are low and failure by conventional norms is likely. In areas of concentrated poverty, therefore, students from poor families legitimize their educational failures by attaching positive value and meaning to outcomes that affluent children label as deviant and unworthy. In adapting to the environment created by concentrated poverty, success in school is devalued, hard work is seen as a sellout, and any display of learning is viewed as distinctly uncool.

At the same time that the concentration of poverty and violence produces distinct subcultures of poverty and affluence, their juxtaposition within a single urban ecology also heightens class awareness and promotes social stereotyping. High rates of crime, delinquency, and social disorder within poor neighborhoods are all too evident to the affluent and harden their negative stereotypes about the poor while inculcating a deep sense of fear of people who exhibit visible markers associated with poverty, which may be physical (height, skin color, hair texture) or cultural (speech, clothing, bearing). In post-industrial societies, such stereotypical fears are exaggerated by their overrepresentation in the media (Fishman and Cavender 1998; Glassner 2000).

The juxtaposition of affluence and poverty also serves to heighten the sense of relative deprivation experienced by the poor and to hone their envy of the rich. Although the vast majority of people in agrarian societies may have been peasants, most never came into contact with members of the nobility, and they had few opportunities to observe directly the discrepancy in living standards. As the poor urbanize and concentrate in post-industrial cities, however, they acquire new opportunities to observe the lifestyles of the privileged, not only through personal observation but through the media. As a result, the concentration of affluence and poverty in cities increases the poor's sense of relative deprivation, which, in turn, is associated with strong feelings of grievance toward the affluent (Sweeney, McFarlin, and Inderrieden 1990; Walker and Smith 2002) and a high likelihood of acting out these sentiments through crime (Blau and Blau 1982). Negative stereotypes of the rich are thus further reinforced and the lines of stratification hardened.

Postmodern Class Warfare

Over the past forty years, class lines have substantially been redrawn in the United States. The Democratic Party's support for the civil rights movement and its attempt to deracialize the welfare state created an opening for conservatives to reverse the ideological trends set in motion during the 1930s. The decision by the Democratic Party to embrace civil rights in the 1960s promoted a mass exodus of southerners from the party, estrangement from blue-collar voters in the North, and the end of the New Deal coalition. On the heels of this realignment, the rules of the American political economy were rewritten to favor the rich at the expense of the middle and lower classes. Unions were weakened, entry-level wages were reduced, access to social protections was curtailed, antipoverty spending was cut back, and taxes on lower-income families were raised while those on upper-income families were reduced, yielding a sharp reduction in the size of the welfare state and a significant decline in the social well-being of most Americans.

The new choreography of rising income inequality and increasing political polarization was reinforced by the emergence of a new geography of inequality characterized by greater class segregation and a spatial concentration of both affluence and poverty. Increasingly the poor have come to live apart from the affluent in communities and neighborhoods inhabited primarily by other poor people, while affluent families have separated themselves from the poor within communities and neighborhoods inhabited by other

209

affluent people. This new geography has served to insulate America's upper classes from the negative externalities stemming from the rise in income inequality while further polarizing the country with respect to ideology. It has also opened the way for a host of mutually reinforcing political, educational, economic, social, and cultural processes to consolidate and operate more effectively to promote even greater inequality, making America's class system perhaps more rigid and unforgiving than it has ever been.

As dire as the foregoing description may seem, it does not fully capture the power of the American stratification system to reproduce advantage and disadvantage across the generations, for the categorical mechanisms of race and class described so far occur within a social world that is also segmented by gender. In addition to understanding the categorical processes of racial and class stratification, it is essential also to comprehend how gender-specific mechanisms of exploitation and opportunity hoarding operate to perpetuate and increase inequality between men and women and how this inequality interacts with inequalities of race and class to engender stratification in the United States.

✍ CHAPTER 6 ✍

ENGENDERING INEQUALITY

Perhaps the oldest and most durable categorical distinction that human beings make is between men and women. All human societies engender the social world by assigning different attributes and expectations to men and women. Although the specific content of male and female roles differs from culture to culture, all human societies make interpersonal distinctions based on the presence or absence of a second X chromosome (Brown 1991). These distinctions are rooted in human biology, of course, which has assigned women responsibility for gestating, bearing, and suckling infants. Given this biological reality, across all cultures women engage in more "caring labor" than men, spending more of their time tending, cooking, cleaning, clothing, washing, nurturing, and otherwise caring for people compared with men (Brown 2000; England and Folbre 1999; Macoby 1998).

Despite this universal division of labor, human societies differ widely with respect to the degree of gender stratification—the differential access of men and women to material, symbolic, and emotional resources. Most hunter-gatherer societies are relatively gender-egalitarian (Sanday 1981). Herding and horticultural societies evince greater levels of stratification between the sexes (Hayden et al. 1986), but it was the advent of agriculture around ten thousand years ago that increased the size and density of human populations to the point where multiple categorical distinctions became possible, thereby increasing the potential for stratification, including that based on gender (Massey 2005a; Sanderson 1999). Until the twentieth century, most sedentary human societies tended to channel resources away from females and toward males, to the point where female life expectancy was pushed below that of males despite a genetic predisposition for longer living (Coale 1991).

The United States constitutes no exception to this legacy of gender inequality (Russell Wright 1997). Indeed, from its inception, America was created as a gender-stratified society. The original U.S. Constitution denied women the right to vote, and by law and custom women remained subject to the control of men in most states. For the bulk of U.S. history, a woman's labor was restricted to the household, where she specialized in caring for others and producing goods and services outside the market. Prior to the twentieth century, fewer than 20 percent of working-age women were gainfully employed, and among married women the share was under 5 percent (Goldin 2006).

The position of women began to change in 1920, when the Nineteenth Amendment to the U.S. Constitution was ratified to grant female suffrage. In that year, only one-quarter of adult women and fewer than 10 percent of married women worked for pay, but in the ensuing decades women entered the labor force in large numbers and came to dominate sectors such as office work. Rising rates of female political and labor force participation after 1920 could easily have led toward gender equality, but they did not. Instead, gender stratification would get much worse before it got better (Goldin 1990).

Twentieth-Century Gender Stratification

The mechanisms devised by human beings to promote gender stratification are different from those used to perpetuate inequalities on the basis of race and class. Whereas elites may frame minorities and the poor as unlikable and incompetent, and thus prime targets for exploitation and exclusion, such a framing cannot very well be used to anchor categorical distinctions based on gender. Husbands have wives, fathers have daughters, brothers have sisters, and sons have mothers to whom they are emotionally attached and with whom they live in intimate association. These emotional bonds preclude the positioning of women as a despised out-group. As a result, gender stratification relies on a different framing, one that positions women as likable and approachable yet exploitable, a tricky balancing act that has given sexism a distinctive attitudinal structure compared with racism and class prejudice.

Ambivalent Sexism

In terms of the social space of intergroup perception discussed in prior chapters, the exploitation of women requires a framing that places them high on the warmth dimension but low on the competence dimension. Such a conceptual mapping can accommodate the greater structural power of men while allowing for their intimate dependence on and association with women (Glick and Fiske 1996). Although males and females inhabit gendered roles that are asymmetric with respect to power and resources, these roles nonetheless exist within structures that are cooperative, most importantly the family. The two sexes are inherently interdependent, relying on one another for material sustenance, companionship, emotional gratification, and reproduction (Glick and Fiske 2001).

Under conditions of such intimate yet asymmetric interdependence, dominant and subordinate actors both have a strong interest in framing social reality such that those in the subordinate group are stereotyped as superior on one fundamental social dimension (warmth) but nonetheless in need of protection owing to a relative lack on the other major social dimension (competence) (see Jackman 1994; Ridgeway 1992, 2006). To measure this distinctive attitudinal profile, Peter Glick and Susan Fiske (1996) created the *ambivalent sexism inventory*, which draws on self-reports of attitudes about gender relations to measure antipathy toward women.

Corresponding to the two basic dimensions of social cognition, the inventory yields two measures of sexism. *Hostile sexism* measures support for the sexual domination and exploitation of women by men and is indicated by agreement with statements such as: "Men will always fight to have greater control in society than women," "A man who is sexually attracted to a woman typically has no morals about doing whatever it takes to get her in bed," and "Most men sexually harass women, even if only in subtle ways, once they are in a position of power over them." *Benevolent sexism*, in contrast, places women on a pedestal as sensitive, caring, and loving but also naive, weak, and vulnerable and thus in need of male protection. Benevolent sexists agree with statements such as: "Women should be cherished and protected by men," "Even if both members of a couple work, the woman ought to be more attentive to taking care of her man at home," and "Men would be lost in this world if women weren't there to guide them" (Glick and Fiske 2001).

The complete inventory contains twenty-two items, each rated on a 0-to-5 scale ranging from "disagree strongly" to "agree strongly." Since its creation, the ambivalent sexism inventory has been applied to a variety of subject populations, yielding reliability measures consistently above .80 and producing a two-dimensional factor structure with goodness-of-fit indices above 0.90 (Glick and Fiske 1996). The associated scales of hostile and benevolent sexism have been validated cross-culturally and shown to correlate in theoretically expected ways with other attitudes and beliefs (Glick and Fiske 2001).

The ambivalent sexism inventory also has a high degree of external validity, evincing remarkably robust correlations with observed levels of gender inequality throughout the world. For example, Glick and his colleagues (2000) assembled samples of subjects from nineteen nations who had been administered the inventory. After deriving subject scores for hostile and benevolent sexism, they computed national averages and used them to predict each country's actual level of gender stratification as measured by the United Nations (1998). Their results showed that average scores on the hostile sexism scale correlated -0.47 with the UN Gender Development Index and -0.53 with the UN Gender Empowerment Index (both significant at $p < .05$). Likewise, average scores on the benevolent sexism scale correlated -0.40 with gender development and -0.43 with gender empowerment across nations (significant at $p < .10$). Even though these samples were small and not nationally representative, the sexist attitudes they measured nonetheless predicted quite reliably the extent of gender stratification within nations.

Glick and Fiske (2001) have also found that male and female ratings on the ambivalent sexism inventory are strongly and positively associated with one another and that the two scales are positively correlated across a variety of subject populations. Given that measures of hostile and benevolent sexism both predict gender inequality, Glick and Fiske concluded that the two forms of sexism go together and complement one another. Women's adherence to benevolent sexism serves to disarm resistance to discrimination and exclusion by giving these actions a benevolent interpretation (they are for the good of women) and thereby obscuring the costs of discrimination and neutralizing resentments that women might otherwise feel (Jackman 1994). Adherence to an ideology of benevolent sexism thus offers women a way of navigating discriminatory social structures without calling the legitimacy of the entire system into question (Ellemers 2001; Wright 2001).

Although benevolent sexism is based on the positive stereotyping of women as warm, caring, and nurturing, Glick and Fiske (2001) found that these positive views were conferred only on women who *conform* to sexist stereotypes. In a study of female subtypes, they found that benevolent sexism strongly predicted feelings about homemakers but not career women, which were predicted instead by hostile sexism (Glick and Fiske 1997). Thus, people with high scores on the benevolent sexism scale evinced positive attitudes toward homemakers, whereas people with high scores on the hostile sexism scale evinced negative views of career women, but not vice versa.

To situate various kinds women in the social space of stereotype content, Thomas Eckes (2002) presented subjects with seventeen labeled female subtypes, including, among others, housewives, secretaries, and "typical women," along with career women, feminists, and "women's libbers." Each subtype was assessed using the competence and warmth scales developed by Fiske and her colleagues (1999), and ratings were subject to a cluster analysis to determine each subgroup's location in the social space of warmth and

Figure 6.1   Stereotype Content Model Applied to Selected
            Female Subtypes

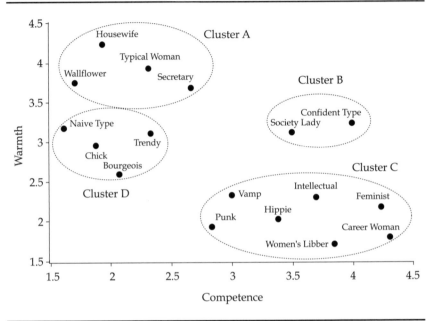

Source: Eckes (2002). Reprinted with permission from Springer-Verlag GmbH.

competence. Figure 6.1 reproduces Eckes's results to show how different subtypes of women are stereotypically perceived within contemporary society.

It is immediately apparent that most of the subtypes cluster in the top left-hand or bottom right-hand quadrants of the social space, zones normally reserved for pitied and envied out-groups. No women really fall into the despised quadrant at the bottom right, and none really fall into the esteemed quadrant at the top left. Those closest to the space normally reserved for despised out-groups are "bourgeois women" and "chicks," and those closest to the space usually occupied by esteemed in-groups are "society ladies" and "confident types." But for the most part the zones associated with esteem and contempt are empty.

Instead, the social spaces associated with pity and envy are crowded. The pitied space of high warmth and low competence is occupied by housewives, wallflowers, secretaries, and "typical women," whereas the envied space of high competence and low warmth is occupied by career women, feminists, intellectuals, and "women's libbers." When it comes to views about women, in other words, stereotypes appear to be bifurcated into envied and pitied images. Unlike stereotypes associated with race and class, there is little room for either out-group contempt or in-group esteem when it comes to gender, underscoring the distinctiveness of sexism's attitudinal foundations.

Occupational Ghettos

Whereas categorical stratification in the United States historically has relied on the spatial segregation of minorities and the poor, separating men and women residentially is not a feasible platform for gender stratification. Males and females share households and living space through large portions of the life cycle. Brothers and sisters live together with mothers and fathers through infancy, childhood, and adolescence, and then after a brief period of household separation in early adulthood, men and women usually come together again for marriage, childbirth, and child-rearing (Macoby 1998).

Rather than separating men and women in physical space, gender stratification rests on their separation in social space—specifically the social space defined by contemporary occupational structures. As already noted, throughout most of recorded history men and women specialized in different kinds of labor, with women engaged in care work within households, mostly without pay, and men engaged in productive labor outside the household, increasingly for pay as time went on. This gendered division of labor is rooted in biology and expressed culturally through an ideology of *gender essentialism*—the belief that men and women are "naturally suited" to different sorts of tasks and responsibilities, with women presumed to be better at tasks involving caring, nurturing, and social exchange (Charles and Grusky 2004, 15).

Until quite recently, occupational segregation mainly involved

217

the allocation of women to tasks within households and men to tasks outside households. In 1870, for example, 95 percent of adult American males worked in the paid labor force, but 85 percent of adult women did not. During working hours, therefore, men and women occupied separate social spheres. Those few women who worked outside the household found themselves sorted into employment niches that paralleled their presumed talent for caring labor, serving others as cooks, cleaners, maids, nurses, and teachers.

Whereas stereotypically female occupations made few demands on upper body strength, those held by men relied on muscle power, yielding a distinction between what Claudia Goldin (1990) has called "brain" versus "brawn" jobs. Prior to the twentieth century, the labor market was dominated by jobs that required more brawn than brains, yielding a "natural" division of labor between men and women and a high degree of occupational segregation. Segregation is commonly measured using the index of dissimilarity, which varies from 0 (men and women are distributed equally across occupational categories) to 100 (men and women have no occupations in common). Male-female dissimilarity indices are plotted in figure 6.2, along with indices of female labor force participation and female concentration in white-collar employment.

In general, dissimilarity values above 60 are considered to be "high," and by this criterion, gender segregation was indeed quite marked before 1900, with values fluctuating between 65 and 70. Of course, few adult women and practically no married women were in the workforce before 1900 to experience this occupational segregation. As more women entered the labor force after the turn of the century, however, a new ideological current increasingly came into play to define occupations socially and stratify them by gender. This second current was *male primacy*, which frames men as more rational, competent, and decisive and thus more deserving of positions of power, influence, and authority than women (Ridgeway 2006). The redefinition of occupations to reflect male primacy after 1900 systematically excluded women from categories carrying greater prestige, authority, and earnings, thereby producing an "occupational ghetto" for women that served to limit their earnings and mobility (Charles and Grusky 2004).

Figure 6.2   Occupational Segregation, Female Labor Force
Participation, and Female Concentration in White-
Collar Jobs, 1860 to 2000

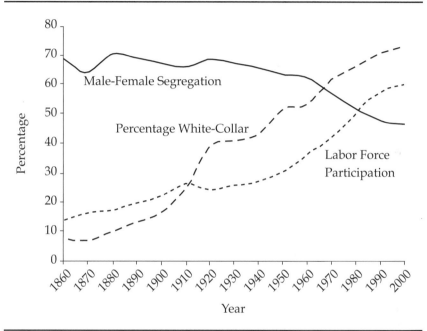

Source: Carter et al. (2006).

Although the level of occupational segregation between men
and women remained fairly constant from 1860 to 1960, the underlying size and structure of the labor market changed dramatically.
Whereas in 1860 the female workforce numbered just 5.2 million,
only 16 percent of whom held white-collar jobs, by 1960 the number of female workers stood at 22.2 million, and 53 percent held
white-collar jobs (see Carter et al. 2006; figure 6.2). Overall, the labor force grew by 144 percent, and the structure of employment
shifted decisively away from agriculture—first toward manufacturing and then toward services.

The fact that gender segregation remained constant despite these
massive shifts suggests that a great deal of boundary work was

done over time to redefine the rules of occupational achievement and earnings. As the relative number of brawn jobs fell and women entered the labor market in record numbers to occupy the growing number of brain jobs, categories of nonmanual work were assigned gendered attributes and identities to maintain high levels of male-female occupational dissimilarity.

Maria Charles and David Grusky (2004) have proposed a two-dimensional measurement model that corresponds to ideologies of gender essentialism and male primacy and conceives of occupational sex segregation as having both horizontal and vertical dimensions. *Horizontal segregation* rests on the notion that men and women are emotionally, mentally, and physically suited for different sorts of jobs, an imperative that is manifested most obviously in the gender divide between manual and nonmanual labor, a distinction that roughly parallels Goldin's (1990) division of occupations into brains and brawn.

Horizontal segregation stems from the cultural definition of males and females as fundamentally and qualitatively different and does not necessarily imply differential access to material, symbolic, or emotional resources. The ordering of occupations by income, prestige, power, and authority and the exclusion of women from positions carrying these attributes defines *vertical segregation*. At the same time as men and women are horizontally segmented into manual and nonmanual positions in conformity with notions of gender essentialism, within each sector women are also allocated to the lowest strata of jobs arranged in a vertical hierarchy, thus reinforcing male primacy. The overall degree of segregation captured by the index of dissimilarity reflects the separation of men and women into positions that are both vertically and horizontally structured.

Figure 6.3 summarizes the Charles-Grusky model schematically. The left side of the graph orders nonmanual or white-collar occupations roughly according to prestige and income, moving from professionals and managers on the left down through clerical, service, and sales occupations to the right. The right-hand portion of the graph likewise arrays manual or blue-collar jobs in rough order of income and prestige, running from crafts on the left down to labor-

Figure 6.3   Charles-Grusky Model of Gender Segregation

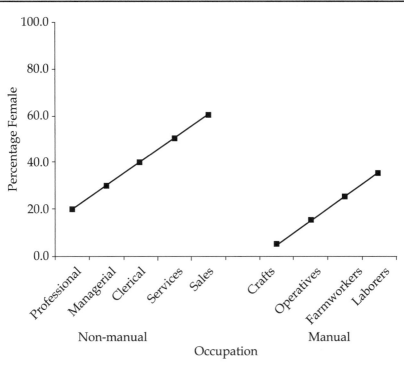

Source: Charles-Grusky (2004).

ers on the right. The y-axis indicates the percentage of women in the different occupational categories. As can be seen, relatively more women work in nonmanual jobs, but within the white-collar sector the presence of women falls as one moves up the ladder of occupational earnings and prestige; the same pattern prevails in the blue-collar sector.

The rise of horizontal segregation in the United States is suggested by the data in figure 6.4, which plots the percentage of female workers in manual and nonmanual jobs from 1860 through 1990. Up through 1900, there was no differentiation between the two sectors. Few women were in the labor force, but they were

Figure 6.4   Percentage of Female Workers in Manual and
Nonmanual Occupations

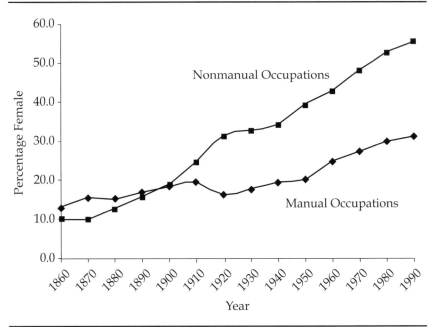

Source: Carter et al. (2006).

equally likely to work in the manual or nonmanual sector. Thereafter, female specialization in white- as opposed to blue-collar jobs
increased at an accelerating rate, producing a widening gap in the
gender composition of the two sectors. Whereas 55 percent of nonmanual workers were female by 1990, only 31 percent of manual
workers were women.

    Figure 6.5 illustrates the rise in vertical gender segregation after
1900. Up through 1900, those few females who worked were just as
likely as men to be employed as managers, proprietors, clerical
workers, or sales workers, and females were actually *overrepre-
sented* in professional occupations compared to their small share in
the labor force. After 1900, however, women came increasingly to
dominate clerical occupations, until by 1990 nearly 80 percent of
clerical workers were female. Women also came to constitute a

Figure 6.5   Percentage of Female Workers in Nonmanual
              Occupations

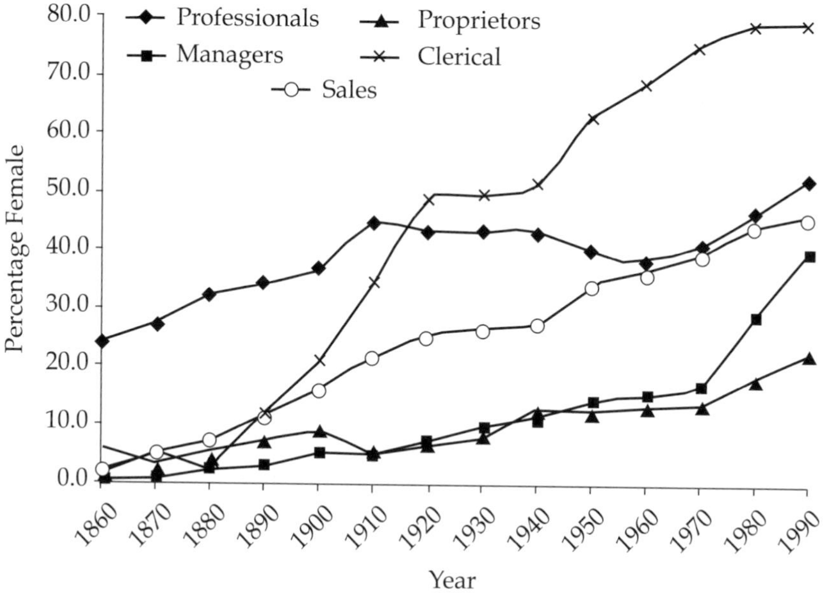

Source: Historical Statistics of the United States Millennial Edition.

growing share of sales workers. After 1910, however, the share of women in professional occupations leveled off and then fell gradually through 1960 as the number of female managers and proprietors grew very slowly and at levels below their rising share of the total labor force, a pattern that lasted until 1970.

The most comprehensive account of the gendered transformation of the American labor market in the twentieth century is that of Goldin (1990). After 1900, industrialization increased the demand for office workers. Managers, professionals, clerks, secretaries, and sales personnel became increasingly important in creating value for business enterprises. To meet the surge in demand for nonmanual workers, legislatures passed new laws mandating school attendance and increased funding for secondary education. As a consequence, levels of high school graduation rose among both males and females, but with factories providing an attractive and lucrative alternative to schooling for boys, their graduation rates lagged behind those of girls.

As factories were mechanized, however, so were offices, creating a new and expanding market for high school graduates. As offices were electrified, devices such as typewriters, mimeographs, stenograph machines, mechanical sorters, and automated billing systems were introduced to make office work more efficient (Goldin 2006). Whereas before offices had been staffed by skilled male secretaries, clerks, and bookkeepers who expected eventually to share in the firm's success as a partner or manager, the new electrified office machines enabled anyone with a high school diploma to manage the flow of paper and information (Goldin 1990). During the 1920s, therefore, office work was deskilled and increasingly allocated not to trusted males but to "office girls" who managed machines.

According to Goldin (2006, 79), this mechanization of the office produced a newly gendered and vertically organized division of labor in the white-collar sector:

> Secretaries no longer kept the secrets of the office. Rather, they took dictation and typed letters. The functions of typist and stenographer became separate in most offices and were no longer bundled with those of a secretary. In large offices … typists were assigned to different pools of varying skill and paid commensurately with the group's typing speed and precision. Similar changes occurred in other sectors of the economy. Retail stores … greatly increased in size … [and] with increased scale, workers were hired to do separate tasks. Saleswomen and salesmen sold the goods, order-clerks placed the orders, stock-clerks handled the inventory, and so on.

The expansion of white-collar employment greatly increased the demand for female workers during the first third of the twentieth century. From 1900 to 1930, female labor force participation increased, the number of working women doubled, and the fraction employed in white-collar jobs went from 16 percent to 42 percent (see figure 6.3). The increase in labor force participation was especially marked among younger women, especially those who were married (Goldin 2006).

Thus, by the 1920s a gender revolution appeared to be in full swing, with women adopting a norm of working after marriage rather than dropping out of the labor force to have children. The age of marriage rose, birthrates fell, women won the right to vote, and they signaled their independence by shortening their skirts and bobbing their hair (Goldin 2006). As young women entered the white-collar workforce straight out of high school, a growing fraction of aspiring professional women also went off to college. By the end of the 1920s, women were well poised to expand their labor force participation—but only if ladders of mobility could be constructed to offer them growth in earnings, responsibility, and prestige.

According to Goldin (2006, 72), the main barrier to greater female labor force participation was that "the 'reservation wage' for married women with children was far higher than was that for other women [so that] earnings would have to exceed the value of 'home time' to entice them to remain employed while raising their children or to reenter the labor force after their children had grown up sufficiently." Unfortunately, although white-collar jobs had the potential for increased earnings and greater job mobility, this potential was never realized because of the gendered reorganization of the white-collar labor market. Instead,

> jobs on the higher rungs of these ladders became closed to women in many office settings, as well as in other parts of the economy. Thus occupations in the white-collar or "brain" sector became "gendered." Because gender became a more significant factor in the labor market, the increased labor-force participation of older married women was delayed by many decades. The "rising significance of gender" ... was accompanied by an increased labor-force participation of young, married women in the early 20th century,... [demonstrating] that young married women were poised to remain in the labor force if only the wage offered to them exceeded their reservation wage. But it did not for quite some time. (Goldin 2006, 72)

This gendering of work opportunities during the 1920s was achieved using a variety of categorical mechanisms. Marriage bars prohibited the hiring of married women and called for the dismissal of any single woman who took a husband; union rules prohibited women from working even at productive tasks suited to their physical capacities; and both prohibitions were applied more extensively during the 1930s in the name of reserving scarce jobs for male "breadwinners" (Goldin 1990). Low-level office jobs such as stenographer, typist, secretary, and filing clerk came to be reserved "for women only," whereas positions as supervisors, managers, partners, and professionals were reserved for men, yielding an impermeable "glass ceiling" that stymied the occupational mobility of women (Goldin 1990, 2006).

A survey conducted by the Women's Bureau of the U.S. Department of Labor in 1940, for example, revealed that 72 percent of firms surveyed (those with at least ten male and ten female employees) reported policies explicitly reserving some positions for men alone, and the same percentage reported the existence of policies reserving positions for women alone. Nearly two-thirds of the firms, 63 percent, stated that they had formal policies that simultaneously reserved some jobs for men and others for women (Goldin 2006). By midcentury, in other words, gender segregation was widely practiced as a matter of explicit policy within American firms.

The prohibition of women from positions with greater earnings and mobility naturally caused a piling up of women in "female" jobs, leading to overcrowding that put downward pressure on women's wages (Bergmann 1974). In addition to this indirect lowering of female earnings through the market, employers also discriminated against women directly, paying them lower wages simply because they were women. In most jobs, wages rise with work experience and job tenure. Indeed, in the blue-collar sector, although men and women earn different starting wages (reflecting their different physical abilities), once hired both experience the same returns to work experience, and the male-female wage gap remains roughly constant over time (Goldin 2006). In contrast, among white-collar workers the initial wage gap between men and women is relatively small, but with experience and job tenure male wages rise much more steeply than those of women, and the size of the wage gap increases steadily over time (Eichengreen 1984; Goldin 1990).

One indicator of the relative importance of wage discrimination in the determination of female earnings is the proportion of the male-female wage gap that remains unexplained after taking into account observable factors such as age, marital status, education, training, work experience, and so on. Around the turn of the century, the share of the wage gap that remained unexplained after accounting for male-female background differences stood at 20 percent. Over the ensuing decades, however, this percentage steadily rose to reach 55 percent by 1940, implying that the level of gender discrimination increased by as much as three times over the first four decades of the twentieth century (Goldin 1990).

Earnings discrimination not only occurred to individual women but was applied to workers in any occupational category that contained a significant share of females. Even after exhaustive controls for the characteristics of workers and jobs are applied, the percentage of women within a particular occupational-industrial category has a strong and significantly negative effect on the earnings of incumbents (England 1992; England, Thompson, and Aman 2001). That is, "female" jobs seem to offer lower wages simply because of the presence of women within them, an effect that led Goldin (2006) to posit a "pollution theory" of discrimination.

In Goldin's model, the entry of women into an occupational category diminishes its prestige for men, either signaling to them that the job has been de-skilled or confirming that less competent workers are being hired (consistent with sexist stereotypes). As a result, the presence of women in a job category symbolically "pollutes" it for men. Relatively few men are willing to enter an occupation in which women predominate. Likewise, men resist the entry of women into male-dominated jobs and occupations that formerly paid well for fear that they will become devalued once women enter them (Goldin 2006). These institutionalized patterns of occupational labeling and gender discrimination were implemented and consolidated during the 1920s and then functioned in self-perpetuating fashion over the next four decades to promote the economic exploitation of working women.

Twenty-First Century Gender Stratification

As noted in earlier chapters, before the civil rights era practices of discrimination and exclusion were not only perfectly legal but commonly accepted and widely practiced. As a result, after a promising initial shift toward gender egalitarianism early in the twentieth century, by 1940 the American labor market was thoroughly engendered with categorical distinctions that suppressed the earnings of women and systematically cut them off from the engines of economic mobility that propelled men upward during the postwar economic boom. In real terms, female earnings remained flat between 1947 and 1967, while men's wages increased sharply, causing the wage gap to increase (as shown in figure 2.6). With the prospects for occupational mobility limited by glass ceilings and earnings constrained by direct and indirect discrimination, women had little incentive to invest in their careers or to devote scarce resources to the acquisition of skills, education, or training.

Under these circumstances, rates of female labor force participation stagnated during the 1950s and 1960s, and women allocated relatively greater amounts of time to homemaking. From 1947 through 1967, birthrates and marriage rates increased and family sizes grew to record levels, yielding an unprecedented period of domesticity and familism that came to be known as the baby boom (Owram 1997). Behind the facade of contented family life, however, lay unresolved tensions and dissatisfactions among women that were suppressed by social pressures and cultural conventions (Coontz 1994).

The various liberation movements of the 1960s overcame these pressures and conventions to give birth to a new era of expanding social and economic rights, not only for African Americans but for all historically oppressed groups (Skrentny 2002). Well-educated women whose careers had been sidetracked by patriarchal mechanisms emerged from the shadows to denounce the culture of domesticity. The opening shot in the revolt was fired in 1963, when

Betty Friedan published *The Feminine Mystique*, a scathing indictment of the cult of suburban family life that drew on conversations with frustrated and resentful classmates of hers from Smith College. In the same year, President Kennedy's Commission on the Status of Women, chaired by Eleanor Roosevelt, issued a report documenting extensive discrimination against women throughout the economy. In response, in 1964 Congress not only banned discrimination on the basis of race but also included gender as a legally protected category. In 1966 feminists formed the National Organization of Women (NOW) to keep up the pressure for change, and in 1968 the Fair Housing Act prohibited discrimination against women in the rental or sale of housing. The Education Amendments of 1972 likewise forbade gender discrimination in education, and the 1974 Equal Credit Opportunity Act outlawed it in lending.

In a few short years between 1964 and 1974, therefore, feminists and their supporters succeeded in overturning the legal basis for most categorical mechanisms of gender stratification, and in doing so they also transformed American public opinion. According to data from the General Social Survey, the percentage of Americans saying they would vote for a woman president grew from 55 percent in 1970 to 90 percent in the late 1990s; the share who approved of working wives went from 55 percent to 80 percent; the share who said women should only be housewives and homemakers fell from 40 percent to 18 percent; the share disagreeing that preschool children suffer when a mother works went from 30 percent to 50 percent; the share disagreeing that it is more important for a woman to help her husband's career went from 42 percent to 80 percent; and the share disagreeing that men make better politicians grew from 50 percent to 70 percent (Davis, Smith, and Marsden 2006).

Americans thus underwent a marked shift in attitudes toward greater support for gender egalitarianism and equal employment opportunities. These trends were accompanied by a marked increase in the rate of female labor force participation, which rose from 30 percent in 1950 to 60 percent in the year 2000. At century's end, some 72 percent of all women were employed in white-collar jobs, and the level of gender segregation in the workforce had declined from dissimilarity levels in the 60s to reach 47 in the year

2000 (see figure 6.3). Over the same period, women's earnings improved markedly relative to those of men. As noted in chapter 2, the female-male earnings ratio rose from just above 0.30 in the early 1960s to 0.57 in 2002 (see figure 2.6). If attention is restricted to full-time workers, the ratio of female-to-male earnings rises to around .80, and if men and women are statistically assigned the same human capital and demographic characteristics, the ratio goes to 0.91 (Blau and Kahn 2004).

These trends are all consistent with a declining significance of gender in the structure, organization, and operation of the U.S. labor market during the latter third of the twentieth century (Blau and Kahn 2006; England 2006; Goldin 2006). However, although gender may be declining in importance as a categorical boundary in U.S. labor markets, it has by no means disappeared. Indeed, Ian Ayres and Peter Siegelman (1995), Claudia Goldin and Cecilia Rouse (2000), William Darity and Patrick Mason (1998), and Douglas Massey and Garvey Lundy (2001) have documented the persistence of discrimination against women in various contemporary markets. That persistent inequalities remain is indicated by the data in figures 6.6 and 6.7, which are based on tabulations prepared by Jerry Jacobs (2001). These figures rank detailed occupational categories by their associated prestige using SEI scores and then divide them into ranked quintiles, with the first quintile corresponding to the lowest-status occupations and the fifth quintile to the highest.

Figure 6.6 shows the percentage of college graduates among male and female workers holding occupations within each status quintile. Not surprisingly, the relative number of college graduates increases sharply as one moves from lowest to highest status. In the first quintile, only 25 percent of workers hold college degrees, whereas in the fifth more than 90 percent do. More relevant for our purposes is the fact that there are no significant differences between male and female workers. Likewise, although occupational status naturally rises from the first to the fifth quintile, the male and female lines are virtually identical, meaning that within quintiles males and females hold equally prestigious occupations.

If there are no significant educational or status differences be-

Figure 6.6   Mean SEI Score and Percentage with College
                  Degree, by Occupational Status Quintile

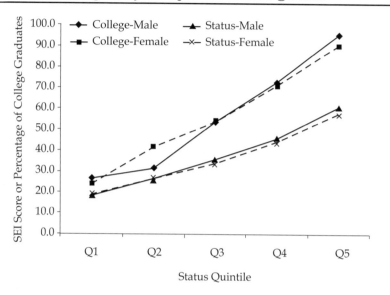

Source: Jacobs (2001).

Figure 6.7   Earnings by Occupational Status

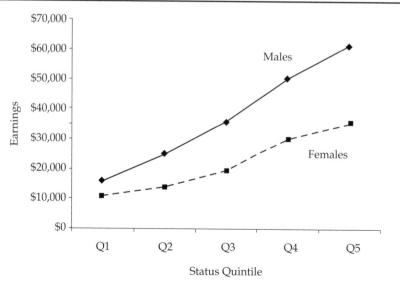

Source: Jacobs (2001).

tween men and women as one moves up the occupational hierarchy, we would not expect to observe much in the way of earnings differences either, but this is not the case. As shown in figure 6.7, although male and female earnings are roughly the same at the bottom of the occupational pyramid, they increasingly diverge as one moves toward the top. Whereas in the lowest-status quintile male workers earn $16,000 compared with $11,000 for women, for a gap of $5,000, the size of the gap steadily increases as one moves up status quintiles. In the second quintile, the gap is $11,000; in the third, it is $16,000; and in the fourth it stands at $20,000. By the fifth quintile, the gap is $26,000, with men earning $60,000 compared with women's $35,000.

Clearly something other than differences in education and occupational status operates to produce these differences. Indeed, Francine Blau and Lawrence Kahn (2004) estimate that 41 percent of the male-female wage gap remains unexplained once male-female differences in education, experience, industrial location, occupation, and other relevant variables are taken into account. This share of unexplained variance is significantly below the 55 percent estimated by Goldin (1990) for 1940, but still well above the 20 percent level prevailing at the beginning of the twentieth century. Although a sizable residual does not prove the existence of discrimination, which may reflect unmeasured male-female differences, it does leave considerable latitude for it to be occurring, and the hypothesis of gender discrimination cannot be eliminated (Blank, Dabady, and Citro 2004).

Among measured factors, some of the earnings gap is explained by the different work histories of men and women: females tend to accumulate less labor market experience because they more often enter and leave the labor market owing to the demands of marriage and childbearing. Given rising levels of female labor force participation by women with children, however, gender differentials in labor market experience have narrowed and presently account for only 16 percent of the gap (Blau and Kahn 2006). Moreover, given that rates of female education and college graduation now exceed those of males, schooling differences cannot be invoked to account for the gender gap in earnings.

Figure 6.8   Contribution to Gender Pay Gap of Measured
               Characteristics

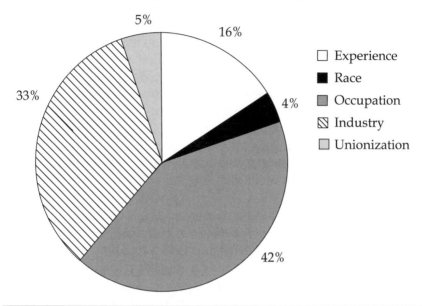

Source: Blau and Kahn (2006).

Figure 6.8 puts aside education and shows the degree to which other measured factors statistically account for observed differences between male and female earnings. As already noted, experience accounts for only 16 percent of the gap, and given the weakened state of unions, as described in the last chapter, it is hardly surprising that unionization accounts for only 5 percent of the gap. Likewise, racial composition explains only 4 percent of the gap, suggesting that women earn roughly the same amounts regardless of race. By far the two most important measured factors accounting for the male-female earnings gap are industrial location (33 percent) and occupation (42 percent), implying that if the distribution of men and women across occupations were somehow equalized, up to three-quarters of the earnings differential would disappear.

In other words, in addition to possible direct wage discrimination against women, which is captured in the residual of Blau and Kahn's (2006) decomposition, the continued segregation of men and women into different occupational-industrial niches plays a prominent role in lowering female earnings compared to those of males. Although segregation levels may have fallen from a dissimilarity of 62 in 1960 to 47 in 2000, the latter figure still implies substantial occupational separation between men and women. Understanding the sources of continued gender segregation in the workforce thus becomes a central issue in attempting to understand earnings stratification between men and women.

A major intellectual puzzle is determining why, given the apparent acceptance of gender egalitarianism by Americans, the decline in gender segregation slowed down so much after 1980 and as of 2000 still remained such that around half of men and women would have to exchange positions to achieve gender balance in the occupational structure. Charles and Grusky (2004) argue that rising support for egalitarianism and equal opportunity does not necessarily challenge ideologies of gender essentialism. One can simultaneously believe that men and women should have equal opportunity and that women and men are nonetheless suited to different sorts of work. They point out that in Sweden, which is among the most egalitarian of all industrial nations and which offers generous family leave packages and child care subsidies, the labor force remains highly segregated by gender. Indeed, the male-female dissimilarity for Sweden stood at 60 in the late 1990s compared with 47 in the United States (Charles and Grusky 2004).

In Sweden, of course, earnings inequality is much lower than in the United States, and medical care is socialized so that a high level of gender segregation carries few implications for the earnings and well-being of women versus men. Although the United States is much less egalitarian than Sweden, Charles and Grusky (2004) hold that the women's rights revolution has played out in very different ways at the top and bottom of America's socioeconomic hierarchy, for a variety of reasons.

First, attitudes about gender vary by education, and egalitarianism has spread more widely and completely among well-educated workers in the managerial and professional classes than in the working classes. Second, because of this fact, open expressions of blatant sexism are no longer publicly acceptable in upper-class circles, and thus the social costs of gender discrimination are higher at the top of the socioeconomic hierarchy. Third, the material costs of discrimination are higher at the top end of the hierarchy because well-educated, upper-middle-class women who believe they have been discriminated against have more resources at their command to fight back. Fourth, positions at the top of the occupational structure are more visible and subject to greater public scrutiny, and thus it is more difficult to discriminate and get away with it. Finally, people who might otherwise wish to discriminate have less room for biased actions because professional and managerial jobs are typically situated within administrative bureaucracies where promotions and pay are determined by objective credentials and standardized procedures.

Figure 6.9 adopts the conceptual approach of Charles and Grusky (2004) to show changes in the percentage of women within various nonmanual and manual occupational categories from 1960 to 2005. It is immediately apparent that there has been much greater movement on the left side of the graph, which corresponds to the white-collar or nonmanual sector. The share of women in professional occupations, for example, which was already relatively high, increased steadily, going from around 36 percent in 1960 to 56 percent in 2005. The growth in female participation in managerial occupations has been even more spectacular, with the share of women rising from 15 percent to 50 percent. Over the same period, the relative share of women in services, sales, and clerical occupations fell modestly, especially after 2000, so that the distribution moved substantially toward the ideal egalitarian configuration of a flat line running close to a fifty-fifty male-female mix. White-collar occupations, in short, have moved substantially toward gender integration in recent years.

In contrast, there has been very little movement on female representation in blue-collar occupations, and what little change we observe has worked to the detriment of women's overall economic welfare, with increases at the bottom rather than the top of the blue-

Figure 6.9   Women in Major Occupational Groups

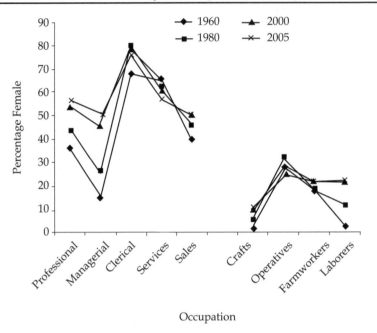

Occupation

Source: U.S. Bureau of the Census, *Statistical Abstract of the United States.*

collar occupational distribution. There has been little or no movement of women into skilled crafts and operative categories, the two most highly remunerated blue-collar occupations. Moreover, although the share of women increased slightly among farmworkers, it rose substantially among unskilled laborers, the lowest and most poorly paid blue-collar job category. From 1960 to 2005, the share of women among laborers increased by a factor of ten, going from 2 percent to 20 percent. Women have gained access to blue-collar jobs, but only those at the bottom of the occupational distribution. Within the blue-collar sector in general, women remain substantially underrepresented compared with their counterparts in the white-collar workforce.

America's Two Gender Systems

Thus, the feminist revolution has played out in quite different ways at the top and bottom of the American class structure. In her presidential address to the Population Association of America, Sara McLanahan (2004) undertook what is to date the most thorough examination of gender and family relations at opposite ends of the socioeconomic spectrum, arguing that recent shifts in the structure of gender relations have been driven by four trends. First, the feminist revolution of the 1960s and 1970s changed American values, offering women identities other than those of wife and mother and valorizing career-oriented behavior to encourage women to invest in education and training. Second, feminism also emphasized independence from men and promoted a new ideal of egalitarian marriage in which household labor would be shared equally by husbands and wives. Third, feminism destigmatized single-motherhood and reduced levels of gender discrimination to open new work opportunities for women that gave them a new ability to support themselves apart from men. Finally, advances in birth control technology gave women control over their own fertility, decoupling sex from marriage and making it possible for them to time major life course events more precisely.

These ideational and technological developments granted new autonomy to women and widened the range of choices in life at the same time that important economic and political transformations altered the context within which these choices were made (McLanahan 2004). The globalization of the economy and its structural shift away from the production of goods and toward the production of knowledge undermined the wages and job prospects of less-educated men while enhancing the earnings and market power of those with greater education. At the same time, political choices made during the 1980s and 1990s lowered the real value of welfare benefits and set time limits on the duration of income transfers.

These structural transformations affected women at the top and bottom of the class structure very differently. Upper-class women streamed into higher education and entered graduate and professional schools in large numbers. The professional and managerial salaries they went on to earn made them very attractive as marital partners in an era of rising inequality, and rates of class endogamy increased (Mare 1991, 1996). Instead of male doctors marrying nurses or male managers marrying secretaries, male and female professionals married one another, often after some period of cohabitation that served as a "trial marriage" to weed out incompatible mates before entering into formal wedlock and childbearing.

These new relationships were made possible by access to cheap and effective birth control, which enabled ambitious women to postpone births until their education was completed and their career begun. Unlimited risk-free sex, along with high household income and a sharing of the burdens involved in raising upper-class children, combined to make marriage a very stable institution for well-educated women. Stability was also enhanced by the elimination of much of the drudgery formerly associated with marriage and family life, for access to two high incomes enabled professional couples to purchase caring labor on the market, paying others to cook, clean, launder, change diapers, and mind children. Meanwhile, housework that was not subcontracted was shared more equally by husbands, who by virtue of their education came to support the ideal of an egalitarian marriage. Freed from the burden of household chores, upper-class women actually ended up spending more time with their children, despite their labor force participation (Bianchi, Robinson, and Milkie 2006).

The situation for women at the other end of the class distribution was much bleaker. The ability of women to control their fertility made it easier for men to shirk parental responsibilities (McLanahan 2004). Before effective contraception, poor women were in a position to extract a promise of marriage from men in return for sexual access, but with the pill's separation of sex from marriage, this bargaining position was effectively eliminated as marriage lost much of its attractiveness to working-class men (see Akerlof, Yellen, and Katz 1996). At the same time, owing to the rise in male joblessness and the stagnation of men's wages, males became less attractive to women as husbands, a situation that was exacerbated once changes in welfare policy pushed poor women into the work-force to make them economically self-sufficient (McLanahan 2004).

With the traditional male role of family provider inaccessible to a growing number of working-class men, they grew more likely than their upper-class counterparts to insist on traditional sex roles in re-lationships, further reducing their attractiveness to women as mates (McLanahan 2004). Given the shortage of men who were by virtue of low income, sexist attitudes, or incarceration socially deemed "unmarriageable," the only realistic path open to poor women seeking a family was bearing children out of wedlock, a choice that was made easier by the disappearance of the stigma as-sociated with single-parenthood. Although marriage with an emo-tionally supportive and financially capable husband remained a valued goal among poor women, having children was "a promise they could keep" when the likelihood of a marriage vow seemed remote (Edin and Kefalas 2005).

McLanahan (2004) confirmed the shifting pattern of gender and family relations in the upper and lower classes by comparing social and economic trends for women at the upper and lower segments of the educational distribution from 1960 through 2000. Although divorce rates rose for both college-educated and non-college-edu-cated women during the 1960s and 1970s and declined during the 1970s and 1980s, the drop was much sharper for educated women, and the gap in divorce rates widened substantially (McLanahan 2004). Whereas the likelihood of divorce during the first ten years of marriage was 14 percent for college-educated women from 1960 to 1964 and 18 percent from 1995 to 1999, the respective figures for non-college-educated women were 19 percent and 33 percent (Mar-tin 2004). The divorce gap between more- and less-educated women, in other words, nearly quadrupled, rising from four to fif-teen points. At present, college-educated women are less likely to be divorced than were non-college-educated women in the early 1960s.

Over the same period, poorly educated women evinced a flat trend in the age of marriage, compared with a rising pattern among well-educated women. By the year 2000, the average age at mar-riage stood at thirty-three for women in the highest educational quartile, compared with only twenty-three among women in the lowest quartile. The frequency of single-motherhood also rose sharply among less-educated women, going from 13 percent in 1960 to 42 percent in 2000 for women in the lowest quartile of schooling. In contrast, the rate of single-parenthood for women in the highest quartile remained constant at 8 percent in both 1960 and 2000 (McLanahan 2004).

As a result of these trends, the children of poorly educated mothers came to spend less time with their fathers compared with the children of well-educated women. In the year 2000, for instance, children of women in the highest educational quartile spent an average of around 1.1 hours per day with their fathers, compared with just 0.7 hours for the children of women in the lowest quartile (Bianchi 2000).

Although rates of labor force participation rose for mothers at all educational levels, the increase was greatest among well-educated women. Between 1960 and 2000, the rate of labor force participation for mothers in the lowest educational quartile rose from 9 percent to 30 percent, but that for mothers in the highest quartile rose from 11 percent to 63 percent. Consistent with these trends, family income for the most-educated women went from a median of $40,000 in 1960 to $68,000 in 2000, whereas family income for women with the least education remained stagnant at around $25,000 (McLanahan 2004).

Clearly, therefore, the combination of structural changes in the political economy and shifting gender roles has produced divergent paths for women at the top and bottom of America's increasingly polarized class distribution. Since 1970, upper-class women have come to enjoy greater access to family income, prestigious occupations, the benefits of stable, egalitarian marriages, and supportive environments for raising children. In contrast, lower-class women have experienced stagnant earnings, rising rates of poverty, limited occupational mobility, and falling access to marriage and its associated supports for children. The interaction of class and gender, in other words, has increasingly pushed the United States toward two very different gender and family systems, one that functions to enhance the social and economic well-being of affluent women and another that limits the material, symbolic, and emotional resources flowing to poor women. Women in the shrinking middle class, meanwhile, find themselves struggling to situate themselves in the former while avoiding relegation to the latter.

❧ Chapter 7 ❧

America Unequal

Stratification does not just happen. It is produced by specific arrangements in human societies that allow exploitation and opportunity hoarding to occur along categorical lines.

An effective system of social stratification requires three basic things: a social structure that divides people into categories on the basis of some combination of achieved and ascribed traits; the labeling of certain of these categories as social out-groups composed of people who are perceived as lacking on two fundamental dimensions of human social evaluation; and the existence of one or more social mechanisms to reserve certain resources for in-group members while extracting other resources from out-group members without full remuneration.

Human beings are cognitively programmed to form conceptual categories and use them to classify the people they encounter. The definition of categorical boundaries and the content of conceptual categories are not, however, automatic. They are learned through instruction and modified by experience. As social beings, people constantly test, extend, and refine the social schemas they carry in their heads, typically through interactions and discussions with other people. Whenever a person works to convince others in society to accept a particular categorization of social reality, the process is called framing.

People are naturally prone to favor frames that give them advantages and privilege their own access to material, symbolic, and emotional resources. Although everyone may prefer a framing of social reality that serves their interests, people with power and resources have more influence than others, and their frames are more likely to be accepted and used in society. Within any social setting, the definition of boundaries and the content of social categories are disproportionately influenced by people at the top of the socioeconomic hierarchy. Although people at the bottom may challenge and resist categorical frames that work against their interests, their ability to control the definition of social reality is constrained by the fact that they have little to offer others to accept their preferred framing.

Any set of socially constructed categories yields a set of social identities that encompass many different attributes and characteristics. Despite this complexity, social groups can be classified along two fundamental dimensions that define the conceptual space of social cognition: warmth and competence. People naturally frame themselves and others like them as both warm (likable, approachable, trustworthy) and competent (efficacious, capable, astute). People perceived in this way are seen as in-group members, or at least as members of groups that are very similar to the in-group. People who are framed as lacking either warmth or competence are socially defined as members of out-groups—as others who are not perceived as "people like us."

Social actors who are seen as warm but not competent fall into the category of pitied out-groups, common examples of which are the sick, the disabled, and the aged. In contrast, people perceived as competent but not warm fall into the category of envied out-groups, the classic examples of which are middleman minorities such as the Chinese in Malaysia, Indians in East Africa, or Jews in medieval Europe. Under normal circumstances, neither of these two kinds of out-groups makes a good candidate for exploitation. Pitied out-groups are not readily exploited because people feel sorry for them, and envied out-groups are not exploited because they usually occupy positions of power and authority by virtue of their competence.

For exploitation to occur smoothly and seamlessly, people in out-groups must be framed as neither competent nor warm—as people who are not likable, approachable, or trustworthy and not efficacious, capable, or astute. The relevant emotion toward out-groups lacking warmth and competence is contempt. People in such groups are despised and perceived as less than fully human at the most fundamental neural level. As a result, they lend themselves to exploitation with relative impunity. Because they are socially despised, they encounter few defenders in society, and because they are perceived as despicable, victimizing them is unlikely to trigger countervailing emotions such as pity or fear.

Paralleling the work of framing in the conceptual realm is the work of boundary definition in the social realm. Boundary work involves actions and behaviors undertaken to differentiate people socially; they are publicly labeled as members of an in- or out-group who thus embody the social traits associated with that category of people. Labeling may occur through informal mechanisms such as gossip, ridicule, shaming, ostracism, praise, or harassment that serves to "put people in their place," or it may be effected formally through regulations and laws such as the one-drop rule and the antimiscegenation laws enacted throughout the South before the civil rights era. Boundary work distinguishes people from one another socially by highlighting interpersonal differences across categorical lines.

Once social groups are created conceptually through framing and reified socially through boundary work, then stratification—the unequal allocation of material, symbolic, and emotional resources among social categories—is accomplished by establishing social mechanisms that operate according to one of two templates: exploitation or opportunity hoarding. Exploitation is the expropriation of resources from an out-group by members of an in-group such that out-group members receive less than full value for the resources they give up. Opportunity hoarding is the monopolization by in-group members of access to a resource so as to keep it for themselves or charge rents to out-group members in return for access. In contemporary American society, the most common form of exploitation is discrimination within markets, and the most common form of opportunity hoarding is exclusion from markets and resource-rich social settings.

Once established, and in the absence of any countervailing social force, mechanisms of discrimination and exclusion tend to persist over time because of two ancillary social processes: emulation, the transfer of stratifying mechanisms from one social setting to another; and adaptation, the structuring of individual actions and expectations in ways that assume the continued operation of a particular stratification system. Together emulation and adaptation institutionalize a system of categorical stratification and make it quite durable over time and across space.

Stratification American-Style

Although, in theory, any socially defined group may be subject to discrimination and exclusion, in the United States categorical inequalities historically have been produced and reproduced along three principal lines: race, class, and gender. African Americans have traditionally been stereotyped as shiftless, dumb, and strong; the poor have been stereotyped as lazy, self-indulgent, and unmotivated; and women have been stereotyped as warm and caring yet lacking in judgment and resolve. Consistent with these prejudicial stereotypes, throughout most of U.S. history minorities, women, and the poor have been denied full social, political, and economic rights. Formal legal rights were not accorded to African Americans until 1869; women were not politically enfranchised until 1920; and poll taxes routinely excluded the poor from political life until the 1960s. Discrimination against women and minorities was not fully outlawed in U.S. markets until the 1970s.

The foregoing chapters have described the framing techniques and boundary-reinforcing mechanisms that function in the United States to enable exploitation and exclusion along categorical lines. African Americans offer by far the clearest historical example of categorical stratification. Slavery institutionalized exploitation and opportunity hoarding to the extreme, of course, and the system of Jim Crow segregation that replaced it was little better. Most white Americans are aware of the history of slavery and legal segregation, but they are less aware of the de facto system of discrimination and exclusion that prevailed in the United States until the 1960s, or the degree to which the U.S. welfare state was itself racialized to exclude African Americans from the wealth-producing engines of postwar America. Whites also remain oblivious to the power of unconscious racism, and most deny the reality of explicit prejudice and discrimination. As a result, they are unwilling to bear the social, economic, and political costs required to end racial stratification.

The dismantling of Jim Crow in the South, the outlawing of discrimination nationwide, and the recognition of black civil rights have failed to produce anything approaching racial equality. After the civil rights era, racial discrimination did not cease—it simply went underground and occurred in more surreptitious ways. Although less observable, clandestine discrimination proved no less effective in undermining the status and welfare of African Americans, yielding high levels of residential segregation and large, persistent black-white gaps in health, education, income, wealth, and occupational achievement.

During the 1970s, new mechanisms of racial exclusion and exploitation arose through the criminal justice system. Crimes likely to be committed by African Americans were singled out for longer sentences, judicial discretion was limited, parole authority was curtailed, and harsher sentencing rules were imposed. Rates of black male incarceration skyrocketed and contributed to a decisive reduction in black earnings and employment, the removal of fathers and husbands from black families, and the spread of family violence and HIV-AIDS throughout the black community.

Although African Americans have historically borne the brunt of America's racial animus, Latinos came in for much harsher treatment in the 1980s. Although Latinos historically have occupied a middle position in the socioeconomic hierarchy between blacks and whites, their status deteriorated markedly during the 1980s and 1990s and now approximates that of African Americans. Latinos from the Caribbean region are often of African ancestry and thus experience the same color prejudice and discrimination as African Americans. By far the most Latinos originate in Mexico, however, and increasingly these people have been framed as a "racialized other" who constitute a serious threat to America's economy, security, and culture. Since the 1980s, categorical stratification against Mexicans has been effected through an increasingly repressive system of immigration and border control.

The militarization of the Mexico-U.S. border after 1986 dramatically lowered the rate of return migration by illegal immigrants, which increased the number of people living north of the border without social, economic, or political rights. Geographically selective border enforcement, meanwhile, deflected migrant flows away from traditional destination areas and helped transform Mexican immigration from a regional into a national phenomenon. As a result, there are now more exploitable Latinos living in more places under more vulnerable circumstances than at any point in American history.

As America's border policies increased the number of residents living in exploitable social circumstances, immigration policies penalized the same people in ever-harsher ways. The criminalization of undocumented hiring increased discrimination against people who "look Hispanic" and "sound foreign" and fomented a broader shift to labor subcontracting that undermined wages and working conditions for all low-skill workers. Avenues for documented entry were systematically reduced by Congress, and social programs were curtailed for legal as well as illegal immigrants. Hispanic children were pushed out of school and into the labor force to raise family incomes enough to sponsor the entry of family members still abroad, and after September 11, police actions against immigrants were extended from the border to the interior of the United States. Not surprisingly, given these trends, during the 1990s Latino incomes fell and poverty rates rose, reaching levels comparable to those historically observed among African Americans.

The foregoing transformations occurred against a backdrop of rising class stratification in the United States. Modifications to U.S. labor law in 1947 and 1959 put the American labor movement on a path of sustained decline compared to other industrial nations, and aggressive anti-union actions undertaken by federal authorities in the 1980s brought unionization levels to record lows. Sharp reductions in the real value of the minimum wage and income transfers, when combined with reduced spending on unemployment and food supplements, sharp cutbacks in access to federal employment, and the imposition of new time limits on welfare receipt, put new economic pressure on middle- and lower-class families and led to rising rates of consumer borrowing despite higher real interest rates and more punitive bankruptcy laws.

As the situation deteriorated for most Americans in the middle and lower reaches of the U.S. socioeconomic hierarchy, things improved markedly for those at the upper end. Progressivity in the American tax structure was largely eliminated as top tax rates were scaled back, taxes on capital gains were reduced, and enforcement efforts were redirected away from the rich and toward the poor. At the same time, regressive payroll taxes were increased, and the tax burden was shifted from the upper to the middle and lower portions of the income distribution. By 2005, levels of inequality with respect to income and wealth had returned to values not seen since the laissez-faire days of the 1920s.

The 1920s were the period in which the foundations for twentieth-century gender inequality were laid. Prior to this era, gender stratification occurred largely outside the market, since few women worked, but as women flooded into the expanding white-collar workforce during the 1920s, a new system of occupational segregation was imposed to confine women to a "pink-collar" ghetto of jobs characterized by low wages and few mobility prospects. In the nonmanual sector, women were excluded from positions of power, authority, and prestige, whereas in the manual sector they were banned from the skilled and unionized job categories reserved for people presumed to be "breadwinners."

Gender segregation was institutionalized throughout the American occupational structure by the 1940s, and given the limitations of their earning power and career prospects, women had few incentives to invest in education, training, or work experience. During the baby boom of the 1950s and 1960s, women put time and effort into family labor rather than the labor market, but resentments and dissatisfactions festered and burst forth in a feminist movement during the 1970s that was successful in outlawing most forms of gender discrimination.

The validation of female employment combined with the stagnation of male wages after 1975 combined to raise the rate of female labor force participation to the point where most women now hold paying jobs, even those with young children. The consequences of this gender revolution have played out in very different ways, however, at the lower and upper ends of the socioeconomic distribution. Jobs in management and the professions have opened up, and women have gained new access to careers in law, medicine, business, and higher education. In an era of lagging male income and rising inequality, the high salaries earned by women in professional and managerial jobs make them attractive as marital partners. Rates of within-class marriage have increased, rates of divorce have fallen, unwed childbearing has fallen, and within families the drudgery of housework has been relieved by the hiring of outside workers and greater sharing with well-educated men who conform more readily than their lower-class counterparts to the ideal of egalitarian marriage. Although a glass ceiling still persists to prevent upper-class women from reaching the top of America's administrative, corporate, and educational hierarchies, in material terms upper-class women and their children are much better off than before.

At the lower end of the socioeconomic distribution, the situation is entirely different. Occupational segregation has remained rigid in the blue-collar workforce, and women without education are confined mostly to unskilled manual and service jobs that offer few chances for mobility and very low pay. Given low earnings and the decoupling of sex from marriage enabled by effective contraception, lower-class women have became less attractive as marriage partners, and as male wages and employment fell, the supply of "marriageable males" was reduced. The end result was a decline in marriage rates, a rise in divorce rates, and an increase in unwed childbearing among lower-class women. In addition, men whose traditional role of breadwinner was increasingly being called into question by stagnant wages and diminishing employment did not so readily adapt to more egalitarian relationships; working-class women continued to do the lion's share of the housework, and their children received smaller investments of paternal time and money.

Figure 7.1   Ratio of 90th to 20th Percentile of Income
Distribution in Selected OECD Nations

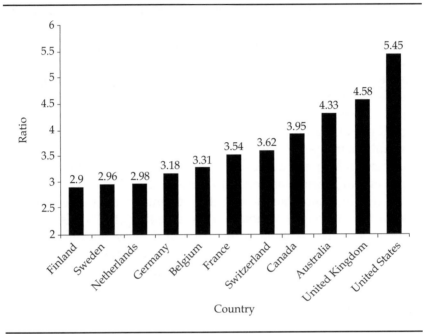

Source: Smeeding (2005).

Stratification at Home and Abroad

Processes of categorical stratification occurring along the lines of race, class, and gender have combined to make the United States the most unequal among advanced industrial nations.

A common way of measuring inequality is by forming the ratio of the ninetieth to the tenth percentile of the income distribution. Figure 7.1 uses data from Smeeding (2005) to show this ratio for selected nations in the Organization for Economic Cooperation and Development (OECD), essentially the "club" for developed nations around the world. These ratios reveal the exceptional nature of American inequality. The American income ratio of 5.45 is well above the average level of 4.0 for OECD nations as a whole and much greater than the ratios that prevail in most European countries. Although not shown in the figure, the only countries that exceed the United States with respect to income inequality are Russia, with a ratio of 8.4, and Mexico, with a ratio of 9.4, both of which are much less developed and characterized by much lower levels of income generally (Smeeding 2005). The United States thus stands out among developed nations for the severity of its inequality.

Rising inequality over the past thirty years has been attributed to a variety of factors, including globalization, technological change, and the segmentation of markets (Danziger and Gottschalk 1995; Levy 1998; Massey 1996). Nonetheless, all countries compete in the same global economy and face the same technological and market conditions, yet the United States is unique among advanced nations in the degree to which it allows these large, macrolevel forces to generate inequality. The end of Jim Crow segregation in the South, the prohibition of open discrimination in the North, and the deracialization of the welfare state paradoxically led to the reinstitution of categorical mechanisms of class stratification that had largely been eliminated during the New Deal. At the same time, older mechanisms of racial and gender stratification did not disappear but evolved to become more subtle and less observable. As discrimination moved underground, new mechanisms for exclusion were built into the criminal justice system for African Americans and into the immigration system for Mexican Americans.

American society can be conceptualized as a three-dimensional social space defined by the axes of race, class, and gender. Gender is easy to define, of course, since the vast majority of people are clearly identifiable as either males or females and statistical data are routinely broken down by sex. Race is more of a social construction, though owing to America's racist legacy, persons of African ancestry have always been well identified in government statistics. The arrival of Asians in the late nineteenth century led to their separate identification as well, and the more recent upsurge in Latin American migration produced a new classification of Latinos, first as "Spanish-surnamed" individuals and after 1970 as "Hispanics." The cross classification of race and Hispanic origin yields five categories: non-Hispanic whites, non-Hispanic blacks, non-Hispanic Asians, Hispanics, and a residual "other" category.

Class is even more of a social construction and difficult to define from available data. Drawing on Marxist and Weberian conceptualizations of class, Erik Wright (1997) distinguished between people on the basis of their relation to the means of production, their relation to authority, their relation to scarce skills, and, among owners, the number of employees. He applied this scheme to classify people using detailed occupational codes. He identified twelve mutually exclusive class categories, which for purposes of parsimony may be collapsed into seven: capitalists and small employers (8 percent of the workforce), the petty bourgeoisie (7 percent), experts and skilled employees with authority (18 percent), nonskilled employees with authority (9 percent), experts without authority (3 percent), skilled employees without authority (14 percent), and unskilled workers without authority (42 percent).

Ideally an assessment of the role played by race, class, and gender would make use of a similar conceptualization of class to analyze changes over time, but such a task is beyond the scope of what can be accomplished here. Instead, for purposes of illustration class is defined by access to human capital—or more specifically, education, the most important resource in today's knowledge-based economy. Figure 7.2 thus proxies the U.S. class structure by dividing people into four groups—college graduates, those with some college, high school graduates, and those with less than a high school education—which when combined with the other categorizations yields a four-by-five-by-two social space of class, race, and gender within which we can examine the distribution of income to assess the basis for U.S. stratification.

Data on personal income were obtained from the 1950 to 2000 censuses and the 2005 Current Population Survey using the Integrated Public Use Microdata Sample (IPUMS). Income was then classified according to the scheme of figure 7.2, and a three-way analysis of variance was performed on the resulting income distribution using the general linear model available from SAS.[1] The resulting main effects of race, class, and gender are plotted by year in

Figure 7.2   Four-by-Five-by-Two Factorial Design for Analysis
                of Variance in U.S. Income Inequality, 1950 to 2005

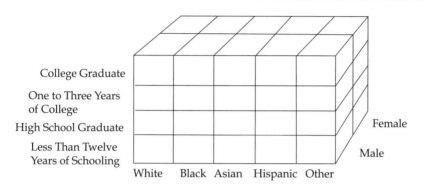

Source: Author's compilation.

figure 7.3. Specifically, this figure shows the percentage of variance in personal income explained by each categorical factor from 1950 to 2005.

As can be seen, in 1950 most of the explained variance in personal income was accounted for by gender. The predominant cleavage in American society was thus between male and female workers, with gender explaining 74 percent of the variance compared with only 18 percent for class (as measured by education) and 4 percent for race. Over the next fifty-five years, however, gender steadily declined as a significant factor in the American stratification system, with the share of variance explaining stratification dropping at a rate of 0.8 percent per year from 1950 to 1980, then accelerating to 1.4 percent per year between 1950 and 1980 before leveling off in 2000 and 2005. Over the entire period, the share of income stratification explained by gender fell from nearly three-quarters in 1950 to less than one-quarter in 2005.

What replaced gender in terms of explanatory power was class: the share of income explained by education went from 18 percent in 1950 to 62 percent in 2005. The percentage of variance explained by race fluctuated somewhat over the period but changed little over-

Figure 7.3 Variance in Personal Income Explained by Race,
Education, and Gender, 1950 to 2005

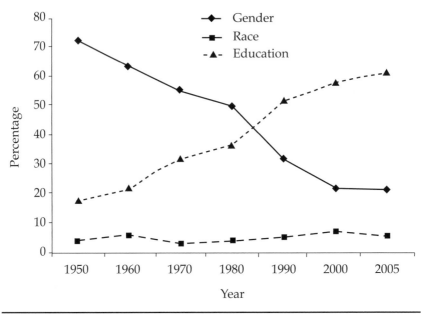

Source: IPUMS.

all, bottoming out in 1970 when it reached 3 percent and then rising
to 8 percent in 2000 before falling back to 7 percent in 2005. Consistent with the conclusions of chapter 6, the interaction between class
and gender also increased in importance over the period, as shown
in figure 7.4, which plots the percentage of variance captured by the
various interactions between race, class, and gender from 1950 to
2005. Although the percentage of variance explained by the class-
gender interaction is small compared to the main effects, its relative
importance nonetheless rose steadily and significantly from 1950
through 2000, going from 3 percent to 7.5 percent before dropping
to 5.5 percent in 2005.

Figure 7.5 repeats the ANOVA using family income instead of
personal income. Although the overall story is similar, the timing of

Figure 7.4   Variance in Personal Income Explained by Race-
               Education-Gender Interactions

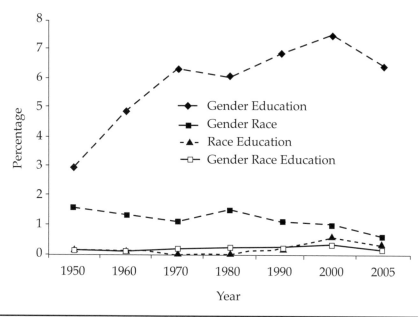

Source: IPUMS.

the changes in categorical importance is different when they are fil-
tered through the American family system, which itself underwent
significant change over the period. The critical year in accounting
for family income appears to be 1980. Until that date, the relative
importance of gender was rising, with the percentage of variance
explained going from 38 percent in 1950 to 51 percent in 1980, while
the share explained by education fluctuated around 40 percent with
no clear trend. After 1980, however, the relative importance of gender in explaining family income dropped markedly, going from 51
percent to 28 percent by 2005, while that explained by education
rose from 40 percent to 61 percent.

Figure 7.6 shows the share of variance in family income ex-

Figure 7.5   Variance in Family Income Explained by Race,
              Education, and Gender

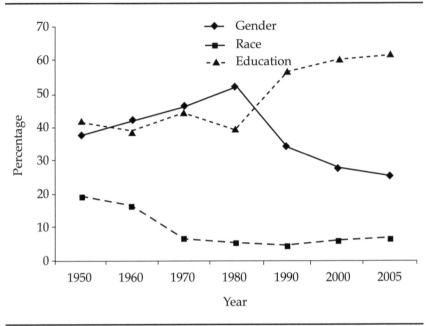

Source: IPUMS.

plained by the various interactions of race, class, and gender at different points in time. As with personal income, there is a very clear increase in the gender-class interaction, but most of the change in categorical importance is observed after 1980, and the decline from 2000 to 2005 is sharper. Unlike the case of personal income, however, there is also evidence of an increase in the race-class interaction after 1980, though in absolute terms it is relatively small.

The Future of Categorical Inequality

American income inequality has thus shifted from stark divisions on the basis of gender to new foundations based on class. That class-based categorical mechanisms have risen to undergird America's

Figure 7.6   Variance in Family Income Explained by Race-
             Education-Gender Interactions

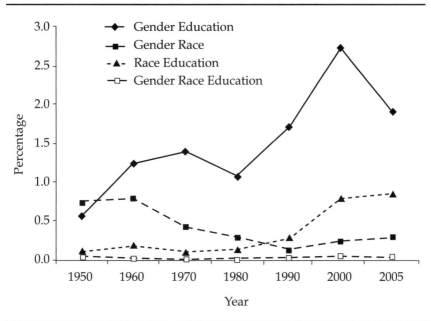

Source: IPUMS.

new system of inequality is also suggested by figure 7.7, which
shows Gini indices of income inequality for selected OECD nations
computed before and after the deduction of taxes. The before-tax
Gini coefficients indicate the amount of raw inequality generated by
capitalist markets in each country, whereas the after-tax Gini indicates the degree of inequality that remains after transfers have been
made to fund the social welfare system in each country. As the gray
bars show, before taxes the United States is no more or no less equal
than any other country. Its pre-tax Gini is .45, only slightly above the
value of .44 in Sweden, .43 in Germany, and .42 in the Netherlands,
but well below the values of .50 and .49 in Belgium and France and
the same as those prevailing in Australia and Britain.

Taxation works in a redistributive direction for all countries, as

Figure 7.7   Gini Index of Income Inequality Before and After
                Taxes in Selected OECD Nations

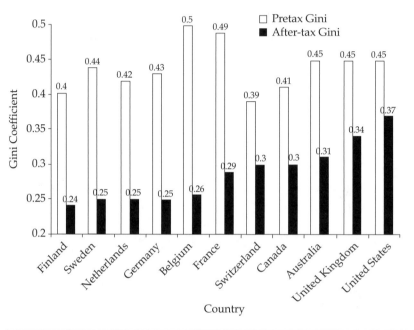

Source: Smeeding (2005).

indicated by the universally lower values for the after-tax Ginis, but the extent of the redistribution is much less in the United States. Its coefficient drops much less as a result of taxation than happens in other countries. The Gini coefficient for income inequality in Belgium, for example, falls from .50 before taxes to just .26 after taxes. The after-tax Gini coefficient is at .30 or below for all countries except Australia, the United Kingdom, and the United States, and in the former two nations the respective figures are .31 and .34, compared with .37 in the United States. Thus, whereas the economy of Belgium produces a distribution of income that is 11 percent more unequal than in the United States before taxes, afterward the institutionalized mechanisms of redistribution yield a distribution that is 22 percent less unequal.

By almost any measure, the United States is unambiguously a more class-stratified place than it was before 1975. The clear increase in class stratification over the past thirty years and the rising share of the variance in income distribution that is explained by education do not mean, however, that race and gender have receded in significance. Indeed, as chapters 2, 3, and 6 have argued, these cleavages continue to function in powerful ways to generate categorical inequalities in the United States. What figures 7.2 to 7.6 indicate is that mechanisms of race and gender stratification increasingly operate through education, the ultimate scarce resource in a knowledge-based economy. Were it possible to define a class variable in the manner of Erik Wright (1997) rather than using education as a proxy, the share of income variance explained by race and gender might well have been larger.

To the extent that education itself is unevenly allocated across categorical boundaries, race and gender are not likely to disappear as salient bases for American stratification. Categorical inequalities in access to quality education are not hard to observe. In terms of race, black males are now more likely to go to prison than to college (Western 2006); the racial segregation of American schools has increased (Orfield and Eaton 1996); and racial differentials in the quality of education have widened (Kozol 2005). Likewise, changes in immigration policy have pushed the children of legal immigrants out of school (Massey 2003) and discouraged school attendance by the children of illegal migrants (Donato, Massey, and Wagner 2006). In terms of class, shifts in welfare policy have made it more difficult for poor people to continue in school (Shaw et al. 2006), while special recruitment programs for athletes and alumni children give the affluent preferential access to elite colleges and universities (Bowen, Kurzweil, and Tobin 2005; Golden 2006; Karabel 2005; Massey and Mooney, forthcoming). In terms of gender, although females now outnumber males in higher education, majors remain quite segregated, with females generally concentrating in lower-earning fields (Jacobs 1996). As long as the quantity and quality of education are so strongly linked to race, class, and gender, categorical mechanisms of stratification will continue to operate with considerable force in the political economy of the United States of America.

NOTES

Chapter 5

1. The author thanks Courtland Smith of the Department of Anthropology at Oregon State University for making available statistics he compiled for his website on poverty and inequality (http://oregonstate.edu/instruct/anth/smith/).
2. The social services included in the tabulation include Aid to Families with Dependent Children (AFDC), general assistance, the Special Supplemental Nutrition Program for Women, Infants, and Children (WIC), work in progress, and other services targeted to low-income Americans.

Chapter 7

1. The author thanks Monica Higgins for assistance in assembling the IPUMS data and estimating the ANOVA.

REFERENCES

Abramovitz, Mimi. 2000. *Under Attack, Fighting Back: Women and Welfare in the United States*. New York: Monthly Review Press.

Achen, Christopher H., and Larry M. Bartels. 2006. "It Feels Like We're Thinking: The Rationalizing Voter and Electoral Democracy." Paper presented to the annual meeting of the American Political Science Association. Philadelphia (August 30–September 3).

Adimora, Adaora A., and Victor J. Schoenbach. 2005. "Social Context, Sexual Networks, and Racial Disparities in Rates of Sexually Transmitted Infections." *Journal of Infectious Diseases* 191(S1): 115–22.

Aguilera, Michael B., and Douglas S. Massey. 2003. "Social Capital and the Wages of Mexican Migrants: New Hypotheses and Tests." *Social Forces* 82(2, December): 671–701.

Akerlof, George A., Janet L. Yellen, and Michael L. Katz. 1996. "An Analysis of Out-of-Wedlock Childbearing in the United States." *Quarterly Journal of Economics* 111(2): 277–317.

Alba, Richard D. 1990. *Ethnic Identity: The Transformation of White America*. New Haven, Conn.: Yale University Press.

Alba, Richard D., and Victor Nee. 2003. *Remaking the American Mainstream: Assimilation and Contemporary Immigration*. Cambridge, Mass.: Harvard University Press.

Allen, Walter, Edward E. Telles, and Margaret Hunter. 2000. "Skin Color, Income, and Education: A Comparison of African Americans and Mexican Americans." *National Journal of Sociology* 12: 129–80.

Altshuler, Alan, William Morrill, Harold Wolman, and Faith Mitchell, eds. 1999. *Governance and Opportunity in Metropolitan America*. Washington, D.C.: National Academies Press.

Anderson, Elijah. 1994. "The Code of the Streets." *Atlantic Monthly* 273(5): 80–94.

———. 1999. *Code of the Street: Decency, Violence, and the Moral Life of the Inner City*. New York: Norton.

Anderson, James, and Dara N. Byrne. 2004. *The Unfinished Agenda of Brown v. Board of Education*. New York: Wiley.

References

Andreas, Peter. 2000. *Border Games: Policing the U.S.-Mexico Divide.* Ithaca, N.Y.: Cornell University Press.

Arce, Carlos S., Edward Murguia, and W. Parker Frisbie. 1987. "Phenotype and Life Chances Among Chicanos." *Hispanic Journal of Behavioral Sciences* 9(1): 19–32.

Ashenfelter, Orley, and George E. Johnson. 1969. "Bargaining Theory, Trade Unions, and Industrial Strike Activity." *American Economic Review* 59(1): 39–55.

Ashenfelter, Orley, George E. Johnson, and John H. Pencavel. 1972. "Trade Unions and the Rate of Change in Money Wages in United States Manufacturing Industry." *Review of Economic Studies* 39(1): 27–54.

Ayres, Ian, and Peter Siegelman. 1995. "Race and Gender Discrimination in Bargaining for a New Car." *American Economic Review* 85(3): 304–21.

Azari-Rad, Hamid, Peter Philips, and Mark J. Prus. 2005. *The Economics of Prevailing Wage Laws.* Burlington, Vt.: Ashgate.

Banaji, Mahzarin R., and Anthony G. Greenwald. 1994. "Implicit Stereotyping and Prejudice." In *The Psychology of Prejudice: The Ontario Symposium,* edited by Mark P. Zanna and James M. Olson. Hillsdale, N.J.: Lawrence Erlbaum.

Banaji, Mahzarin R., and Curtis Hardin. 1996. "Automatic Stereotyping." *Psychological Science* 7: 136–41.

Banner, Stuart. 2002. *The Death Penalty: An American History.* Cambridge, Mass.: Harvard University Press.

Bargh, John A. 1989. "Conditional Automaticity: Varieties of Automatic Influence in Social Perception and Cognition." In *Unintended Thought,* edited by James S. Uleman and John A. Bargh Bargh. New York: Guilford Press.

———. 1996. "Automaticity in Social Psychology." In *Social Psychology: Handbook of Basic Principles,* edited by E. Tory Higgins and Arie W. Kruglanski. New York: Guilford.

———. 1997. "The Automaticity of Everyday Life." In *The Automaticity of Everyday Life: Advances in Social Cognition,* edited by Robert S. Weyer Jr. Mahwah, N.J.: Lawrence Erlbaum.

Bartels, Larry M. 2004. "Partisan Politics and the U.S. Income Distribution." Working paper. Princeton, N.J.: Princeton University, Department of Politics.

———. 2005a. "Homer Gets a Tax Cut: Inequality and Public Policy in the American Mind." *Perspectives on Politics* 3(1): 15–31.

———. 2005b. "Economic Inequality and Political Representation." Working paper, Department of Politics and Woodrow Wilson School of Public and International Affairs, Princeton University.

Barth, Fredrik. 1969. *Ethnic Groups and Boundaries: The Social Organization of Culture Difference.* Boston: Little, Brown.

———. 1981. *Process and Form in Social Life.* London: Routledge and Kegan Paul.

Bartley, Numan. 1975. *Southern Politics and the Second Reconstruction.* Baltimore: Johns Hopkins University Press.

Baugh, John. 1983. *Black Street Speech: Its History, Structure, and Survival.* Austin: University of Texas Press.

Bauman, John F. 1987. *Public Housing, Race, and Renewal: Urban Planning in Philadelphia, 1920–1974.* Philadelphia: Temple University Press.

Bean, Frank D., B. Lindsay Lowell, and Lowell J. Taylor. 1988. "Undocumented Mexican Immigrants and the Earnings of Other Workers in the United States." *Demography* 25(1): 35–52.

Bean, Frank D., and Marta Tienda. 1987. *The Hispanic Population of the United States.* New York: Russell Sage Foundation.

Beck, Warren A. 1969. *New Mexico: A History of Four Centuries.* Norman: University of Oklahoma Press.

Becker, Gary S. 1975. *Human Capital: A Theoretical and Empirical Analysis with Special Reference to Education.* Chicago: University of Chicago Press.

———. 1991. *A Treatise on the Family.* Cambridge, Mass.: Harvard University Press.

Bergmann, Barbara. 1974. "Occupational Segregation, Wages, and Profits When Employers Discriminate by Race or Sex." *Eastern Economic Journal* 1(2): 103–10.

Berry, Brian J. L. 1973. *The Human Consequences of Urbanization.* New York: St. Martin's Press.

Bertrand, Marianne, and Sendhil Mullainathan. 2004. "Are Emily and Greg More Employable Than Lakisha and Jamal? A Field Experiment on Labor Market Discrimination." *American Economic Review* 94(4): 991–1013.

Biagi, Shirley, and Marilyn Kern-Foxworth. 1997. *Facing Difference: Race, Gender, and Mass Media.* New York: Pine Science Press.

Bianchi, Suzanne M. 2000. "Maternal Employment and Time with Children: Dramatic Change or Surprising Continuity?" *Demography* 37(4): 401–14.

Bianchi, Suzanne M., John P. Robinson, and Melissa A. Milkie. 2006. *Changing Rhythms of American Family Life.* New York: Russell Sage Foundation.

Bianchi, Suzanne M., and Daphne Spain. 1986. *American Women in Transition.* New York: Russell Sage Foundation.

References

Black, Harold A., and Robert L. Schweitzer. 1985. "A Canonical Analysis of Mortgage Lending Terms: Testing for Lending Discrimination at a Commercial Bank." *Urban Studies* 22: 13–20.

Blank, Rebecca M., Marilyn Dabady, and Constance F. Citro, eds. 2004. *Measuring Racial Discrimination*. Washington, D.C.: National Academies Press.

Blau, Francine D., and Lawrence M. Kahn. 2004. "The U.S. Gender Pay Gap in the 1990s: Slowing Convergence." Working paper 10853. Washington, D.C.: National Bureau of Economic Research.

———. 2006. "The Gender Pay Gap: Going, Going . . . But Not Gone." In *The Declining Significance of Gender?* edited by Francine D. Blau, Mary C. Brinton, and David B. Grusky. New York: Russell Sage Foundation.

Blau, Peter M. 1977. *Inequality and Heterogeneity: A Primitive Theory of Social Structure*. New York: Free Press.

Blau, Peter M., and Judith R. Blau. 1982. "The Cost of Inequality: Metropolitan Structure and Violent Crime." *American Sociological Review* 47(1): 114–29.

Bluestone, Barry, and Mary Huff Stevenson. 2000. *The Boston Renaissance: Race, Space, and Economic Change in an American Metropolis*. New York: Russell Sage Foundation.

Bobo, Lawrence D. 1989. "Keeping the Linchpin in Place: Testing the Multiple Sources of Opposition to Residential Integration." *International Review of Social Psychology* 2: 305–23.

———. 2001. "Racial Attitudes and Relations at the Close of the Twentieth Century." In *America Becoming: Racial Trends and Their Consequences*, vol. 1, edited by Neil Smelser, William Julius Wilson, and Faith Mitchell. Washington, D.C.: National Academies Press.

Bobo, Lawrence D., and Devon Johnson. 2000. "Racial Attitudes in a Prismatic Metropolis: Mapping Identity, Stereotypes, Competition, and Views on Affirmative Action." In *Prismatic Metropolis: Inequality in Los Angeles*, edited by Lawrence D. Bobo, Melvin L. Oliver, James H. Johnson Jr., and Abel Valenzuela Jr. New York: Russell Sage Foundation.

Bobo, Lawrence D., and James R. Kluegel. 1993. "Opposition to Race Targeting: Self-interest, Stratification, Ideology, or Racial Attitudes?" *American Sociological Review* 58(4): 443–64.

———. 1997. "Status, Ideology, and Dimensions of Whites' Racial Beliefs and Attitudes." In *Racial Attitudes in the 1990s: Continuities and Change*, edited by Steven J. Tuch and Jack A. Martin. Westport, Conn.: Praeger.

Bobo, Lawrence D., James R. Kluegel, and Ryan A. Smith. 1997. "Laissez-

Faire Racism: The Crystallization of a Kinder, Gentler, Antiblack Ideology." In *Racial Attitudes in the 1990s: Continuities and Change*, edited by Steven J. Tuch and Jack A. Martin. Westport, Conn.: Praeger.

Bobo, Lawrence D., and Michael P. Massagli. 2001. "Stereotyping and Urban Inequality." In *Urban Inequality: Evidence from Four Cities*, edited by Alice O'Connor, Chris Tilly, and Lawrence D. Bobo. New York: Russell Sage Foundation.

Bobo, Lawrence D., and Camille Zubrinsky. 1996. "Attitudes Toward Residential Integration: Perceived Status Differences, Mere In-group Preference, or Racial Prejudice?" *Social Forces* 74(3): 883–909.

Bodenhausen, Galen V., and Meryl Lichtenstein. 1987. "Social Stereotypes and Information-Processing Strategies: The Impact of Task Complexity." *Journal of Personality and Social Psychology* 52: 871–80.

Bodenhausen, Galen V., and Robert S. Wyer. 1985. "Effects of Stereotypes on Decision Making and Information-Processing Strategies." *Journal of Personality and Social Psychology* 48(2): 267–82.

Bolte, Charles G., and Louis Harris. 1947. *Our Negro Veterans*. New York: Public Affairs Committee.

Bonilla-Silva, Eduardo. 2003. *Racism Without Racists: Color-Blind Racism and the Persistence of Racial Inequality in the United States*. Lanham, Md.: Rowman and Littlefield.

Borjas, George J. 1984. "The Impact of Immigrants on the Earnings of the Native-Born." In *Immigration: Issues and Policies*, edited by Vernon R. Briggs Jr. and Marta Tienda. Salt Lake City: Olympus Publishing.

———. 1987. "Immigrants, Minorities, and Labor Market Competition." *Industrial and Labor Relations Review* 40(3): 382–92.

———. 1993. "The Impact of Immigration on the Employment Opportunities of Natives." In *The Changing Course of Immigration*. Paris: Organization for Economic Cooperation and Development.

———. 1994. "The Economics of Immigration." *Journal of Economic Literature* 32(4): 1667–1717.

———. 1995. "Assimilation and Changes in Cohort Quality Revisited: What Happened to Immigrant Earnings in the 1980s?" *Journal of Labor Economics* 13(2): 201–45.

———. 1997. "The Economic Impact of Mexican Immigration." In *Coming Together: Mexico-U.S. Relations*, edited by Barry P. Bosworth, Susan M. Collins, and Nora Claudia Lustig. Washington, D.C.: Brookings Institution Press.

———. 1999. *Heaven's Door: Immigration Policy and the American Economy*. Princeton, N.J.: Princeton University Press.

References

———. 2004. "Food Insecurity and Public Assistance." *Journal of Public Economics* 88(7-8): 1421–43.

Borjas, George J., Richard B. Freeman, and Lawrence F. Katz. 1992. "On the Labor Market Effects of Immigration and Trade." In *Immigration and the Workforce: Economic Consequences for the United States and Source Areas*, edited by George J. Borjas and Richard B. Freeman. Chicago: University of Chicago Press.

———. 1996. "Searching for the Effect of Immigration on the Labor Market." *American Economic Review* 86(2): 246–51.

Borjas, George J., and Marta Tienda. 1987. "The Economic Consequences of Immigration." *Science* (February 6): 645–51.

———. 1993. "The Employment and Wages of Legalized Immigrants." *International Migration Review* 27(4): 712–47.

Bourdieu, Pierre. 1986. "The Forms of Capital." In *Handbook of Theory and Research for the Sociology of Education*, edited by John G. Richardson. New York: Greenwood Press.

Bourgois, Philippe. 2003. *In Search of Respect: Selling Crack in El Barrio*, 2nd ed. New York: Cambridge University Press.

Bowen, William G., and Derek Bok. 1998. *The Shape of the River: Long-term Consequences of Considering Race in College and University Admissions*. Princeton, N.J.: Princeton University Press.

Bowen, William G., Martin A. Kurzweil, and Eugene M. Tobin. 2005. *Equity and Excellence in American Higher Education*. Charlottesville: University Press of Virginia.

Bradbury, Katharine L., Karl E. Case, and Constance R. Dunham. 1989. "Geographic Patterns of Mortgage Lending in Boston, 1982–1987." *New England Economic Review* (September–October): 3–30.

Brandolini, Andrea., and Timothy M. Smeeding. Forthcoming. "Inequality: International Evidence." *New Palgrave Dictionary of Economics*, edited by William A. Darrity et al. New York: Palgrave-MacMillan.

Breland, Hunter M., James Maxey, Gail T. McLure, Michael J. Valiga, Michael A. Boatwright, and Veronica L. Ganley. 1995. *Challenges in College Admissions: A Report of a Survey of Undergraduate Admissions Policies, Practices, and Procedures*. Princeton, N.J.: Educational Testing Service.

Brodkin, Karen. 1999. *How Jews Became White Folks and What That Says About Race in America*. New Brunswick, N.J.: Rutgers University Press.

Brown, Donald E. 1991. *Human Universals*. New York: McGraw-Hill.

———. 2000. "Human Universals and Their Implications." In *Being Humans: Anthropological Universality and Particularity in Transdisciplinary Perspectives*, edited by Neil Roughly. New York: Walter de Gruyter.

Buchanan, Patrick J. 2006. *State of Emergency: The Third World Invasion and Conquest of America*. New York: Thomas Dunne Books.

Burtless, Gary, and Timothy B. Smeeding. 2001. "The Level, Trend, and Composition of Poverty." In *Understanding Poverty*, edited by Sheldon Danziger and Robert H. Haveman. New York: Russell Sage Foundation.

Calavita, Kitty. 1992. *Inside the State: The Bracero Program, Immigration, and the INS*. New York: Routledge.

Card, David. 1996. "The Effects of Unions on the Structure of Wages: A Longitudinal Analysis." *Econometrica* 64(4): 597–679.

Cardoso, Lawrence A. 1980. *Mexican Emigration to the United States, 1897–1931: Socioeconomic Patterns*. Tucson: University of Arizona Press.

Carr, James H., and Isaac F. Megbolugbe. 1993. "The Federal Reserve Bank of Boston Study on Mortgage Lending Revisited." *Journal of Housing Research* 4(2): 277–313.

Carrigan, William D. 2004. *The Making of a Lynching Culture: Violence and Vigilantism in Central Texas, 1836–1916*. Urbana: University of Illinois Press.

Carrigan, William D., and Clive Webb. 2003. "The Lynching of Persons of Mexican Origin or Descent in the United States, 1848 to 1928." *Journal of Social History* 37(2): 411–38.

Carruthers, Bruce G., and Sarah L. Babb. 2000. *Economy/Society: Markets, Meanings, and Social Structure*. Thousand Oaks, Calif.: Pine Forge Press.

Carter, Rita. 1998. *Mapping the Mind*. Berkeley: University of California Press.

Carter, Susan B., Scott Sigmund Gartner, Michael R. Haines, Alan L. Olmstead, Richard Sutch, and Gavin Wright. 2006. *Historical Statistics of the United States Millennial Edition*. New York: Cambridge University Press.

Castells, Manuel. 1996. *The Rise of the Network Society*. Cambridge: Blackwell.

———. 1997. *The Power of Identity*. Cambridge: Blackwell.

Chandler, Tetrius, and Gerald Fox. 1974. *3,000 Years of Urban Growth*. New York: Academic Press.

Chant, Colin, and David Goodman. 1999. *Pre-industrial Cities and Technology*. London: Routledge.

Charles, Camille Z. 2000. "Neighborhood Racial Composition Preferences: Evidence from a Multiethnic Metropolis." *Social Problems* 47(3): 379–407.

———. 2002. "Comfort Zones: Immigration, Assimilation, and the Neighborhood Racial-Composition Preferences of Latinos and Asians." Paper presented to the annual meeting of the American Sociological Association. Chicago (August 16–19).

References

———. 2003. "The Dynamics of Racial Residential Segregation." *Annual Review of Sociology* 29: 167–207.

———. 2006. *Won't You Be My Neighbor?* New York: Russell Sage Foundation.

Charles, Maria, and David B. Grusky. 2004. *Occupational Ghettos: The Worldwide Segregation of Women and Men*. Stanford, Calif.: Stanford University Press.

Chavez, Leo R. 2001. *Covering Immigration: Population Images and the Politics of the Nation*. Berkeley: University of California Press.

Chiswick, Barry R. 1984. "Illegal Aliens in the United States Labor Market: An Analysis of Occupational Attainment and Earnings." *International Migration Review* 18(3): 714–32.

Clayton, Obie, Jr., Christopher R. Geller, Sahadeo Patram, Travis Patton, and David L. Sjoquist. 2000. "Racial Attitudes and Perceptions in Atlanta." In *The Atlanta Paradox*, edited by David L. Sjoquist. New York: Russell Sage Foundation.

Coale, Ansley J. 1991. "Excess Female Mortality and the Balance of the Sexes in the Population: An Estimate of the Number of 'Missing Females.'" *Population and Development Review* 17(3): 517–23.

Cobb-Clark, Deborah A., Clinton R. Shiells, and B. Lindsay Lowell. 1995. "Immigration Reform: The Effects of Employer Sanctions and Legalization on Wages." *Journal of Labor Economics* 13(3): 472–98.

Coleman, James S. 1988. "Social Capital in the Creation of Human Capital." *American Journal of Sociology* 94(suppl.): S95–120.

Collins, Patricia Hill. 2004. *Black Sexual Politics: African Americans, Gender, and the New Racism*. New York: Taylor and Francis.

Common Cause. 2003. *Prospecting for Access: How the Bush Pioneers Shaped Public Policy*. Washington, D.C.: Common Cause.

Cook, Sherburne F., and Woodrow Borah. 1979. *Essays in Population History*, vol. 3: *Mexico and California*. Berkeley: University of California Press.

Coontz, Stephanie. 1994. *The Way We Never Were: American Families and the Nostalgia Trap*. New York: Random House.

Corneo, Giacoma, and Claudia Lucifora. 1997. "Wage Formation Under Union Threat Effects: Theory and Empirical Evidence." *Labor Economics* 4(3): 265–92.

Cross, Harry, Genevieve Kenney, Jane Mell, and Wendy Zimmermann. 1990. *Employer Hiring Practices: Differential Treatment of Hispanic and Anglo Job Seekers*. Washington, D.C.: Urban Institute Press.

Damasio, Antonio R. 1994. *Descartes' Error: Emotion, Reason, and the Human Brain*. New York: Putnam.

————. 1999. *The Feeling of What Happens: Body and Emotion in the Making of Consciousness*. New York: Harcourt Brace.

Daniels, Roger. 1988. *Asian America: Chinese and Japanese in the United States Since 1850*. Seattle: University of Washington Press.

Danziger, Sheldon, and Peter Gottschalk. 1995. *America Unequal*. New York: Russell Sage Foundation.

Darity, William A., Jr., and Patrick L. Mason. 1998. "Evidence on Discrimination in Employment: Codes of Color, Codes of Gender." *Journal of Economic Perspectives* 12(2): 63–90.

Dates, Jennifer, and William Barlow. 1983. *Split Image: African Americans in the Mass Media*. Washington, D.C.: Howard University Press.

Davies, Glynn. 2002. *A History of Money: From Ancient Times to the Present Day*. Cardiff: University of Wales Press.

Dávila, Alberto, José Pagán, and Montserrat Vladrich Grau. 1998. "The Impact of IRCA on the Job Opportunities and Earnings of Mexican-American and Hispanic-American Workers." *International Migration Review* 32(1): 79–95.

Davis, James A., Tom W. Smith, and Peter V. Marsden. 2004. *General Social Survey Cumulative File 1972–2004 Cumulative File, Release 2*. Chicago: National Opinion Research Center (producer); Storrs, Conn.: Roper Center for Public Opinion Research (distributor).

Davis, Mike. 1998. *Ecology of Fear: Los Angeles and the Imagination of Disaster*. New York: Metropolitan Books.

Dawes, Robyn M. 1998. "Behavioral Decision Making and Judgment." In *The Handbook of Social Psychology*, edited by Daniel T. Gilbert, Susan T. Fiske, and Gardner Lindzey. Boston: McGraw-Hill.

Dawes, Robyn M., and Reid Hastie. 2001. *Rational Choice in an Uncertain World: The Psychology of Judgment and Decision Making*. Newbury Park, Calif.: Sage Publications.

Dedman, Bill. 1988. "The Color of Money." *Atlanta Journal and Constitution*, May 4.

————. 1989. "Blacks Denied S&L Loans Twice as Often as Whites." *Atlanta Journal and Constitution*, January 22.

De León, Arnoldo. 1993. *Mexican Americans in Texas: A Brief History*. Wheeling, Ill.: Harlan Davidson.

Denton, Nancy A., and Douglas S. Massey. 1989. "Racial Identity Among Caribbean Hispanics: The Effect of Double Minority Status on Residential Segregation." *American Sociological Review* 54(5): 790–808.

Devine, Fiona, and Mary C. Waters. 2004. *Social Inequalities in Comparative Perspective*. New York: Blackwell.

271

Devine, Patricia G. 1989. "Stereotypes and Prejudice: Their Automatic and Controlled Components." *Journal of Personality and Social Psychology* 56: 5–18.

Donald, Merlin. 1991. *Origins of the Modern Mind: Three States in the Evolution of Culture and Cognition*. Cambridge, Mass.: Harvard University Press.

Donaldson, Gary A. 1999. *The Second Reconstruction: A History of the Modern Civil Rights Movement*. Melbourne, Fla.: Krieger.

Donato, Katharine M., Jorge Durand, and Douglas S. Massey. 1992a. "Stemming the Tide? Assessing the Deterrent Effects of the Immigration Reform and Control Act." *Demography* 29(2): 139–57.

———. 1992b. "Changing Conditions in the U.S. Labor Market: Effects of the Immigration Reform and Control Act of 1986." *Population Research and Policy Review* 11(3): 93–115.

Donato, Katharine M., and Douglas S. Massey. 1993. "Effect of the Immigration Reform and Control Act on the Wages of Mexican Migrants." *Social Science Quarterly* 74(3): 523–41.

Donato, Katharine M., Douglas S. Massey, and Brandon Wagner. 2006. "The Chilling Effect: Public Service Usage by Mexican Migrants to the United States." Paper presented to the annual meeting of the Population Association of America. Los Angeles (March 30–April 1).

Doss, Richard C., and Alan M. Gross. 1994. "The Effects of Black English and Code-Switching on Intraracial Perceptions." *Journal of Black Psychology* 29: 282–93.

Dovidio, John F., and Samuel L. Gaertner. 2004. "Aversive Racism." In *Advances in Experimental Social Psychology* 36: 1–51. San Diego, Calif.: Academic Press.

Dow, Mark. 2004. *American Gulag: Inside U.S. Immigration Prisons*. Berkeley: University of California Press.

Drake, St. Clair, and Horace R. Cayton. 1945. *Black Metropolis: A Study of Life in a Northern City*. New York: Harcourt, Brace, and Co.

Dray, Phillip. 2002. *At the Hands of Persons Unknown: The Lynching of Black America*. New York: Random House.

Dreier, Peter, John Mollenkopf, and Todd Swanstrom. 2001. *Place Matters: Metropolitics for the Twenty-first Century*. Lawrence: University of Kansas Press.

Duany, Jorge. 1998. "Reconstructing Racial Identity: Ethnicity, Color, and Class Among Dominicans in the United States and Puerto Rico." *Latin American Perspectives* 25(3): 147–72.

Dubber, Markus D. 2001. "Policing Possession: The War on Crime and the

End of Criminal Law." *Journal of Criminal Law and Criminology* 91(4): 829–996.

Dubofsky, Jean E. 1969. "Fair Housing: A Legislative History and a Perspective." *Washburn Law Journal* 8: 149–66.

Duncan, Otis D., and Beverly Duncan. 1957. *The Negro Population of Chicago: A Study of Residential Succession*. Chicago: University of Chicago Press.

Dunn, Timothy J. 1996. *The Militarization of the U.S.-Mexico Border, 1978–1992: Low-Intensity Conflict Doctrine Comes Home*. Austin: University of Texas, Center for Mexican American Studies.

Durand, Jorge. 1997. "Les Nouveaux Scénarios de l'immigration Mexicaine aux Etats-Unis. *Revue Tiers Monde* 150: 359–69.

Durand, Jorge, and Patricia Arias. 2000. *La Experiencia Migrante: Iconografía de la Migración México-Estados Unidos*. México, DF: Altexto.

Durand, Jorge, and Douglas S. Massey. 2003. "The Costs of Contradiction: U.S. Immigration Policy 1986–1996." *Latino Studies* 1: 233–52.

Durand, Jorge, Douglas S. Massey, and Emilio A. Parrado. 1999. "The New Era of Mexican Migration to the United States." *Journal of American History* 86(2): 518–36.

Eckes, Thomas. 2002. "Paternalistic and Envious Gender Stereotypes: Testing Predictions from the Stereotype Content Model." *Sex Roles* 47(3-4): 99–114.

Edin, Kathryn, and Maria Kefalas. 2005. *Promises I Can Keep: Why Poor Women Put Motherhood Before Marriage*. Berkeley: University of California Press.

Edin, Kathryn, Timothy J. Nelson, and Rechell Paranal. 2004. "Fatherhood and Incarceration as Potential Turning Points in the Criminal Careers of Unskilled Men." In *Imprisoning America: The Social Effects of Mass Incarceration*, edited by Mary Pattillo, David Weiman, and Bruce Western. New York: Russell Sage Foundation.

Edmonston, Barry, Sharon M. Lee, and Jeffrey S. Passel. 2002. "Recent Trends in Intermarriage and Immigration and the Effects on the Future Racial Composition of the U.S. Population." In *The New Race Question: How the Census Counts Multiracial Individuals*, edited by Joel Perlmann and Mary C. Waters. New York: Russell Sage Foundation.

Edsall, Thomas B., and Mary D. Edsall. 1991. *Chain Reaction: The Impact of Race, Rights, and Taxes on American Politics*. New York: Norton.

Eichengreen, Barry. 1984. "Experience and the Male-Female Earnings Gap in the 1890s." *Journal of Economic History* 44(3): 822–34.

Ellemers, Naomi. 2001. "Individual Upward Mobility and the Perceived Legitimacy of Intergroup Relations." In *The Psychology of Legitimacy: Emerg-*

ing Perspectives on Ideology, Justice, and Intergroup Relations, edited by John T. Jost and Brenda Majors. New York: Cambridge University Press.

Emerson, Michael O., George Yancy, and Karen Chai. 2001. "Does Race Matter in Residential Segregation? Exploring the Preferences of White Americans." *American Sociological Review* 66(6): 922–35.

England, Paula. 1992. *Comparable Worth: Theories and Evidence*. New York: Aldine de Gruyter.

———. 2005. "Emerging Theories of Care Work." *Annual Review of Sociology* 31: 381–99.

———. 2006. "Toward Gender Equality: Progress and Bottlenecks." In *The Declining Significance of Gender?* edited by Francine D. Blau, Mary C. Brinton, and David B. Grusky. New York: Russell Sage Foundation.

England, Paula, and Nancy Folbre. 1999. "The Cost of Caring." *Annals of the American Academy of Political and Social Sciences* 561(Jan.): 39–51.

England, Paula, Jennifer Thompson, and Carolyn Aman. 2001. "The Sex Gap in Pay and Comparable Worth: An Update." In *Sourcebook on Labor Markets: Evolving Structures and Processes*, edited by Ivar Berg and Arne L. Kalleberg. New York: Plenum.

Entman, Robert M., and Andrew Rojecki. 2000. *The Black Image in White Minds: Media and Race in America*. Chicago: University of Chicago Press.

Espenshade, Thomas J. 1990. "Undocumented Migration to the United States: Evidence from a Repeated Trials Model." In *Undocumented Migration to the United States: IRCA and the Experience of the 1980s*, edited by Frank D. Bean, Barry Edmonston, and Jeffrey S. Passel. Washington, D.C.: Urban Institute Press.

———. 1994. "Does the Threat of Apprehension Deter Undocumented U.S. Immigration?" *Population and Development Review* 20(4): 871–92.

Espenshade, Thomas J., Chang Y. Chung, and Joan L. Walling. 2004. "Admission Preferences for Minority Studies, Athletes, and Legacies at Elite Universities." *Social Science Quarterly* 85(5): 1422–46.

Espino, Rodolfo, and Michael M. Franz. 2002. "Latino Phenotypic Discrimination Revisited: The Impact of Skin Color on Occupational Status." *Social Science Quarterly* 83(2): 612–23.

Farkas, George, and Paula England. 1986. *Households, Employment, and Gender: A Social, Economic, and Demographic View*. New York: Aldine.

Farley, Reynolds, and Walter T. Allen. 1989. *The Color Line and the Quality of Life in America*. New York: Russell Sage Foundation.

Farley, Reynolds, Sheldon Danziger, and Harry J. Holzer. 2000. *Detroit Divided*. New York: Russell Sage Foundation.

Feagin, Joe R. 1994. "A House Is Not a Home: White Racism and U.S.

Housing Practices." In *Residential Apartheid: The American Legacy*, edited by Robert D. Bullard, J. Eugene Grigsby III, and Charles Lee. Los Angeles: CAAS Publications.

Feagin, Joe R., and Melvin P. Sikes. 1994. *Living with Racism: The Black Middle-Class Experience*. Boston: Beacon Press.

Fischer, Claude S. 1975. "Toward a Subcultural Theory of Urbanism." *American Journal of Sociology* 80(6): 1319–41.

———. 1995. "The Subcultural Theory of Urbanism: A Twentieth-Year Assessment." *American Journal of Sociology* 101(3): 543–77.

Fischer, Claude S., Gretchen Stockmayer, Jon Stiles, and Michael Hout. 2004. "Distinguishing the Geographic Levels and Social Dimensions of U.S. Metropolitan Segregation, 1960–2000." *Demography* 41(1): 37–59.

Fischer, Mary J., and Douglas S. Massey. 2004. "The Social Ecology of Racial Discrimination." *City and Community* 3: 221–43.

Fischer, Mary J., and Marta Tienda. 2006. "Redrawing Spatial Color Lines: Hispanic Metropolitan Dispersal, Segregation, and Economic Opportunity." In *Hispanics and the Future of America*, edited by Marta Tienda and Faith Mitchell. Washington, D.C.: National Academies Press.

Fishman, Mark, and Gray Cavender. 1998. *Entertaining Crime: Television Reality Programs*. New York: Aldine de Gruyter.

Fiske, Susan T. 1998. "Stereotyping, Prejudice, and Discrimination." In *The Handbook of Social Psychology*, 4th ed., vol. 1, edited by Daniel T. Gilbert, Susan T. Fiske, and Gardner Lindzey. New York: McGraw-Hill.

———. 2004. *Social Beings: A Core Motives Approach to Social Psychology*. New York: Wiley.

Fiske, Susan T., Peter Cluck, Amy Cuddy, and J. Xu. 1999. "Ambivalent Content of Stereotypes Predicted by Social Structure: Status and Competition Predict Competence and Warmth." Paper presented to the twenty-second general meeting of the European Association of Experimental Social Psychology. Oxford (July).

Fiske, Susan T., Amy J. C. Cuddy, Peter Glick, and Jun Xu. 2002. "A Model of (Often Mixed) Stereotype Content: Competence and Warmth Respectively Follow from Perceived Status and Competition." *Journal of Personality and Social Psychology* 82(6): 878–902.

Fiske, Susan T., and Shelly E. Taylor. 1991. *Social Cognition*, 2nd ed. New York: McGraw-Hill.

Fix, Michael, and Wendy Zimmermann. 2004. "The Legacy of Welfare Reform for U.S. Immigrants." In *International Migration: Prospects and Policies in a Global Market*, edited by Douglas S. Massey and J. Edward Taylor. Oxford: Oxford University Press.

References

Fligstein, Neil. 2001. *The Architecture of Markets: An Economic Sociology of Twenty-first-Century Capitalist Societies*. Princeton, N.J.: Princeton University Press.

Folbre, Nancy. 2001. *The Invisible Heart: Economics and Family Values*. New York: New Press.

Foner, Eric. 1988. *Reconstruction: America's Unfinished Revolution, 1863–1877*. New York: Harper & Row.

Frank, Thomas. 2004. *What's the Matter with Kansas? How Conservatives Won the Heart of America*. New York: Metropolitan Books.

Freeman, Richard B. 1993. "How Much Has De-unionization Contributed to the Rise in Male Earnings Inequality?" In *Uneven Tides: Rising Inequality in America*, edited by Sheldon Danziger and Peter Gottschalk. New York: Russell Sage Foundation.

———. 2001. "The Rising Tide Lifts . . .?" In *Understanding Poverty*, edited by Sheldon Danziger and Robert H. Haveman. New York: Russell Sage Foundation.

Freeman, Richard B., and James Medoff. 1984. *What Do Unions Do?* New York: Basic Books.

Friedman, Milton. 1956. *A Restatement of the Quantity Theory of Money*. Chicago: University of Chicago Press.

Friedman, Samantha, and Gregory D. Squires. 2005. "Does the Community Reinvestment Act Help Minorities Access Traditionally Inaccessible Neighborhoods?" *Social Problems* 52(2): 209–31.

Friedman, Thomas. 2000. *The Lexus and the Olive Tree: Understanding Globalization*. New York: Farrar, Straus and Giroux.

———. 2005. *The World Is Flat: A Brief History of the Twenty-first Century*. New York: Farrar, Straus and Giroux.

Fry, Richard, B. Lindsay Lowell, and Elhum Haghighat 1995. "The Impact of Employer Sanctions on Metropolitan Wage Rates." *Industrial Relations* 34 (July): 464–84.

Fuchs, Lawrence H. 1990. "The Corpse That Would Not Die: The Immigration Reform and Control Act of 1996." *Revue Européenne des Migrations Internationales* 6(1): 111–27.

Galbraith, John Kenneth. 1958. *The Affluent Society*. Boston: Houghton Mifflin.

Galster, George C. 1990a. "Racial Discrimination in Housing Markets During the 1980s: A Review of the Audit Evidence." *Journal of Planning Education and Research* 9(2): 165–75.

———. 1990b. "Racial Steering by Real Estate Agents: Mechanisms and Motives." *Review of Black Political Economy* 19: 39–63.

———. 1990c. "Racial Steering in Urban Housing Markets: A Review of the Audit Evidence." *Review of Black Political Economy* 18: 105–29.

Gamble, Clive. 1999. *The Paleolithic Societies of Europe*. Cambridge: Cambridge University Press.

Gieryn, Thomas F. 1983. "Boundary-Work and the Demarcation of Science from Non-science: Strains and Interests in Professional Ideologies of Scientists." *American Sociological Review* 48(6): 781–95.

Gilbert, Martin. 2001. *History of the Twentieth Century*. New York: Morrow.

Gilens. Martin. 1999. *Why Americans Hate Welfare*. Chicago: University of Chicago Press.

———. 2003. "How the Poor Became Black: The Racialization of American Poverty in the Mass Media." In Sanford F. Schram, Joe Soss, and Richard C. Fording, eds., *Race and the Politics of Welfare Reform*. Ann Arbor: University of Michigan Press.

———. 2005. "Inequality and Democratic Responsiveness." *Public Opinion Quarterly* 69(5): 778–96.

Gilliam, Franklin D., Jr., and Shanto Iyengar. 2000. "Prime Suspects: The Influence of Local Television News on the Viewing Public." *American Journal of Political Science* 44(3, July): 560–73.

Gittinger, Ted, and Allen Fisher. 2004. "LBJ Champions the Civil Rights Act of 1964, Part 2." *Prologue* 36(2, Summer). Available at National Archives, http://www.archives.gov/publications/prologue/2004/summer/civil-rights-act-2.html.

Glassner, Barry. 2000. *The Culture of Fear: Why Americans Are Afraid of the Wrong Things*. New York: Basic Books.

Glick, Peter, and Susan T. Fiske. 1996. "The Ambivalent Sexism Inventory: Differentiating Hostile and Benevolent Sexism." *Journal of Personality and Social Psychology* 70: 491–52.

———. 1997. "Hostile and Benevolent Sexism: Measuring Ambivalent Sexist Attitudes Toward Women." *Psychology of Women Quarterly* 21(1): 119–35.

———. 2001. "Ambivalent Sexism." In *Advances in Experimental Social Psychology*, vol. 33, edited by Mark P. Zanna. Thousand Oaks, Calif.: Academic Press.

Glick, Peter, et al. 2000. "Beyond Prejudice as Simple Antipathy: Hostile and Benevolent Sexism Across Cultures." *Journal of Personality and Social Psychology* 79(5): 763–75.

Golden, Daniel. 2003. "Family Ties: Preference for Alumni Children in College Admission Draws Fire." *Wall Street Journal,* January 15.

———. 2006. *The Price of Admission: How America's Ruling Class Buys Its*

Way into Elite Colleges—And Who Gets Left Outside the Gates. New York: Crown.

Goldin, Claudia. 1990. *Understanding the Gender Gap: An Economic History of American Women.* New York: Oxford University Press.

———. 2006. "The Rising (and Then Declining) Significance of Gender." In *The Declining Significance of Gender?* edited by Francine D. Blau, Mary C. Brinton, and David B. Grusky. New York: Russell Sage Foundation.

Goldin, Claudia, and Robert A. Margo. 1992. "The Great Compression: The U.S. Wage Structure at Midcentury." *Quarterly Journal of Economics* 107(1): 1–34.

Goldin, Claudia, and Cecilia Rouse. 2000. "Orchestrating Impartiality: The Impact of 'Blind' Auditions on Female Musicians." *American Economic Review* 90(4): 715–41.

Gomez, Christina. 2000. "The Continual Significance of Skin Color: An Exploratory Study of Latinos in the Northeast." *Hispanic Journal of the Behavioral Sciences* 22(1): 94–103.

Graham, Richard. 1990. *The Idea of Race in Latin America: 1870–1940.* Austin: University of Texas Press.

Granovetter, Mark S. 1973. "The Strength of Weak Ties." *American Journal of Sociology* 78(6): 1360–80.

———. 1974. *Getting a Job: A Study of Contacts and Careers.* Cambridge, Mass.: Harvard University Press.

———. 1985. "Economic Action and Social Structure: The Problem of Embeddedness." *American Journal of Sociology* 91(3): 481–510.

Grebler, Leo, Joan Moore, and Ralph Guzman. 1970. *The Mexican-American People: The Nation's Second Largest Minority.* New York: Free Press.

Grossman, James R. 1989. *Land of Hope: Chicago, Black Southerners, and the Great Migration.* Chicago: University of Chicago Press.

Gutierrez, David. 1995. *Walls and Mirrors: Mexican Americans, Mexican Immigrants, and the Politics of Ethnicity.* Berkeley: University of California Press.

Guzman, Betsy. 2001. *The Hispanic Population 2000: Census 2000 Brief.* Washington: U.S. Government Printing Office.

Hall, Peter A., and David Soskice. 2001. *Varieties of Capitalism: The Institutional Foundations of Comparative Advantage.* Oxford: Oxford University Press.

Hammett, Theodore M., Mary P. Harmon, and William Rhodes. 2002. "The Burden of Infectious Disease Among Inmates of and Releases from U.S. Correctional Facilities." *American Journal of Public Health* 92(11): 1789–94.

Harris, Lasana T., and Susan T. Fiske. 2006. "Dehumanizing the Lowest of the Low: Neuroimaging Responses to Extreme Outgroups." *Psychological Science* 17(10): 847–53.

Harrison, Bennett. 1995. *Lean and Mean: The Changing Landscape of Corporate Power in the Age of Flexibility*. New York: Basic Books.

Harrison, Bennett, and Barry Bluestone. 1988. *The Great U-Turn: Corporate Restructuring and the Polarizing of America*. New York: Basic Books.

Hart, John Mason. 1987. *Revolutionary Mexico: The Coming and Process of the Mexican Revolution*. Berkeley: University of California Press.

Harvey, David. 1991. *The Condition of Postmodernity: An Inquiry into the Origins of Cultural Change*. New York: Blackwell.

Hatton, Timothy J., and Jeffrey G. Williamson. 1998. *The Age of Mass Migration: Causes and Economic Impact*. Oxford: Oxford University Press.

Hayden, Brian, Michael Deal, Aubrey Cannon, and Joanna Casey. 1986. "Ecological Determinants of Women's Status Among Hunter-Gatherers." *Human Evolution* 1(5): 449–74.

Heckman, James J., and Brook S. Payner. 1989. "Determining the Impact of Federal Antidiscrimination Policy on the Economic Status of Blacks: A Study of South Carolina." *American Economic Review* 79(1): 138–77.

Henry, Sally M. 2006. *The New Bankruptcy Code*. Washington, D.C.: National Bar Association.

Herivel, Tara, and Paul Wright. 2003. *Prison Nation: The Warehousing of America's Poor*. New York: Routledge.

Heyman, Josiah M. 1995. "Putting Power in the Anthropology of Bureaucracy: The Immigration and Naturalization Service at the Mexico-United States Border." *Current Anthropology* 36(2): 261–87.

Higginbotham, A. Leon. 1980. *In the Matter of Color: The Colonial Period*. New York: Oxford University Press.

———. 1996. *Shades of Freedom: Racial Politics and Presumptions of the American Legal Process*. New York: Oxford University Press.

Higham, John. 1955. *Strangers in the Land: Patterns of American Nativism, 1860–1925*. New Brunswick, N.J.: Rutgers University Press.

Hirsch, Arnold R. 1983. *Making the Second Ghetto: Race and Housing in Chicago, 1940–1960*. Cambridge: Cambridge University Press.

Hochschild, Jennifer L. 1995. *Facing Up to the American Dream: Race, Class, and the Soul of the Nation*. Princeton, N.J.: Princeton University Press.

Hoefer, Michael, Nancy Rytina, and Christopher Campbell. 2006. "Estimates of the Unauthorized Immigrant Population Residing in the United States: January 2005." *Population Estimates* (August). Washington: Department of Homeland Security, Office of Immigration Statistics.

Hoffman, Abraham. 1974. *Unwanted Mexican Americans in the Great Depres-*

sion: Repatriation Pressures, 1929–1939. Tucson: University of Arizona Press.

Holtzman, Linda. 2001. *Media Messages: What Film, Television, and Popular Music Teach Us About Race, Class, Gender, and Sexual Orientation*. New York: M. E. Sharpe.

Holzer, Harry J. 1996. *What Employers Want: Job Prospects for Less-Educated Workers*. New York: Russell Sage Foundation.

———. 2001. "Racial Differences in Labor Market Outcomes Among Men." In *America Becoming: Racial Trends and Their Consequences*, vol. 2, edited by Neil Smelser, William Julius Wilson, and Faith Mitchell. Washington, D.C.: National Academies Press.

Holzer, Harry J., Stephen Raphael, and Michael A. Stoll. 2004. "Will Employers Hire Former Offenders? Employer Preferences, Background Checks, and Their Determinants." In *Imprisoning America: The Social Effects of Mass Incarceration*, edited by Mary Pattillo, David Weiman, and Bruce Western. New York: Russell Sage Foundation.

Howell, Cameron, and Sarah E. Turner. 2004. "Legacies in Black and White: The Racial Composition of the Legacy Pool." *Research in Higher Education* 45(4): 325–51.

Hula, Richard D. 1981. "Public Needs and Private Investment: The Case of Home Credit." *Social Science Quarterly* 62: 685–703.

———. 1982. "The Allocation of House Credit: Market Versus Nonmarket Factors." *Journal of Urban Affairs* 6: 151–65.

Human Rights Watch. 1991. *Prison Conditions in the United States: A Human Rights Watch Report*. Washington, D.C.: Human Rights Watch.

Huntington, Samuel P. 2004. "The Hispanic Challenge." *Foreign Policy* 153 (March–April): 30–45.

Hurwitz, Jonathan M., and Mark A. Peffley. 1997. "Public Perceptions of Race and Crime: The Role of Racial Stereotypes." *American Journal of Political Science* 41(2): 375–401.

Iceland, John, and Rima Wilkes. 2006. "Does Socioeconomic Status Matter? Race, Class, and Residential Segregation." *Social Problems* 53(2, May): 248–73.

Ignatiev, Noel. 1996. *How the Irish Became White*. New York: Routledge.

Ivins, Molly, and Lou Dubose. 2003. *Bushwhacked: Life in George W. Bush's America*. New York: Random House.

Jackman, Mary R. 1994. *The Velvet Glove: Paternalism and Conflict in Gender, Class, and Race Relations*. Berkeley: University of California Press.

Jackson, Kenneth T. 1985. *Crabgrass Frontier: The Suburbanization of the United States*. New York: Oxford University Press.

Jacobs, David, and Jason T. Carmichael. 2001. "The Politics of Punishment Across Time and Space: A Pooled Time-Series Analysis of Imprisonment Rates." *Social Forces* 80(1): 61–91.

Jacobs, David, and Ronald E. Helms. 1996. "Toward a Political Model of Incarceration: A Time-Series Examination of Multiple Explanations for Prison Admission Rates." *American Journal of Sociology* 102(2): 323–57.

Jacobs, Jerry A. 1996. "Gender Inequality in Higher Education." *Annual Review of Sociology* 22: 153–85.

———. 2001. "Evolving Patterns of Sex Segregation." In *Sourcebook of Labor Markets: Evolving Structures and Processes*, edited by Ivar Berg and Arne L. Kalleberg. New York: Plenum.

Jacobson, Matthew F. 1999. *Whiteness of a Different Color: European Immigrants and the Alchemy of Race*. Cambridge, Mass.: Harvard University Press.

Jacobson-Hardy, Michael. 1998. *Behind the Razor Wire: Portrait of a Contemporary American Prison System*. New York: New York University Press.

Jaffe, Abraham J., Ruth M. Cullen, and Thomas D. Boswell.1980. *The Changing Demography of Spanish Americans*. New York: Academic Press.

James, Harold. 2001. *The End of Globalization: Lessons from the Great Depression*. Cambridge, Mass.: Harvard University Press.

Johnson, Elizabeth I., and Jane Waldfogel. 2004. "Children of Incarcerated Parents: Multiple Risks and Children's Living Arrangements." In *Imprisoning America: The Social Effects of Mass Incarceration*, edited by Mary Pattillo, David Weiman, and Bruce Western. New York: Russell Sage Foundation.

Johnson, Rucker C., and Steven Raphael. 2005. "The Effects of Male Incarceration Dynamics on AIDS Infection Rates Among African-American Women and Men." Working paper. Berkeley: University of California, Goldman School of Public Policy Studies.

Johnston, Lloyd D., P. M. O'Malley, J. G. Bachman, and J. E. Schulenberg. 2004. *Monitoring the Future Survey Results on Drug Use 1975–2003*. Bethesda, Md.: National Institute on Drug Abuse.

Jones, Edward E., and Richard E. Nisbett. 1972. "The Actor and the Observer: Divergent Perceptions of the Causes of Behavior." In *Attribution: Perceiving the Causes of Behavior*, edited by Edward E. Jones, S. Valin, and B. Weiner. Morristown, N.J.: General Learning Press.

Kahneman, Daniel. 2003. "Maps of Bounded Rationality: Psychology for Behavioral Economics." *American Economic Review* 93(5): 1449–75.

Kahneman, Daniel, and Amos Tversky. 1973. "On the Psychology of Prediction." *Psychological Review* 80: 237–5l.

————. 1979. "Prospect Theory: An Analysis of Decisions Under Risk." *Econometrica* 47(2): 313–27.

————. 2000. *Choices, Values, and Frames.* New York: Cambridge University Press.

Kalleberg, Arne L., Michael Wallace, and Lawrence R. Raffalovich. 1984. "Accounting for Labor's Share: Class and Income Distribution in the Printing Industry." *Industrial and Labor Relations Review* 37(3): 486–42.

Kamen, Al. 1990. "Central America Is No Longer the Central Issue for Americans." *Austin American Statesman*, October 21.

Karabel, Jerome. 2005. *The Chosen: The Hidden History of Admission and Exclusion at Harvard, Yale, and Princeton.* New York: Houghton Mifflin.

Karlin, Carolyn A., Paula England, and Mary Richardson. 2002. "Why Do 'Women's Jobs' Have Low Pay for Their Educational Level?" *Gender Issues* 20: 3–22.

Kasarda, John D. 1995. "Industrial Restructuring and the Changing Location of Jobs." In *State of the Union: America in the 1990s,* edited by Reynolds Farley. New York: Russell Sage Foundation.

Katz, Michel B. 1986. *In the Shadow of the Poorhouse: A Social History of Welfare in America.* New York: Basic Books.

Katznelson, Ira. 2005. *When Affirmative Action Was White: An Untold History of Racial Inequality in Twentieth-Century America.* New York: Norton.

Kawachi, Ichiro, and Bruce P. Kennedy. 2002. *The Health of Nations: Why Inequality Is Harmful to Your Health.* New York: New Press.

Keister, Lisa A. 2000. *Wealth in America: Trends in Inequality.* New York: Cambridge University Press.

Kelly, Robert L. 1995. *The Foraging Spectrum: Diversity in Hunter-Gatherer Lifeways.* Washington, D.C.: Smithsonian Institution Press.

Kennedy, Robert F., Jr. 2006. "Was the 2004 Election Stolen?" *Rolling Stone* (July). Available at: http://www.rollingstone.com/news/story/10432334/was_the_2004_election_stolen.

Kenwood, A. George, and Alan L. Lougheed. 1999. *The Growth of the International Economy 1820–2000.* London: Routledge.

Kenworthy, Lane. 2004. *Egalitarian Capitalism: Jobs, Incomes, and Growth in Affluent Countries.* New York: Russell Sage Foundation.

Kilbourne, Barbara, Paula England, George Farkas, Kurt Beron, and Dorothea Weir. 1994. "Returns to Skills, Compensating Differentials, and Gender Bias: Effects of Occupational Characteristics on the Wages of White Women and Men." *American Journal of Sociology* 100(3): 689–719.

Kinder, Donald R., and David O. Sears. 1981. "Prejudice and Politics: Symbolic Racism Versus Threats to the Good Life." *Journal of Personality and Social Psychology* 40: 414–31.

Kirschenman, Joleen, and Kathryn M. Neckerman. 1991. "'We'd Love to Hire Them, but …': The Meaning of Race for Employers." In *The Urban Underclass*, edited by Christopher Jencks and Paul E. Peterson. Washington, D.C.: Brookings Institution Press.

Kitano, Harry H. L. 1969. *Japanese Americans: The Evolution of a Subculture*. Englewood Cliffs, N.J.: Prentice-Hall.

Klein, Robert W. 1995. *The Impact of Loss Costs on Homeowners' Insurance Markets*. Kansas City, Mo.: National Association of Insurance Commissioners.

———. 1997. "Availability and Unaffordability in Urban Homeowners' Insurance Markets." In *Insurance Redlining: Disinvestment, Reinvestment, and the Evolving Role of Financial Institutions*, edited by Gregory D. Squires. Washington, D.C.: Urban Institute Press.

Kluegel, James R., and Lawrence D. Bobo. 2001. "Perceived Group Discrimination and Policy Attitudes: The Sources and Consequences of the Race and Gender Gaps." In *Urban Inequality: Evidence from Four Cities*, edited by Alice O'Connor, Chris Tilly, and Lawrence D. Bobo. New York: Russell Sage Foundation.

Kluegel, James R., and Eliot R. Smith. 1986. *Beliefs About Inequality*. Chicago: Aldine de Gruyter.

Kohut, Andrew, and Roberto Suro. 2006. *No Consensus on Immigration Quandary or Proposed Fixes*. Washington, D.C.: Pew Research Center for the People and the Press and Pew Hispanic Center.

Konner, Melvin. 2002. *The Tangled Wing: Biological Constraints on the Human Spirit*. New York: Henry Holt.

Kossoudji, Sherrie A. 1992. "Playing Cat and Mouse at the U.S.-Mexican Border." *Demography* 29(2): 159–80.

Kozol, Jonathan. 1991. *Savage Inequalities: Children in America's Schools*. New York: Crown.

———. 2005. *The Shame of the Nation: The Restoration of Apartheid Schooling in America*. New York: Crown.

Krebs, Christopher P. 2002. "High-Risk HIV Transmission Behavior in Prison and the Prison Subculture." *The Prison Journal* 82(1): 19–49.

Krivo, Lauren J., and Robert L. Kaufman. 1999. "How Low Can It Go? Declining Black-White Segregation in a Multiethnic Context." *Demography* 36(1): 93–109.

Krivo, Lauren J., and Ruth D. Peterson. 1996. "Extremely Disadvantaged Neighborhoods and Urban Crime." *Social Forces* 75(2): 619–48.

References

Krugman, Paul. 2003. *The Great Unraveling: Losing Our Way in the New Century*. New York: Norton.

Kuhn, Peter, and Arthur Sweetman. 1998. "Wage Loss Following Displacement: The Role of Union Coverage." *Industrial and Labor Relations Review* 51(3): 384–99.

Kuper, Adam. 1999. *Culture: The Anthropologists' Account*. Cambridge, Mass.: Harvard University Press.

Labov, William. 1972. *Language in the Inner City: Studies in the Black English Vernacular*. Philadelphia: University of Pennsylvania Press.

Labov, William, and Wendell A. Harris. 1986. "De Facto Segregation of Black and White Vernaculars," in David Sankoff, ed., *Current Issues in Linguistic Theory 53: Diversity and Diachrony*. Amsterdam: John Benjamins Publishing.

Lakoff, George. 2002. *Moral Politics : How Liberals and Conservatives Think*. Chicago: University of Chicago Press.

Lakoff, George, and Mark Johnson. 2003. *Metaphors We Live By*. Chicago: University of Chicago Press.

Lamont, Michèle. 2000. *The Dignity of Working Men: Morality and the Boundaries of Race, Class, and Immigration*. Cambridge, Mass.: Harvard University Press.

Lamont, Michèle, and Vireg Molnar. 2002. "The Study of Boundaries in the Social Sciences." *Annual Review of Sociology* 28: 167–95.

Landry, Bart. 1987. *The New Black Middle Class*. Berkeley: University of California Press.

LeDoux, Joseph. 1996. *The Emotional Brain: The Mysterious Underpinnings of Emotional Life*. New York: Simon & Schuster.

———. 2002. *Synaptic Self: How Our Brains Become Who We Are*. New York: Viking.

Lee, Sharon M., and Barry Edmonston. 2005. "New Marriages, New Families: U.S. Racial and Hispanic Intermarriage." *Population Bulletin* 60(2). Washington, D.C.: Population Reference Bureau.

Lee, Tiane L., and Susan T. Fiske. 2006. "Not an Out-group, Not Yet an In-group: Immigrants in the Stereotype Content Model." *International Journal of Intercultural Relations* 30(6, November): 751–68.

Legomsky, Stephen H. 2000. "Fear and Loathing in Congress and the Courts: Immigration and Judicial Review." *Texas Law Review* 78: 1612–20.

Leicht, Kevin T. 1989. "On the Estimation of Union Treat Effects." *American Sociological Review* 54(6): 1035–47.

Lemann, Nicholas. 1991. *The Promised Land: The Great Black Migration and How It Changed America.* New York: Knopf.

Leslie, Lisa M., V. S. Constantine, and Susan T. Fiske. 2006. "The Princeton Quartet: How Are Stereotypes Changing?" Unpublished paper. Princeton, N.J.: Princeton University, Department of Psychology.

Lester, Paul M., and Susan D. Ross. 2003. *Images That Injure: Pictorial Stereotypes in the Media.* New York: Praeger.

Levitan, Sar A., and Karen A. Cleary. 1973. *Old Wars Remain Unfinished: The Veterans Benefits System.* Baltimore: Johns Hopkins University Press.

Levy, Frank. 1998. *The New Dollars and Dreams: American Incomes and Economic Change.* New York: Russell Sage Foundation.

Lieberman, Robert. 1998. *Shifting the Color Line: Race and the American Welfare State.* Cambridge, Mass.: Harvard University Press.

Lieberson, Stanley. 1985. *Making It Count: The Improvement of Social Research and Theory.* Berkeley: University of California Press.

Lieberson, Stanley, and Mary C. Waters. 1988. *From Many Strands: Ethnic and Racial Groups in Contemporary America.* New York: Russell Sage Foundation.

Lind, Michael. 2002. *Made in Texas: George W. Bush and the Southern Takeover of American Politics.* New York: Basic Books.

Lomnitz, Larissa. 1975. *Cómo Sobreviven los Marginados.* México, DF: Siglo Veintiuno.

Lomnitz, Larissa, and Marisol Pérez-Lizaur. 1987. *A Mexican Elite Family, 1820–1980: Kinship, Class, and Culture.* Princeton, N.J.: Princeton University Press.

Lowell, B. Lindsay, and Zhongren Jing. 1994. "Unauthorized Workers and Immigration Reform: What Can We Ascertain from Employers?" *International Migration Review* 28(3): 427–48.

Lowell, B. Lindsay, Jay Teachman, and Zhongren Jing. 1995. "Unintended Consequences of Immigration Reform: Discrimination and Hispanic Employment." *Demography* 32(4): 617–28.

Lynch, William H. 1997. "NAACP v. American Family." In *Insurance Redlining: Disinvestment, Reinvestment, and the Evolving Role of Financial Institutions*, edited by Gregory D. Squires. Washington, D.C.: Urban Institute Press.

Lynch, James P., and William J. Sabol. 2004. "Effects of Incarceration on Informal Control in Communities." In *Imprisoning America: The Social Effects of Mass Incarceration*, edited by Mary Pattillo, David Weiman, and Bruce Western. New York: Russell Sage Foundation.

References

MacLachlan, Colin M., and William H. Beezley. 2003. *El Gran Pueblo: A History of Greater Mexico*, 3rd ed. New York: Prentice-Hall.

Macmillan, Ross. 2001. "Violence and the Life Course: The Consequences of Victimization for Personal and Social Development." *Annual Review of Sociology* 27: 1–22.

Macoby, Eleanor E. 1998. *The Two Sexes: Growing Up, Coming Apart.* Cambridge, Mass.: Harvard University Press.

Macrae, C. Neil, and Galen V. Bodenhausen. 2000. "Social Cognition: Thinking Categorically About Others." *Annual Review of Psychology* 51: 93–120.

Maddison, Angus. 2001. *The World Economy: Historical Statistics.* Paris: Organization for Economic Cooperation and Development.

Maddrick, Jeffrey. 1995. *The End of Affluence: The Causes and Consequences of America's Economic Dilemma.* New York: Random House.

Maki, Mitchell T., Harry M. Kitano, and S. Megan Berthold. 1999. *Achieving the Impossible Dream: How Japanese Americans Obtained Redress.* Urbana: University of Illinois Press.

Manning, Robert D. 2000. *Credit Card Nation: The Consequences of America's Addiction to Credit.* New York: Basic Books.

Marable, Manning. 1984. *Race, Reform, and Rebellion: The Second Reconstruction in Black America, 1945–1982.* Oxford: University of Mississippi Press.

Mare, Robert D. 1991. "Five Decades of Educational Assortative Mating." *American Sociological Review* 56(1): 15–32.

———. 1996. "Demography and the Evolution of Educational Inequality." In *Social Differentiation and Social Inequality: Theoretical and Empirical Inquiries: Essays in Honor of John C. Pock*, edited by James Baron, David B. Grusky, and Donald Treiman. Boulder, Colo.: Westview.

Marks, Carole. 1989. *Farewell, We're Good and Gone: The Great Black Migration.* Bloomington: Indiana University Press.

Martin, Philip L. 1996. *Promises to Keep: Collective Bargaining in California Agriculture.* Ames, I.A.: Iowa State University Press.

Martin, Philip L., and J. Edward Taylor. 1991. "Immigration Reform and Farm Labor Contracting in California." In *The Paper Curtain: Employer Sanctions' Implementation, Impact, and Reform*, edited by Michael Fix. Washington, D.C.: Urban Institute Press.

Martin, Steven P. 2004. "Growing Evidence for a Divorce Divide? Education and Marital Dissolution Rates in the United States Since the 1970s." Working Papers: Series on Social Dimensions of Inequality. New York: Russell Sage Foundation.

Mason, Patrick L. 2004. "Annual Income, Hourly Wages, and Identity

Among Mexican-Americans and Other Latinos." *Industrial Relations* 43(4): 817–26.

Massey, Douglas S. 1987. "Do Undocumented Migrants Earn Lower Wages Than Legal Immigrants? New Evidence from Mexico." *International Migration Review* 21(2): 236–74.

———. 1990. "American Apartheid: Segregation and the Making of the Underclass." *American Journal of Sociology* 96(2): 329–57.

———. 1996. "The Age of Extremes: Concentrated Affluence and Poverty in the Twenty-first Century." *Demography* 33(4): 395–412.

———. 2001. "Segregation and Violent Crime in Urban America." In *Problem of the Century: Racial Stratification in the United States*, edited by Elijah Anderson and Douglas S. Massey. New York: Russell Sage Foundation.

———. 2003. "The American Side of the Bargain." In *Reinventing the Melting Pot: The New Immigrants and What It Means to Be American*, edited by Tamar Jacoby. New York: Basic Books.

———. 2004. "Segregation and Stratification: A Biosocial Perspective." *DuBois Review: Social Science Research on Race* 1(1): 1–19.

———. 2005a. *Strangers in a Strange Land: Humans in an Urbanizing World.* New York: Norton.

———. 2005b. *Return of the L-Word: A Liberal Vision for the New Century.* Princeton, N.J.: Princeton University Press.

———. 2005c. "Racial Discrimination in Housing: A Moving Target." *Social Problems* 52(2): 148–51.

———. 2005d. "Backfire at the Border: Why Enforcement Without Legalization Cannot Stop Illegal Immigration." *Trade Policy Analyses* 29. Washington, D.C.: Cato Institute, Center for Trade Policy Studies.

Massey, Douglas S., Rafael Alarcón, Jorge Durand, and Humberto González. 1987. *Return to Aztlan: The Social Process of International Migration from Western Mexico.* Berkeley: University of California Press.

Massey, Douglas S., and Katherine Bartley. 2005. "The Changing Legal Status Distribution of Immigrants: A Caution." *International Migration Review* 39(2): 469–84.

Massey, Douglas S., and Brooks Bitterman. 1985. "Explaining the Paradox of Puerto Rican Segregation." *Social Forces* 64(2): 306–31.

Massey, Douglas S., and Rebecca M. Blank. Forthcoming. "Assessing Racial Discrimination: Methods and Measures." In *Fairness in the Housing Market*, edited by John Goering. Lanham, Md.: Rowman and Littlefield.

Massey, Douglas S., Gretchen A. Condran, and Nancy A. Denton. 1987. "The Effect of Residential Segregation on Black Social and Economic Well-being." *Social Forces* 66(1): 29–56.

References

Massey, Douglas S., and Nancy A. Denton. 1988. "The Dimensions of Residential Segregation." *Social Forces* 67(2): 281–315.

———. 1989. "Hypersegregation in U.S. Metropolitan Areas: Black and Hispanic Segregation Along Five Dimensions." *Demography* 26(3): 373–93.

———. 1993. *American Apartheid: Segregation and the Making of the Underclass.* Cambridge, Mass.: Harvard University Press.

Massey, Douglas S., Katharine M. Donato, and Zai Liang. 1990. "Effects of the Immigration Reform and Control Act of 1986: Preliminary Data from Mexico." In *Undocumented Migration to the United States: IRCA and the Experience of the 1980s,* edited by Frank D. Bean, Barry Edmonston, and Jeffrey S. Passel. Washington, D.C.: Urban Institute Press.

Massey, Douglas S., Jorge Durand, and Nolan J. Malone. 2002. *Beyond Smoke and Mirrors: Mexican Immigration in an Era of Economic Integration.* New York: Russell Sage Foundation.

Massey, Douglas S., and Mitchell E. Eggers. 1990. "The Ecology of Inequality: Minorities and the Concentration of Poverty 1970–1980." *American Journal of Sociology* 95(5): 1153–88.

———. 1993. "The Spatial Concentration of Affluence and Poverty During the 1970s." *Urban Affairs Quarterly* 29(2): 299–315.

Massey, Douglas S., and Kristin E. Espinosa. 1997. "What's Driving Mexico-U.S. Migration? A Theoretical, Empirical, and Policy Analysis." *American Journal of Sociology* 102(4): 939–99.

Massey, Douglas S., and Mary J. Fischer. 1999. "Does Rising Income Bring Integration? New Results for Blacks, Hispanics, and Asians in 1990." *Social Science Research* 28(3): 316–26.

———. 2000. "How Segregation Concentrates Poverty." *Ethnic and Racial Studies* 23(4): 670–91.

———. 2003. "The Geography of Inequality in the United States, 1950–2000." In *Brookings-Wharton Papers on Urban Affairs 2003,* edited by William G. Gale and Janet Rothenberg Pack. Washington, D.C.: Brookings Institution Press.

Massey, Douglas S., and Andrew B. Gross. 1991. "Explaining Trends in Residential Segregation 1970–1980." *Urban Affairs Quarterly* 27(1): 13–35.

Massey, Douglas S., Andrew B. Gross, and Mitchell E. Eggers. 1991. "Segregation, the Concentration of Poverty, and the Life Chances of Individuals." *Social Science Research* 20: 397–420.

Massey, Douglas S., and Garvey J. Lundy. 2001. "Use of Black English and Racial Discrimination in Urban Housing Markets: New Methods and Findings." *Urban Affairs Review* 36(March): 470–96.

Massey, Douglas S., and Margarita Mooney. Forthcoming. "The Effects of America's Three Affirmative Action Programs on Academic Performance." *Social Problems.*

Massey, Douglas S., Magaly Sanchez, and Jere R. Behrman. 2006. *Chronicle of a Myth Foretold: The Washington Consensus in Latin America.* Philadelphia: American Academy of Political and Social Science.

Massey, Douglas S., and Audrey Singer. 1995. "New Estimates of Undocumented Mexican Migration and the Probability of Apprehension." *Demography* 32(2): 203–11.

Mazón, Mauricio. 1984. *The Zoot-Suit Riots: The Psychology of Symbolic Annihilation.* Austin: University of Texas Press.

McCarty, Nolan, Keith T. Poole, and Howard Rosenthal. 2006. *Polarized America: The Dance of Ideology and Unequal Riches.* Cambridge, Mass.: MIT Press.

McConahay, J. B. 1983. "Modern Racism and Modern Discrimination: The Effects of Race, Racial Attitudes, and Context on Simulated Hiring Decisions." *Personality and Social Psychology Bulletin* 9(4): 551–58.

McLanahan, Sara. 2004. "Diverging Destinies: How Children Are Faring Under the Second Demographic Transition." *Demography* 41(4): 607–27.

McLanahan, Sara, and Gary D. Sandefur. 1994. *Growing Up with a Single Parent.* Cambridge, Mass.: Harvard University Press.

Metcalf, George R. 1988. *Fair Housing Comes of Age.* New York: Greenwood Press.

Miller, Mark Crispin. 2005. "None Dare Call It Stolen: Ohio, the Election, and America's Servile Press." *Harper's* (August). Available at: http://www.harpers.org/ExcerptNoneDare.html.

Mills, C. Wright. 1956. *The Power Elite.* New York: Oxford University Press.

Miringoff, Marc, and Marque-Luisa Miringoff. 1999. *The Social Health of the Nation: How America Is Really Doing.* New York: Oxford University Press.

Montalvo, Frank F., and Edward Codina. 2001. "Skin Color and Latinos in the United States." *Ethnicities* 1: 321–41.

Montgomery, Mark R. Richard Stren, Barney Cohen, and Holly E. Reed. 2003. *Cities Transformed: Demographic Change and its Implications in the Developing World.* Washington, D.C.: National Academies Press.

Moore, Nina M. 2000. *Governing Race: Policy, Process, and the Politics of Race.* New York: Praeger.

Morales, Patricia. 1982. *Indocumentados Mexicanos.* México, DF: Editorial Grijalvo.

Moss, Philip, and Chris Tilly. 2001. *Stories Employers Tell: Race, Skill, and Hiring in America.* New York: Russell Sage Foundation.

289

References

Munnell, Alicia H., Lynn E. Browne, James McEnearney, and Geoffrey M. B. Tootell. 1996. "Mortgage Lending in Boston: Interpreting HMDA Data." *American Economic Review* 86(1): 25–53.

Myrdal, Gunnar. 1944. *An American Dilemma: The Negro Problem and Modern Democracy*, vol. 1. New York: Harper & Row.

National Fair Housing Alliance. 2002. *2002 Fair Housing Trends Report*. Washington, D.C.: National Fair Housing Alliance.

Neubeck, Kenneth J., and Noel A. Cazenave. 2001. *Welfare Racism: Playing the Race Card Against America's Poor*. New York: Routledge.

Neumark, David, and Michael L. Wachter. 1995. "Union Effects on Nonunion Wages: Evidence from Panel Data on Industries and Cities." *Industrial and Labor Relations Review* 49(1): 20–38.

Nevins, Joseph. 2001. *Operation Gatekeeper: The Rise of the "Illegal Alien" and the Making of the U.S.-Mexico Boundary*. New York: Routledge.

Newell, Allen, and Herbert A. Simon. 1972. *Human Problem Solving*. Englewood Cliffs, N.J.: Prentice-Hall.

Nurse, Anne M. 2004. "Returning to Strangers: Newly Paroled Young Fathers and Their Children." In *Imprisoning America: The Social Effects of Mass Incarceration*, edited by Mary Pattillo, David Weiman, and Bruce Western. New York: Russell Sage Foundation.

Obregón Pagán, Eduardo. 2003. *Murder at the Sleepy Lagoon: Zoot Suits, Race, and Riot in Wartime L.A.* Chapel Hill: University of North Carolina Press.

Ogbu, John U. 1978. *Minority Education and Caste: The American System in Cross-cultural Perspective*. New York: Academic Press.

———. 1991. "Minority Responses and School Experiences." *Journal of Psychohistory* 18: 433–56.

Ogburn, William F. 1922. *Social Change with Respect to Culture and Original Nature*. Chicago: B. W. Huebsch.

Orfield, Myron. 2002. *American Metropolitics: The New Suburban Reality*. Washington, D.C.: Brookings Institution Press.

Orfield, Gary, and Susan E. Eaton. 1996. *Dismantling Desegregation: The Quiet Reversal of Brown v. Board of Education*. New York: New Press.

O'Rourke, Kevin H., and Jeffrey G. Williamson. 1999. *Globalization and History: The Evolution of a Nineteenth-Century Atlantic Economy*. Cambridge, Mass.: MIT Press.

Owram, Doug. 1997. *Born at the Right Time: A History of the Baby Boom Generation*. Toronto: University of Toronto Press.

Packard, Gerald M. 2002. *American Nightmare: The History of Jim Crow*. New York: St. Martin's Press.

Pager, Devah. 2003. "The Mark of a Criminal Record." *American Journal of Sociology* 108(5): 937–75.

Pager, Devah, and Lincoln Quillian. 2005. "Walking the Talk: What Employers Say Versus What They Do." *American Sociological Review* 70(3): 355–80.

Pager, Devah, and Bruce Western. 2006. "Race at Work: Realities of Race and Criminal Record in the New York City Job Market." Paper presented to the New York City Commission on Human Rights "Conference on the Realities of Race and Criminal Record in the New York City Job Market." New York (December 9, 2005).

Palast, Greg. 2002. *The Best Democracy Money Can Buy: An Investigative Reporter Exposes the Truth About Globalization, Corporate Cons, and High-Finance Fraudsters.* New York: Pluto Press.

Panksepp, Jaak. 1998. *Affective Neuroscience: The Foundations of Human and Animal Emotions.* New York: Oxford University Press.

Passel, Jeffrey, and Karen A. Woodrow. 1987. "Change in the Undocumented Alien Population in the United States, 1979–1983." *International Migration Review* 21(4): 1304–34.

Pattillo, Mary, David Weiman, and Bruce Western, eds. 2004. *Imprisoning America: The Social Effects of Mass Incarceration.* New York: Russell Sage Foundation.

Pearce, Diana M. 1979. "Gatekeepers and Homeseekers: Institutional Patterns in Racial Steering." *Social Problems* 26(3): 325–42.

Pels, Rebecca B. 1995. "The Pressures of PATCO: Strikes and Stress in the 1980s." *Essays in History* 37. Corcoran Department of History at the University of Virginia. Available at: http://etext.lib.virginia.edu/journals/EH/EH37/Pels.html.

Perlmutter, Phillip. 1999. *Legacy of Hate: A Short History of Ethnic, Religious, and Racial Prejudice in America.* New York: M. E. Sharp.

Petersen, William E. 1971. *Japanese Americans: Oppression and Success.* New York: Random House.

Pettigrew, Thomas. 1979. "Racial Change and Social Policy." *Annals of the American Academy of Political and Social Science* 441: 114–31.

Phillips, Julie A., and Douglas S. Massey. 1999. "The New Labor Market: Immigrants and Wages After IRCA." *Demography* 36(2): 233–46.

Phillips, Kevin. 1969. *The Coming Republican Majority.* New York: Arlington.

———. 2002. *Wealth and Democracy: A Political History of the American Rich.* New York: Broadway Books.

Piketty, Thomas, and Emmanuel Saez. 2003. "Income Inequality in the

United States, 1913–1998." *Quarterly Journal of Economics* 118(1): 2003, 1–39. Data updated through 1994 at: http://elsa.berkeley.edu/~saez/TabFig2004.xls.

Piven, Frances Fox, and Richard A. Cloward. 1977. *Poor People's Movements: Why They Succeed, How They Fail.* New York: Pantheon.

Pol, Louis G., Rebecca F. Guy, Randy E. Ryker, and William C. S. Chan. 1981. "Anticipated Discrimination in the Home Lending Market." *Housing and Society* 8: 3–11.

Portes, Alejandro, and Min Zhou. 1993. "The New Second Generation: Segmented Assimilation and Its Variants." *Annals of the American Academy of Political and Social Science* 530: 74–96.

Preston, Samuel H. 1984. "Children and the Elderly: Divergent Paths for America's Dependents." *Demography* 21(4): 435–57.

Public Campaign. 2003. "The Road to Clean Elections" (documentary). See Public Campaign website: http://www.publicampaign.org/publications/index.htm.

Purnell, Thomas, William Idsardi, and John Baugh. 1999. "Perceptual and Phonetic Experiments on American English Dialect Identification." *Journal of Language and Social Psychology* 18(1): 10–30.

Purnick, Joyce. 2006. "Stricter Voting Laws Carve Latest Partisan Divide." *New York Times*, September 26.

Quadagno, Jill. 1994. *The Color of Welfare: How Racism Undermined the War on Poverty.* New York: Oxford University Press.

———. 2005. *One Nation, Uninsured: Why the U.S. Has No National Health Insurance.* New York: Oxford University Press.

Quillian, Lincoln, and Devah Pager. 2001. "Black Neighbors, Higher Crime? The Role of Racial Stereotypes in Evaluations of Neighborhood Crime." *American Journal of Sociology* 107(3): 717–67.

Quint, Michael. 1991. "Racial Disparity in Mortgages Shown in U.S. Data." *New York Times*, November 14.

Radford, Benjamin. 2003. *Media Mythmakers: How Journalists, Activists, and Advertisers Mislead Us.* Amherst, N.Y.: Prometheus Books.

Reisler, Mark. 1976. *By the Sweat of Their Brow: Mexican Immigrant Labor in the United States 1900–1940.* Westport, Conn.: Greenwood Press.

Relethford, John H., Michael P. Stern, Sharon P. Gaskill, and Helen P. Hazuda. 1983. "Social Class, Admixture, and Skin Color Variation in Mexican Americans and Anglo-Americans Living in San Antonio, Texas." *American Journal of Physical Anthropology* 61: 97–102.

Reskin, Barbara F. 2003. "Including Mechanisms in Our Models of Ascriptive Inequality." *American Sociological Review* 68(1): 1–21.

Ricardo, David. 1996. *Principles of Political Economy and Taxation*. New York: Prometheus Books.

Richeson, Jennifer A., and Sophie Trawalter. 2005. "Why Do Interracial Interactions Impair Executive Function? A Resource Depletion Account?" *Journal of Personality and Social Psychology* 88: 934–97.

Ridgeway, Cecilia L. 1992. *Gender, Interaction, and Inequality*. New York: Springer-Verlag.

———. 2006. "Gender as an Organizing Force in Social Relations: Implications for the Future of Inequality." In *The Declining Significance of Gender?* edited by Francine D. Blau, Mary C. Brinton, and David B. Grusky. New York: Russell Sage Foundation.

Ridley, Stanley E., James A. Bayton, and Janice H. Outtz. 1989. "Taxi Service in the District of Columbia: Is It Influenced by Patron's Race and Destination?" Paper prepared for the Washington, D.C., Lawyers' Committee for Civil Rights Under the Law (June).

Rifkin, Jeremy. 1995. *The End of Work: The Decline of the Global Labor Force and the Dawn of the Postmarket Era*. New York: Putnam.

Riosmena, Fernando. 2004. "Return Versus Settlement Among Undocumented Mexican Migrants, 1980 to 1996." In *Crossing the Border: Research from the Mexican Migration Project*, edited by Jorge Durand and Douglas S. Massey. New York: Russell Sage Foundation.

Ritter, Richard J. 1997. "Racial Justice and the Role of the U.S. Department of Justice in Combating Insurance Redlining." In *Insurance Redlining: Disinvestment, Reinvestment, and the Evolving Role of Financial Institutions*, edited by Gregory D. Squires. Washington, D.C.: Urban Institute Press.

Roach, Jack L., and Janet K. Roach. 1978. "Mobilizing the Poor: Road to a Dead End." *Social Problems* 26: 160-71.

Robinson, Chris. 1989. "The Joint Determination of Union Status and Union Wage Effects." *Journal of Political Economy* 97(3): 639–67.

Rodriguez, Clara. 1991. "The Effect of Race on Puerto Rican Wages." In *Hispanics in the Labor Force*, edited by Edwin Melendez, Clara Rodriguez, and Janis B. Figueroa. New York: Plenum Press.

Roediger, David R. 1991. *The Wages of Whiteness: Race and the Making of the American Working Class*. New York: Verso Books.

Rome, Dennis. 2004. *Black Demons: The Media's Depiction of the African American Male Criminal Stereotype*. New York: Praeger.

Rosenfeld, Jake. 2006. "Desperate Measures: Strikes and Wages in Post-Accord America." *Social Forces* 85(1): 235–66.

———. Forthcoming. "Widening the Gap: The Effect of Declining Unionization on Managerial and Worker Pay, 1983–2000." *Research in Social Stratification and Mobility.*

Ross, Lee R., D. Greene, and P. House. 1977. "The False Consensus Effect: An Egocentric Bias in Social Perception and Attribution Processes." *Journal of Experimental Social Psychology* 13: 279–301.

Ross, Stephen L., and Margery A. Turner. 2004. "Other Things Being Equal: A Paired Testing Study of Discrimination in Mortgage Lending." *Journal of Urban Economics* 55: 278–97.

Ross, Stephen L., and John Yinger. 2002. *The Color of Credit: Mortgage Discrimination, Research Methodology, and Fair-Lending Enforcement.* Cambridge, Mass.: MIT Press.

Royce, Edward Cary. 1993. *The Origins of Southern Sharecropping.* Philadelphia: Temple University Press.

Saltman, Juliet. 1979. "Housing Discrimination: Policy Research, Methods, and Results." *Annals of the American Academy of Political and Social Science* 441: 186–96.

Sampson, Robert J., Jeffrey Morenoff, and Felton Earls. 1999. "Beyond Social Capital: Spatial Dynamics of Collective Efficacy for Children." *American Sociological Review* 64(5): 633–60.

Sampson, Robert J., Stephen Raudenbush, and Felton Earls. 1997. "Neighborhoods and Violent Crime: A Multilevel Study of Collective Efficacy." *Science* 277: 918–24.

Sanchez, George I. 1995. *Becoming Mexican American: Ethnicity, Culture, and Identity in Chicano Los Angeles, 1900–1945.* New York: Oxford University Press.

Sanday, Peggy R. 1981. *Female Power and Dominance: On the Origins of Sexual Inequality.* Pittsburgh: University of Pittsburgh Press.

Sanderson, Stephen K. 1999. *Social Transformations: A General Theory of Historical Development.* Lanham, Md.: Rowman and Littlefield.

Schaefer, Richard T. 2005. *Racial and Ethnic Groups*, 10th ed. Upper Saddle River, N.J.: Prentice-Hall.

Schlosser, Eric. 1998. "The Prison Industrial Complex." *Atlantic Monthly* (December): 51–57.

Scholz, John Karl, and Kara Levine. 2001. "The Evolution of Income Support Policy in Recent Decades." In *Understanding Poverty*, edited by Sheldon H. Danziger and Robert H. Haveman. New York: Russell Sage Foundation.

Schultz, Jay D. 1997. "Homeowners Insurance Availability and Agent Location." In *Insurance Redlining: Disinvestment, Reinvestment, and the*

Evolving Role of Financial Institutions, edited by Gregory D. Squires. Washington, D.C.: Brookings Institution Press.

Schultz, Theodore W. 1963. *The Economic Value of Education*. New York: Columbia University Press.

Schuman, Howard, Charlotte Steeh, Lawrence D. Bobo, and Maria Krysan. 1998. *Racial Attitudes in America: Trends and Interpretations*. Cambridge, Mass.: Harvard University Press.

Schwemm, Robert G. 1989. "The Limits of Litigation Under the Housing Act of 1968." In *The Fair Housing Act After Twenty Years*, edited by Robert G. Schwemm. New Haven, Conn.: Yale Law School.

Sentencing Project. 2006. "Felony Disenfranchisement Laws in the United States." Sentencing Project Publications. Available at: http://www.sentencingproject.org/pubs_05.cfm.

Shaw, Kathleen M., Sara Goldrick-Rab, Christopher Mazzeo, and Jerry Jacobs. 2006. *Putting Poor People to Work: How the Work-First Idea Eroded College Access for the Poor*. New York: Russell Sage Foundation.

Shlay, Anne B. 1983. "Not in That Neighborhood: The Effects of Population and Housing on the Distribution of Mortgage Finance Within the Chicago SMSA from 1980 to 1983." *Social Science Research* 17: 137–63.

Silver, Christopher, and John V. Moeser. 1995. *The Separate City: Black Communities in the Urban South, 1940–1968*. Lexington: University of Kentucky Press.

Simon, Herbert A. 1981. *Sciences of the Artificial*, 2nd ed., rev. and enl. Cambridge, Mass.: MIT Press.

Singer, Audrey, and Douglas S. Massey. 1998. "The Social Process of Undocumented Border Crossing." *International Migration Review* 32(3): 561–92.

Sjoberg, Gideon. 1960. *The Pre-industrial City: Past and Present*. Glencoe, Ill.: Free Press.

Skrentny, John D. 1996. *The Ironies of Affirmative Action: Politics, Culture, and Justice in America*. Chicago: University of Chicago Press.

———. 2002. *The Minority Rights Revolution*. Cambridge, Mass.: Harvard University Press.

Smedley, Brian D., Adrienne Y. Stith, and Alan R. Nelson. 2002. *Unequal Treatment: Confronting Racial and Ethnic Disparities in Health Care*. Washington, D.C.: National Academies Press.

Smeeding, Timothy M. 2005. "Public Policy, Economic Inequality, and Poverty: The United States in Comparative Perspective." *Social Science Quarterly* 86(5): 955–83.

References

———. 2006. "Poor People in Rich Nations: The United States in Comparative Perspective." *Journal of Economic Perspectives* 20: 69–90.

Smeeding, Timothy M., Michael O'Higgins, and Lee Rainwater. 1994. *Poverty, Inequality, and Income Distribution in Comparative Perspective: The Luxembourg Income Study*. Lanham, Md.: University Press of America.

Smith, Courtland. 2006. Website on Poverty and Inequality. Oregon State University, Department of Anthropology. http://oregonstate.edu/instruct/anth/smith/.

Smith, James P. 1988. "Poverty and the Family." In *Divided Opportunities: Minorities, Poverty, and Social Policy*, edited by Gary D. Sandefur and Marta Tienda. New York: Plenum.

Smith, Robin, and Michelle DeLair. 1999. "New Evidence from Lender Testing: Discrimination at the Pre-application Stage." In *Mortgage Lending Discrimination: A Review of Existing Evidence*, edited by Margery A. Turner and Felicity Skidmore. Washington, D.C.: Urban Institute Press.

Smith, Rogers M. 1997. *Civic Ideals: Conflicting Visions of Citizenship in U.S. History*. New Haven, Conn.: Yale University Press.

Smith, Shana L., and Cathy Cloud. 1997. "Documenting Discrimination by Homeowners Insurance Companies Through Testing." In *Insurance Redlining: Disinvestment, Reinvestment, and the Evolving Role of Financial Institutions*, edited by Gregory D. Squires. Washington, D.C.: Urban Institute Press.

Sniderman, Paul M., and Edward G. Carmines. 1997. *Reaching Beyond Race*. Cambridge, Mass.: Harvard University Press.

Sniderman, Paul M., and Thomas Piazza. 1993. *The Scar of Race*. Cambridge, Mass.: Harvard University Press.

Sorensen, Elaine, and Frank D. Bean. 1994. "The Immigration Reform and Control Act and the Wages of Mexican-Origin Workers: Evidence from Current Population Surveys." *Social Science Quarterly* 75(1): 1–17.

Spear, Allan H. 1967. *Black Chicago: The Making of a Negro Ghetto: 1890–1920*. Chicago: University of Chicago Press.

Squires, Gregory D., and Jan Chadwick. 2006. "Linguistic Profiling: A Continuing Tradition of Discrimination in the Home Insurance Industry." *Urban Affairs Review* 41: 400–15.

Squires, Gregory D., Sally O'Conner, and Josh Silver. 2001. "The Unavailability of Information on Insurance Unavailability: Insurance Redlining and the Absence of Geocoded Disclosure Data." *Housing Policy Debate* 12: 347–42.

Squires, Gregory D., and William Velez. 1987. "Insurance Redlining and the Transformation of an Urban Metropolis." *Urban Affairs Quarterly* 23(September): 63–83.

Squires, Gregory D., William Velez, and Karl E. Taeuber. 1991. "Insurance Redlining, Agency Location, and the Process of Urban Disinvestment." *Urban Affairs Quarterly* 26(4): 567–88.

Stack, Carol B. 1974. *All Our Kin: Strategies for Survival in a Black Community*. New York: Harper & Row.

Stangor, Charles, L. Lynch, C. Duan, and B. Glass. 1992. "Categorization of Individuals on the Basis of Multiple Social Features." *Journal of Personality and Social Psychology* 62(2): 207–18.

Sullivan, Theresa A., Elizabeth Warren, and Jay Lawrence Westbrook. 2000. *The Fragile Middle Class: Americans in Debt*. New Haven, Conn.: Yale University Press.

Svallfors, Stefan. 2005. *Analyzing Inequality: Life Chances and Social Mobility in Comparative Perspective*. Stanford, Calif.: Stanford University Press.

Swartz, James E., Arthur J. Lurigio, and Dana A. Weiner. 2004. "Correlates of HIV Risk Behavior Among Prison Inmates: Implications for Tailored AIDS Prevention Programming." *The Prison Journal* 84(4): 486–504.

Swedberg, Richard. 2003. *Principles of Economic Sociology*. Princeton, N.J.: Princeton University Press.

Sweeney, Paul D., Dean B. McFarlin, and Edward J. Inderrieden. 1990. "Using Relative Deprivation Theory to Explain Satisfaction with Income and Pay Level: A Multistudy Examination." *Academy of Management Journal* 33(2): 423–36.

Taeuber, Karl E., and Alma F. Taeuber. 1965. *Negroes in Cities: Residential Segregation and Neighborhood Change*. Chicago: Aldine de Gruyter.

Taggart, Harriet Tee, and Kevin W. Smith. 1981. "Redlining: An Assessment of the Evidence of Disinvestment in Metropolitan Boston." *Urban Affairs Quarterly* 17: 91–107.

Taylor, J. Edward. 1996. "IRCA's Effects in California Agriculture." In *Immigration Reform and U.S. Agriculture*, edited by Philip L. Martin, W. Huffman, R. Emerson, and J. Edward Taylor. Oakland: California Division of Agriculture and Natural Resources.

Taylor, J. Edward, Philip L. Martin, and Michael Fix. 1997. *Poverty Amid Prosperity: Immigration and the Changing Face of Rural California*. Washington, D.C.: Urban Institute Press.

Taylor, J. Edward., and Dawn Thilmany. 1993. "Worker Turnover, Farm

Labor Contractors, and IRCA's Impact on the California Farm Labor Market." *American Journal of Agricultural Economics* 75(2): 350–60.

Taylor, Shelly E., Susan T. Fiske, Nancy L. Etcoff, and Audrey J. Ruderman. 1978. "Categorical Bases of Person Memory and Stereotyping." *Journal of Personality and Social Psychology* 36: 778–93.

Telles, Edward E. 2005. *Race in Another America: The Significance of Skin Color in Brazil.* Princeton, N.J.: Princeton University Press.

Telles, Edward E., and Edward Murguia. 1990. "Phenotypic Discrimination and Income Differences Among Mexican Americans." *Social Science Quarterly* 71(4): 682–96.

Tienda, Marta, and Audrey Singer. 1995. "Wage Mobility of Undocumented Workers in the United States." *International Migration Review* 29(1): 112–38.

Tilly, Charles. 1998. *Durable Inequality.* Berkeley: University of California Press.

Tilly, Louise A. 1994. *Industrialization and Gender Inequality.* Washington, D.C.: American Historical Association.

Timmer, Ashley S., and Jeffrey G. Williamson. 1998. "Immigration Policy Prior to the 1930s: Labor Markets, Policy Interactions, and Globalization Backlash." *Population and Development Review* 24(4): 739–72.

Tolnay, Stewart, and Elwood M. Beck. 1995. *A Festival of Violence: An Analysis of the Lynching of African-Americans in the American South, 1882–1930.* Urbana: University of Illinois Press.

Tonry, Michael. 1996. *Malign Neglect: Race, Crime, and Punishment in America.* New York: Oxford University Press.

Turner, Margery A., Michael Fix, and Raymond J. Struyk. 1991. *Opportunities Denied, Opportunities Diminished: Racial Discrimination in Hiring.* Washington, D.C.: Urban Institute Press.

Turner, Margery A., Fred Freiberg, Erin B. Godfrey, Carla Herbig, Diane K. Levy, and Robert E. Smith. 2002. *All Other Things Being Equal: A Paired Testing Study of Mortgage Lending Institutions.* Washington: U.S. Department of Housing and Urban Development.

Turner, Margery A., Stephen L. Ross, George C. Galster, and John Yinger. 2002. *Discrimination in Metropolitan Housing Markets: National Results from Phase I.* Washington: U.S. Department of Housing and Urban Development.

Uchitelle, Louis. 2006. *The Disposable American: Layoffs and Their Consequences.* New York: Knopf.

Uggen, Christopher, and Jeff Manza. 2004. "Lost Voices: The Civic and Political Views of Disenfranchised Felons." In *Imprisoning America: The So-*

cial Effects of Mass Incarceration, edited by Mary Pattillo, David Weiman, and Bruce Western. New York: Russell Sage Foundation.

United Nations. 1998. *Human Development Report 1998*. New York: Oxford University Press.

University of Pennsylvania. 2005. "Penn Alumni: Admissions for Legacies: Statistics." Available at: http://www.alumni.upenn.edu/aca/admissionstats.html (accessed June 26, 2005).

U.S. Bureau of the Census. 2006. "The Hispanic Population in the United States: 2004 Detailed Tables." Available at: http://www.census.gov/population/www/socdemo/hispanic/cps2004.html (accessed August 4, 2006).

U.S. General Accounting Office. 1990. *Immigration Reform: Employer Sanctions and the Question of Discrimination*. Washington: U.S. Government Printing Office.

———. 1997. "Death Penalty Sentencing: Research Indicates Pattern of Racial Disparities." In *The Death Penalty in America: Current Controversies*, edited by Hugo A. Bedau. New York: Oxford University Press.

U.S. Immigration Commission. 1911. *Immigrants in Industries*, part 25, *Japanese and Other Immigrant Races in the Pacific Coast and Rocky Mountain States: Agriculture*. Washington: U.S. Government Printing Office.

Van Kerkhove, Barbara. 2005. *The Homeowners Insurance Gap: How Race and Neighborhood Composition Explain Cost and Access Disparities in Rochester and Monroe County, New York*. Rochester: Greater Upstate Law Project.

Wacquant, Loic. 2000. "The New 'Peculiar Institution': On the Prison as a Surrogate Ghetto." *Theoretical Criminology* 4(3): 377–89.

———. 2001. "Deadly Symbiosis: When Ghetto and Prison Meet and Mesh." In *Mass Imprisonment: Social Causes and Consequences*, edited by David Garland. Thousand Oaks, Calif.: Sage Publications.

Wade, Peter. 1997. *Race and Ethnicity in Latin America*. London: Pluto Press.

Waite, Linda J., and Maggie Gallagher. 2000. *The Case for Marriage: Why Married People Are Happier, Healthier, and Better Off Financially*. New York: Doubleday.

Waldrep, Christopher. 1998. *Roots of Disorder: Race and Criminal Justice in the American South, 1817–1880*. Urbana: University of Illinois Press.

Walker, Iain, and Heather J. Smith. 2002. *Relative Deprivation: Specification, Development, and Integration*. Cambridge: Cambridge University Press.

Warren, Elizabeth, and Amelia Warren Tyagi. 2003. *The Two-Income Trap: Why Middle-Class Mothers and Fathers Are Going Broke*. New York: Basic Books.

Warren, Robert, and Jeffrey S. Passel. 1987. "A Count of the Uncountable:

References

Estimates of Undocumented Aliens Counted in the 1980 United States Census." *Demography* 24(3): 375–93.

Waters, Mary C. 1990. *Ethnic Options: Choosing Identities in America*. Berkeley: University of California Press.

Webster, Chris, Georg Glasze, and Klaus Frantz. 2002. "The Global Spread of Gated Communities." *Environment and Planning B* 29(3): 315–20.

Weiss, Michael J. 1988. *The Clustering of America*. New York: Harper & Row.

———. 2000. *The Clustered World: How We Live, What We Buy, and What It All Means About Who We Are*. Boston: Little, Brown.

Western, Bruce. 1997. *Between Class and the Market: Postwar Unionization in the Capitalist Democracies*. Princeton, N.J.: Princeton University Press.

———. 2006. *Punishment and Inequality in America*. New York: Russell Sage Foundation.

White, Michael J. 1980. *Urban Renewal and the Residential Structure of the City*. Chicago: Community and Family Studies Center.

Whitley, Richard. 1999. *Divergent Capitalisms: The Social Structuring and Change of Business Systems*. Oxford: Oxford University Press.

Wienk, Ronald, Cliff Reid, John Simonson, and Fred Eggers. 1979. *Measuring Racial Discrimination in American Housing Markets: The Housing Market Practices Survey*. Washington: U.S. Department of Housing and Urban Development.

Wilkes, Rima, and John Iceland. 2004. "Hypersegregation in the Twenty-first Century: An Update and Analysis." *Demography* 41(1): 23–36.

Williams, Jonathan. 1998. *Money: A History*. New York: St. Martin's Press.

Williams, Richard A., Reynold Nesiba, and Eileen Diaz McConnell. 2005. "The Changing Face of Mortgage Lending." *Social Problems* 52: 181–208.

Williams-Leon, Teresa. 2002. "Check All That Apply: Trends and Perspectives Among Asian-Descent Multiracials." In *New Faces in a Changing America: Multiracial Identity in the Twenty-first Century*, edited by Loretta I. Winters and Herman L. DeBose. Thousand Oaks, Calif.: Sage Publications.

Williamson, Jeffrey G. 1980. *American Inequality: A Macroeconomic History*. New York: Academic Press.

Wirth, Louis. 1928. *The Ghetto*. Chicago: University of Chicago Press.

Wissoker, Douglas A., Wendy Zimmermann, and George Galster. 1998. *Testing for Discrimination in Home Insurance*. Washington, D.C.: Urban Institute Press.

Woodrow-Lafield, Karen. 1998. "Estimating Authorized Immigration." Pp. 619-82 in *Migration Between Mexico and the United States, Binational*

Study, Volume 2: Research Reports and Background Materials. Washington: U.S. Commission on Immigration Reform

Woodward, C. Vann. 1955. *The Strange Career of Jim Crow.* New York : Oxford University Press.

Wormser, Richard. 2003. *The Rise and Fall of Jim Crow.* New York: St. Martin's Press.

Wright, Erik O. 1997. *Class Counts: Comparative Studies in Class Analysis.* New York: Cambridge University Press.

Wright, Russell O. 1997. *Life and Death in the United States: Statistics on Life Expectancies, Diseases and Death Rates for the Twentieth Century.* Jefferson, N.C.: McFarland & Co.

Wright, Stephen C. 2001. "Restricted Intergroup Boundaries: Tokenism, Ambiguity, and the Tolerance of Injustice." In *The Psychology of Legitimacy: Emerging Perspectives on Ideology, Justice, and Intergroup Relations,* edited by John T. Jost and Brenda Majors. New York: Cambridge University Press.

Yinger, John. 1986. "Measuring Racial Discrimination with Fair Housing Audits: Caught in the Act." *American Economic Review* 76(5): 991–93.

———. 1989. "Measuring Discrimination in Housing Availability." Final research report no. 2 to the U.S. Department of Housing and Urban Development. Washington, D.C.: The Urban Institute.

———. 1991. *Housing Discrimination Study: Incidence and Severity of Unfavorable Treatment.* Washington: U.S. Department of Housing and Urban Development, Office of Policy Development and Research.

———. 1995. *Closed Doors, Opportunities Lost: The Continuing Costs of Housing Discrimination.* New York: Russell Sage Foundation.

Zajonc, Robert B. 1998. "Emotions." In *The Handbook of Social Psychology,* edited by Daniel T. Gilbert, Susan T. Fiske, and Gardner Lindzey. Boston: McGraw-Hill.

Zamora, Emilio. 1993. *The World of the Mexican Worker in Texas.* College Station: Texas A&M Press.

Zimmermann, Wendy, and Michael Fix. 1998. *Declining Immigrant Applications for Medi-Cal and Welfare Benefits in Los Angeles County.* Washington, D.C.: Urban Institute Press.

Zolberg, Aristide R. 2006. *A Nation by Design: Immigration Policy in the Fashioning of America.* New York: Russell Sage Foundation.

INDEX

Boldface numbers refer to figures and tables.